History of Computing

Founding Editor
Martin Campbell-Kelly, University of Warwick, Coventry, UK

Series Editor
Gerard Alberts, University of Amsterdam, Amsterdam, The Netherlands

Advisory Board
Jack Copeland, University of Canterbury, Christchurch, New Zealand
Ulf Hashagen, Deutsches Museum, Munich, Germany
John V. Tucker, Swansea University, Swansea, UK
Jeffrey R. Yost, University of Minnesota, Minneapolis, USA

The History of Computing series publishes high-quality books which address the history of computing, with an emphasis on the 'externalist' view of this history, more accessible to a wider audience. The series examines content and history from four main quadrants: the history of relevant technologies, the history of the core science, the history of relevant business and economic developments, and the history of computing as it pertains to social history and societal developments.

Titles can span a variety of product types, including but not exclusively, themed volumes, biographies, 'profile' books (with brief biographies of a number of key people), expansions of workshop proceedings, general readers, scholarly expositions, titles used as ancillary textbooks, revivals and new editions of previous worthy titles.

These books will appeal, varyingly, to academics and students in computer science, history, mathematics, business and technology studies. Some titles will also directly appeal to professionals and practitioners of different backgrounds.

More information about this series at http://www.springer.com/series/8442

Valérie Schafer • Benjamin G. Thierry

Editors

Connecting Women

Women, Gender and ICT in Europe
in the Nineteenth and Twentieth Century

 Springer

Editors
Valérie Schafer
Institute for Communication Sciences
(CNRS, Paris-Sorbonne, UPMC)
Paris, France

Benjamin G. Thierry
Université Paris-Sorbonne
Institute for Communication Sciences
(CNRS, Paris-Sorbonne, UPMC)
Paris, France

ISSN 2190-6831
History of Computing
ISBN 978-3-319-36484-1
DOI 10.1007/978-3-319-20837-4

ISSN 2190-684X (electronic)

ISBN 978-3-319-20837-4 (eBook)

Springer Cham Heidelberg New York Dordrecht London
© Springer International Publishing Switzerland 2015
Softcover re-print of the Hardcover 1st edition 2015

Printed on acid-free paper

Springer International Publishing AG Switzerland is part of Springer Science+Business Media (www.springer.com)

Foreword

Women, gender, and information and communication technologies – a grouping of terms that would have made an utterly impossible and impenetrable title only a few decades ago. In their current meanings, these words simply did not exist. Genders were grammatical categories and the French *genres* a matter of literature; information, communication, and technology were discrete elements, far from the iconic acronym ICT; and history as well as technology afforded women an equal level of invisibility. More crucially, associating these terms into a coherent angle of research would have not been feasible. Research teams focusing on gender and women's history very rarely met with academics interested in the history of technological innovation: both groups had to devote most of their time and efforts to developing and asserting their existence. Today, with an undeniable institutional and historiographical legitimacy, these fields of research can connect, as they did in Paris at the May 2014 symposium organized by the LabEx EHNE. In this volume are presented the results of a convergence of approaches, the meeting of minds and experiences, and connections through and beyond the variety of methodologies and interests.

Since the 1970s, women's history has returned to visibility the half of humankind which at best had been present if partially hidden in the world and times of men, at worst forgotten. While this is not the place for a full account of its historiography,[1] women's history, it must be noted, was before all else a social history of women, making its own the themes of the *Nouvelle Histoire*. In the first instance, labor and conflicts, education, and women's bodies were analyzed as spaces where male domination exerts itself, but also as the locus of emancipation. The necessary objective was to assert, against stereotypes, the separation of "the woman" from the object of nature: historicize "her body" and therefore historicize medicine, maternity, and sexuality. One essential step was to extract women from the archives; mostly written by men, they seemed at first glance to have very little to say of women. Oral history made it possible to fill in the "silences of history" for the more recent periods; archives were helpful, chiefly for the fields where women had

---

[1] See, for example, Thébaud, Françoise, 2007. *Ecrire l'histoire des femmes et du genre*. Lyon: ENS Ed.

a strong presence – schools and health-care careers, often very far from technology. Indeed, technology seemed to be a field of men: why explore it when looking for women? Then again, why not? From the history of technologies[2] to the history of innovation, approaches to materiality have grown and diversified.[3] This historiography has integrated the study of large technical systems, of practices and usages, as well as political economy and the social construction of technological systems. Combining social and cultural history, this field of research takes into account all the stakeholders – not only the "key players" but all the agents of history in their diversity and the variety of their actions, from the "informed" groups of involved users to the general public. Within this history, through the new spaces and territories it discovers in its study of networks and apparatus, the history of information and communication technologies has its own intellectual space, where new approaches can develop freely.

The choice of words and concept has had a definite impact on the complex trajectories of these approaches. When "sex" – the natural and biological differentiation, in addition to the sexuality, present in both French and English – had to be separated from a cultural and social distinction between men and women, French researchers weighted their options ("social sex relations," "sex difference," "social sex") before settling for the English word "gender" and later the French *genre*, which still remains controversial. Since the early 1970s, France has added to its language the new words needed to describe new domains – like *télématique* for innovations such as the national videotext *Minitel* system and *informatique* for both computer science and information technology. The English phrase information and communication technology was first used in the 1980s; its French equivalent, *Technologie de l'information et de la communication*, testifies to the convergence of previously separate domains, induced by the development of digital technologies. The corresponding acronyms are widely used in both languages: ICT and TIC are commonly found in the technological domain, but also in education, where transmission of knowledge must always find new forms and where technological and social mutations must be followed. To both fields, a stigma seems to be attached – the shame of a common "anglophone original sin?" In 2014, while "gender" seemed a naughty word that the French Ministry for National Education endeavored to erase discretely, the British government, taking the advice of the Royal Society,[4] replaced the phrase "ICT" and its "negative connotations" by "computing."[5]

---

[2] Pestre, Dominique (ed. in collaboration with Yves Cohen), 1998. *Histoire des techniques. Annales, Histoires, Sciences Sociales* 4/5.

[3] Griset, Pascal and Yves Bouvier, 2012. *De l'histoire des techniques à l'histoire de l'innovation. Tendances de la recherche française en histoire contemporaine* (From the History of Technologies to the History of Innovation. Trends of French Eschare in Contemporary History). *Histoire, économie et société*, HES 2: 29–43.

[4] Royal Society, 2012. Shut down or restart? The way forward for computing in UK schools: 18. "The term 'ICT' should no longer be used as it has attracted too many negative connotations."

[5] https://www.gov.uk/government/publications/national-curriculum-in-england-computing-programmes-of-study. Accessed 15 March 2015.

Nevertheless, the history of women, gender, and information and communication technology, as it appears in these pages, makes a strong case in favor of the combination of approaches. The study of the field does not amount to tracking down the presence of women in ICTs – a compensatory history against which Charlotte Bunch and Mary Hunt, and later Janet Abbate, have warned researchers; instead, it is the investigation into why this domain was and still is too often considered masculine. Albeit in unbalanced proportions, men and women are agents of the conception, production, and use of these technologies. Yet, in terms of dynamics, the lesser visibility of women leads to a very stereotyped image of their agency. Small, nimble hands carry out simple, repetitive tasks, from switchboard operators to computer girls; feminine voices are fit for phone receptionists and the sensual overtones of evening radio shows. In contrast, men understand tools, master technologies, and control networks. A closer look at reality shows a much more complex world, where the "demoiselles du téléphone" (female "switches") are everything but passive when it comes to their social condition, as Dominique Pinsolle tells us; where Spanish *radios libres* (free radios) are a vehicle of female activism, as José Emilio Pérez Martinez describes; and where the glass ceiling and pipeline shrinkage in computer science careers are historical constructs, as shown by Giuditta Parolini's research on the Rothamsted Statistics Department since the 1920s.

Since the last years of the twentieth century, researchers have described a number of aspects of what can be analyzed as another mode of male domination. Their perspective follows the deconstruction of culturally persistent images and relies on the study of the various domains of information and communication technologies, from their conception – here, in the chapter on computing, by Martina McDonell and Chantal Morley – to their representations, as exemplified by the works of Marion Dalibert and Simona de Iulio. These approaches are necessary if the "glass slipper" is ever to be shattered, as Catherine Ashcraft and Karen Lee Ashcraft suggest. The variety of sources used in this book (institutional archives and archives of research centers, oral testimonies and the press, as well as born-digital heritage, in the chapter by Alexie Geers) is an invitation to travel from one scale to another, from individuals to groups to networks. The range of sources also allows the reader to consider the many aspects of what has been at play, over the last two centuries, in the relation between women and men. Relegation to subordinate positions and contestation; pioneering personalities; female, feminine, and/or feminist uses of information technologies; and the relations between gender and occupational identities: the issues and questions are as abundant today as they were in the first days of the telegraph, presented by Simone M. Müller in her research.

From the cultural and societal standpoints, the conceptual issues are crucial. However, they should not make us forget that, beyond all the forms of academic debate, any approach – in any domain – where any group of agents of the development of a field is overlooked, overestimated, undervalued, or forgotten, is bound to be incomplete and distorted.

This is the reason why, within the long-term project of a new history of Europe, it appears as imperative to process and study in conjunction the issues of European fluxes as products of a material civilization and the questions raised by a continent where sex and gender relations are an integral part of a common history. *Connecting Women. Women, Gender, and ICT in Europe* is a human connection of themes and histories; one can only hope that its promising research will lead to new explorations.

Paris, France   Pascal Griset
22 April 2015   Fabrice Virgili

Preface

Both sides of the Atlantic marked the year 2015 with a celebration of the bicentennial of the birth of Ada Augusta Byron, best known as Ada Lovelace. The polemics over her contribution, referred to "Deleting Ada Lovelace from the history of computing,"[1] fortunately do not deter her standing as a symbol of women's contributions in the history of computing, as shown by the ADA Awards, for instance.

Women's contributions to the field are also being recognized in the proliferation of academic initiatives. In 2015, the annual meeting of the Congrès de la Société Informatique de France (SIF, Convention of Computing Society in France) focused entirely on the theme of "Women and Computing" before an audience composed primarily of computer scientists concerned about the two-decade decline of women in the field.[2]

Historical work allows us to recover the significant female presence that existed in computing research and industry until the 1980s, as we have seen in the work of Tom Misa (2010),[3] Janet Abbate (2012),[4] Nathan Ensmenger (2010),[5] or Mary Hicks (2010),[6] to name but a few. This trend in historical research leads us to view women's current peripheral status as neither structural nor static.

Certainly, great care is required to avoid amalgams that could introduce an artificial continuity that has no evidentiary basis between human computers, keypunch operators, or today's women laborers in computing (with all the diversity within the milieus of

---

[1] The Ada Initiative, 2013, http://adainitiative.org/2013/08/deleting-ada-lovelace-from-the-history-of-computing/Accessed 5 March 2015.

[2] Margolis, Jane, and Allan Fisher. 2001. *Unlocking the clubhouse*. Cambridge, MA: The MIT Press.

[3] Misa, Thomas J. (ed.). 2010. *Gender codes: why women are leaving computing?* Hoboken: Wiley and IEEE Computer Society.

[4] Abbate, Janet. 2012. *Recoding gender: women's changing participation in computing*. Cambridge, MA: The MIT Press.

[5] Ensmenger, Nathan. 2010. *The computer boys take over: computers, programmers and the politics of technical expertise*. Cambridge, MA: The MIT Press.

[6] Hicks, Mary. 2010. Only the clothes changed: women operators in British computing and advertising, 1950–1970. *IEEE Annals of the History of Computing* 32(4): 5–17.

industry, public and private research, education, etc.). Therefore, creating a dialogue that includes different periods, spaces, and ICTs, from the telegraph with Simone M. Müller to computing with Chantal Morley and Martina McDonnell, may make this all the more difficult. But the choice to embrace multiplicity seemed relevant from several angles.

In the first place, it is true that the field of computing has evolved: the understanding of women's historical role in computing, e.g., punch cards, calculations carried out for research, "work-from-home" programmers in the 1960s for companies like those created by Elsie Shutt or Stephanie Shirley,[7] and office automation, must maintain skepticism of hasty or linear genealogies. Therefore, is a historical gaze that is focused solely on the history of computing equipped to capture topics of such pronounced diversity? Delphine Gardey's work has shown how the history of office automation should also be included in a broader history of women's professionalization, looking upstream of the first computers and including a reflection on the "material remains (technical and cognitive) of companies producing immateriality".[8] Karen Lee Ashcraft and Catherine Ashcraft's chapter, which draws a parallel between occupational identities in aviation and the ICT sector, invites an expanded analysis beyond the bounds of ICT, so as to understand the structure of women's spheres of professionalization. If computing serves to highlight specific forms of female professionalization, an analysis of women's labor sheds light on the distribution of professional activities in computing's different spheres, be it design, use, or training.

Are the female undervalued tasks in computing in the 1950s so dissimilar to the case of the *demoiselles du téléphone*, France's phone operators in the early 1900s studied by Dominique Pinsolle, with all the nuanced parallels that could be drawn? Such examples invite us to reconsider the notion of clerical workers,[9] the differentiation between blue-collar and white-collar workers and low-status jobs in the long history of women in technology. In her chapter, Giuditta Parolini describes the women in the Rothamsted Statistics Department as blue-collar workers and takes on a detailed analysis of the symbolic hierarchy of tasks in the field of data processing. The diachronic exploration of agencies is complex but allows access to social, economic, and symbolic configurations that are in a state of perpetual change.

Finally, in terms of uses, studying forms of empowerment extends beyond the history of computing. As the papers of José Emilio Pérez Martínez and Alexie Geers attest, feminist currents, and more broadly women's discourse, have long seized upon the media as spaces for expression, well before the advent of the Internet and blogs. The same can be said of representations, as shown by Marion Dalibert and Simona De Iulio's cross-analysis of ICTs, gender, and youth. By focusing our attention on the history of communications rather than on technology alone,

---

[7] Abbate 2012.

[8] Gardey, Delphine. 2008. *Écrire, calculer, classer. Comment une révolution de papier a transformé les sociétés contemporaines (1800–1940)*. Paris: La Découverte.

[9] Davis, Margery W. 1988. Women clerical workers and the typewriter: the writing machine. In *Technology and women's voices. Keeping in touch*, ed. Cheris Kramarae, 23–32. London: Routledge & Kegan Paul.

it becomes relevant to expand the field of study beyond the computer to comprehend uses of communication media in their full diversity, from the telephone's one-to-one context to the Web's many-to-many forums.

We shift the gaze by encompassing objects that disciplinary fields and chronological divisions traditionally keep distant, so that analyses achieving unity through the study of gendered relations to technology, to information, and to communications may be compared and placed together.

Gender studies, media history, and the history of computing may come from fields with little academic overlap (separate laboratories, historiographies and epistemologies, etc.), but they are not hermetically sealed from each other. This book's choice to operate by crossing approaches and subjects of research, and by convening researchers from diverse horizons around a common topic, is part of the Sorbonne University's LabEx EHNE initiative.[10] This grouping of several research labs around the topic *Ecrire une nouvelle histoire de l'Europe* (Writing a New History of Europe) permitted us to cross-pollinate approaches around the concepts of innovation, technology, gender, and women's history and to invite our colleagues to consider these subjects and their mutual relations within the contemporary European space.[11]

As much by their approaches, methods, and sources as by their results, the contributors of this book, into ten contributions and three parts – *Networks and Empowerment, Gendered Representations*, and *ICT and Professionalization* – connect gender, women, and ICT in Europe from a long-term diachronic perspective, enlightening some gender infrastructures of the information age, as noted by Delphine Gardey in her conclusive chapter.

Paris, France   Valérie Schafer
                                                                                                            Benjamin G. Thierry

References

Abbate, Janet. 2012. *Recoding gender: women's changing participation in computing.* Cambridge, MA: The MIT Press.
Davis, Margery W. 1988. Women clerical workers and the typewriter: the writing machine. In *Technology and women's voices. Keeping in touch*, ed. Cheris Kramarae, 23–32. London: Routledge & Kegan Paul.
Ensmenger, Nathan. 2010. *The computer boys take over: computers, programmers and the politics of technical expertise.* Cambridge, MA: The MIT Press.

---

[10] http://www.labex-ehne.fr

[11] First in a symposium held at the Institute for Communication Sciences in Paris in May 2014, co-organized with Delphine Diaz, Arielle Haakenstad, and Régis Schlagdenhauffen with support from LabEx EHNE, Profs. Eric Bussière and Pascal Griset, and Fabrice Virgili and, later in this book, with the support of Gerard Alberts and Springer around the *History of Computing* collection.

Gardey, Delphine. 2008. *Écrire, calculer, classer. Comment une révolution de papier a transformé les sociétés contemporaines (1800–1940)*. Paris: La Découverte.

Hicks, Mary. 2010. Only the clothes changed: women operators in British computing and advertising, 1950–1970. *IEEE Annals of the History of Computing* 32(4): 5–17.

Margolis, Jane, and Allan Fisher. 2001. *Unlocking the clubhouse*. Cambridge, MA: The MIT Press.

Misa, Thomas J. (ed.). 2010. *Gender codes: why women are leaving computing?* Hoboken: Wiley and IEEE Computer Society.

Acknowledgment

We wish to thank for their continued support over the course of this project the LabEx EHNE, especially its director Professor Eric Bussière, Professor Pascal Griset, and Dr Fabrice Virgili. We sincerely thank the authors of the texts, Gerard Alberts, and our publisher Springer for their confidence in the project, as well as Laura Kraftowitz and Xavier Blandin for their remarkable translations of several of the texts. We are grateful for the friendship of Delphine Diaz, Arielle Haakenstad, and Régis Schlagdenhauffen, our co-organizers of the international conference on Women, Gender and ICT in Europe, held in May 2014 in the Institute for Communication Sciences (CNRS, Paris-Sorbonne, UPMC). We would like to thank all of those who were part of its scientific committee: Gerard Alberts, Alec Badenoch, Isabelle Berrebi-Hoffmann, Niels Brügger, Frédéric Clavert, Delphine Gardey, Pascal Griset, Sandra Laugier, Christophe Lécuyer, Ilana Löwy, Cécile Méadel, Ruth Oldenziel, Jean-Claude Ruano-Borbalan, and Fabrice Virgili. Finally, our sincere thanks to all participants of the conference who, even if they are not all present in the volume, all contributed to this collective reflection.

We wish to thank...

Contents

Chapter 1
Connecting Gender, Women and ICT in Europe: A Long-Term Perspective

Valérie Schafer and Benjamin G. Thierry

Abstract Cross-analysing the problem of ICT with women and gender's roles on a long-term perspective, as this collective book aspires to do, may seem challenging. As described in some pioneering historical works, the very notion of computing as a construct calls for a nuanced understanding. Great care is required to avoid amalgams that could introduce an artificial continuity that has no evidentiary basis between human computers, keypunch operators or today's women labourers in computing (with all the diversity within the milieus of industry, public and private research, education, etc.). Therefore, creating a dialogue that includes diverse ICTs, diverse contexts and various European countries may make this all the more difficult. But the choice to embrace multiplicity seemed relevant from several angles that are discussed in this introductory chapter.

Les Petites Filles modèles	*Good Little Girls*
Ne jouent plus à la poupée	*Do not play with dolls*
Ne jouent plus à la marelle	*Do not play hopscotch*
A la corde à chat perché	*Or tag or ball*
Branchées grâce au Minitel	*Connected through theMinitel*
Sur le marché financier	*To the stock market*
Les Petites Filles modèles	*Good Little Girls*
S'amusent à boursicoter	*Play at investing*
C'est à ce jeu qu'elles excellent	*At this game they excel*
Fruit de la modernité	*This fruit of modernity*
Ah la belle ah la belle ah la belle société (…)	*Oh high oh high oh high society [...]*
Jean Ferrat (1991)	*Jean Ferrat (1991)*[a]

[a]Translation by L. Kraftowitz

V. Schafer (✉)
Institute for Communication Sciences, (CNRS, Paris-Sorbonne, UPMC),
20, rue Berbier-du-Mets, 75013 Paris, France
e-mail: valerie.schafer@cnrs.fr

B.G. Thierry
Université Paris-Sorbonne, Institute for Communication Sciences,
(CNRS, Paris-Sorbonne, UPMC), 20, rue Berbier-du-Mets, 75013 Paris, France
e-mail: Benjamin.thierry@paris-sorbonne.fr

© Springer International Publishing Switzerland 2015
V. Schafer, B.G. Thierry (eds.), *Connecting Women*, History of Computing,
DOI 10.1007/978-3-319-20837-4_1

In his book *Gender Codes: Why Women Are LeavingComputing*, Tom Misa describes how the computing industry's initial trend of increasing female participation[1] was followed by its net reversal, an unprecedented event in labour history.[2] The field of computing, which seemed 'woman friendly' according to Lois Mandel's 1967 description in *Cosmopolitan*,[3] witnessed a unique reversal as it lost its female members over the last twenty years. The ACM-W began worrying about this phenomenon and exploring its causes, from pipeline shrinkage to media representation, as early as 2002, in its report, 'An ACM-W Literature Review on Women in Computing'.[4]

The general public in turn discovers this little-known history, which disrupts the historical canon that carved out a place for men while consigning women to oblivion.[5] The British series *The Bletchley Circle* depicted women in Bletchley Park during the Second World War who, though overshadowed by Alan Turing, made contributions to the counterintelligence operations of the British computer centre.[6] The same can be seen in the recent *Imitation Game* with Keira Knightley's portrayal of Joan Clarke, who serves as a foil in the romanticised story of Bletchley Park, but still draws attention to the historical figure's true role as a talented cryptanalyst.

Social networks also demonstrate these trends. One example is the success of the Twitter hashtag *#FeministHackerBarbie* that called for a *détournement* of the Barbie book *I Can Be a Computer Engineer*, thanks to Kathleen Tuite's initiative. This independent computerprogrammer based near Santa Cruz created a website[7] where people could 'hack' the original book and express their creativity, humour and also anger against the stereotypes that were developed in the 'official book'. 'In the past few days, her Feminist Hacker Barbie has blossomed into a full-blown and extremely funny Internet meme with thousands of captions'.[8]

These examples echo historians' efforts to reverse women's under-representation[9] and recent decades of invisibility, however, without placing them into a compensatory

---

[1] Light, Jennifer S. 1999. When computers were women. *Technology and Culture* 40(3): 455–483.

[2] Misa, Thomas J. (ed.). 2010. *Gender codes: why women are leaving computing?* Hoboken: Wiley/IEEE Computer Society.

[3] Ensmenger, Nathan. 2010a. *The computer boys take over: computers, programmers and the politics of technical expertise*. Cambridge, MA: MIT Press.

[4] Gürer, Denise, and Tracy Camp. 2002. An ACM-W literature review on women in computing. *SIGCSE Bulletin* 34(2): 121–127.

[5] Ashcraft, Catherine. 2014. *Increasing the participation of women and underrepresented minorities in computing: missing perspectives and new directions*. Orlando: National Science Foundation Computer Science Education Summit.

[6] Burman, Annie. 2013. *Gendering decryption – decrypting gender: the gender discourse of labour at Bletchley Park 1939–1945*. MA thesis, Uppsala University.

[7] https://computer-engineer-barbie.herokuapp.com. Accessed 4 March 2015

[8] McMillan, R. 2014. *Feminist Hacker Barbie is just what our little girls need*. Wired. 21 Nov 2014.

[9] Cohoon, Joanne, and William Aspray (eds.). 2006. *Women and information technology: research on under-representation*. Cambridge, MA: MIT Press.

history, as Janet Abbate, following Charlotte Bunch and Mary Hunt, warns against.[10] Other fields such as educational studies also try to modify representations of 'hegemonic masculinity', like the figures of the nerd and the geek that gradually served to conflate the image of the programmer with that of men.[11]

Despite the ostensible self-evidence of such a remark, it is worth remembering that the interest in women's role in computing – e.g. the publication of *Gender Codes*[12] and *Recoding Gender*[13] – was only recently made possible by the development of research in computing history, a recent field that draws on the dynamic of a growing international community and of gender studies. In recent years, these rapprochements have generated fruitful cross-analyses, like Jennifer S. Light's article on the ENIAC Girls in *Gender & Technology*.[14]

The interest in women's role in computing on both sides of the Atlantic coincides with similar interest from other disciplines, particularly the Information and Communication Sciences and Education Sciences,[15] as well as with a general interest in ICTs as seen in numerous French academic special issues, like 'Le sexe du téléphone' (Phone sex), in *Réseaux* (2000); 'Une communication sexuée' (A sexual communication), published in 2003 in the same journal; 'TIC et genre' (Gender and ICT), published in *TIC&Société* in 2011; and 'Recherches au féminin en Sciences de l'information et de la communication' (Research on the feminine in the information and communication sciences), published in 2014 in the *Revue Française des Sciences de l'Information et de la Communication* (French Review of Information and Communication Sciences).

Cross-analysing the problem of ICT with women's roles, as this work aspires to do, may seem challenging. As described in the works of Tom Misa, Tom Haigh or Nathan Ensmenger, the very notion of computing as a construct requires a nuanced understanding. Indeed, computing is not homogeneous but encompasses multiple realities, as Thomas Haigh points out in the article 'Masculinity and the Machine Man':

> First, computing is not a single kind of work but a collection of hugely diverse jobs across many industries [...]. The rhetoric of computing as a single profession first surfaced in the 1960s. [...] We should follow the advice of the late Mike Mahoney to look 'at histories of computing (s)' rather than a single 'history of computing'. Thinking of computing as a single area of activity makes it hard to understand why women were inventing programming in the 1940s but made up only a small proportion of the corporate computing

---

[10] Abbate, J. 2012. *Recoding gender: women's changing participation in computing*. Cambridge, MA: The MIT Press.

[11] Collet, Isabelle. 2011. Effet de genre: le paradoxe des études d'informatique. *tic&société* 5: 1. http://ticetsociete.revues.org/955. Accessed 14 Mar 2015.

[12] Misa 2010.

[13] Abbate 2012.

[14] Lerman, N., R.O. Nina, and A.P. Mohun (eds.). 2003. *Gender and technology: a reader*. Baltimore: John Hopkins University Press.

[15] Bourdeloie, Hélène, and Virginie Julliard. 2013. La question du genre et des TNIC au prisme du dialogue de la sociologie et de la sémiotique. *Episteme* 9: 243–270. Collet, Isabelle. 2006. *L'informatique a-t-elle un sexe? Hackers, mythes et réalités*. Paris: L'Harmattan. Margolis, Jane, and Allan Fisher. 2001. *Unlocking the clubhouse*. Cambridge, MA: MIT Press.

workforce a decade later. This situation looks very different if we conceptualize programming as a task carried out in many different social contexts, or in Mahoney's terms, in multiple Computing each with its own history. Why would we expect the accountant in charge of an insurance company's project to staff its electronic data processing department in the mid-1950s to be guided by the fact that participants in the experimental military academic ENIAC project believed female mathematicians to have an aptitude for translating mathematical methods into switch and wire configurations?.[16]

While the successive generations of ICT have overlapped and hybridised, the history of women and that of gender are certainly not synonymous, and the notion of Europe has also considerably evolved from the end of the nineteenth century until today, inviting consideration of their complex and changing relationships.

1.1 From the Telegraph to Phone Lines to Online Networks: Women Connecting Through Heterogeneity

This book meets the challenge of heterogeneity by bringing together eight various cases, as much by their approaches, methods and sources as by their results, that shed light on the relationship of gender, women and ICT in Europe from a long-term diachronic perspective.

1.1.1 Framing ICT

It is difficult to pin down the number of jobs emerging directly and strictly from the sectors of computing or more broadly of ICT today. But the inclusion of professional activities that more broadly inform women's investment in ICT seems to in turn shed light on their investment in computing. In this, we follow Kristina Haralanova's conclusion in her master's thesis, 'L'apport des femmes dans le développement du logiciel libre' (Women's contribution to open source software development), defended at the University of Quebec at Montreal in 2010:

> We find that women perform many activities in and for open source coding. These activities are not related to programming source code but are considered peripheral to programming. On the other hand, while some women are active in open source software communities, others are virtually absent from these appropriation and development groups, placing themselves principally within communities unassociated with open source software. In our study, female participants represent the key persons integrating software within a community because of the activities they undertake, like awareness-raising among decision makers to migrate to open source [...].

> - female participants carry out activities that are not viewed as contributions because they do not directly impact coding (e.g. its promotion and the organisation of workshops and trainings on open source advocacy);

---

[16] Haigh, T. 2010. Masculinity and the machine man. In *Gender codes: why women are leaving computing?* ed. Thomas J. Misa, 51–71. Hoboken: Wiley/IEEE Computer Society.

- they work in spaces that are invisible to the open source community (their primary role being to provide open source to others).

Finally, we wish to conclude with the proposition that the more we consider open source as a social movement not limited to a technical project, the more visible women will be.[17]

The question of women's long-term invisibility and place in the periphery of the information sector deserves a historical analysis. From the telegraph to the social networks, while there are issues relevant to women and technology in terms of use, representation and professionalisation, not all the various technologies are necessarily linked by continuities. So what is the common thread between the *demoiselles du téléphone* and twentieth-century programmers?

In Alexie Geers' analysis of *MarieClaire* magazine and 'feminine' blogs, comparing these two forms of expression geared primarily towards women, significant differences arise, reflecting the change of medium from paper to digital, as well as the changing nature of the producer and receiver of information. Blogs' thematic aggregation of common topics, or the creation of reading lists using hypertext to invite a potentially more fragmented or circuitous reading style, need not obscure the fact that many women's magazines, like any form of writing, may also allow for widely varying readings.[18] Nevertheless, there is a fundamental, structural and organisational shift between the two mediums and their structures of authorship, access and readership. But we may also find common codes and approaches, like recurring themes, a voluntarily gendered content and 'female complicity' between columnists and readers.

Women's magazines[19] and blogs provoke questions that are at once common and specific, and we might cite similar contradictions with the telephone, television and computers, three technologies that are also evoked in this collection. What are the commonalities between the *demoiselles du téléphone* working in France during the telecommunications state monopoly in the early twentieth century, as explored by Dominique Pinsolle; the Spanish free radio that fed the climate of freedom during the post-Franco period, as analysed by José Emilio Pérez Martínez; and the progressive approach to computerisation adopted by British, Danish and French policymakers in the second half of the twentieth century, as Chantal Morley and Martina McDonnell explore?

Indeed, technology distributors and consumers are not comparable. Between an exclusive and elite object like the telephone in the first half of the twentieth century in France, the widespread distribution of public radio in Spain in the 1980s and the evolution of computing from mainframe to mini- to microcomputers over a rela-

---

[17] Haralanova, Kristina. 2010. *L'apport des femmes dans le développement du logiciel libre*. Master en communication. Montréal: Université du Québec. http://www.archipel.uqam.ca/3873/. Accessed 20 Mar 2015.

[18] Cavallo, Gugliemo, and Roger Chartier. 2001. *Histoire de la lecture dans le monde occidental*. Paris: Editions du Seuil. Chartier, Roger. 2003. *Pratiques de la lecture*. Paris: Payot.

[19] On *Elle* magazine, see Blandin, Claire. 2014. Les discours sur la sexualité dans la presse féminine: le tournant des années 1968. In *Sexualités*, ed. Etienne Armand Amato, Fred Pailler, and Valérie Schafer, 82–87. *Hermès* 69.

tively short period, technology users, like the contexts in which they operate, vary greatly.

But connecting these technologies is not purely rhetorical if we seek a long-term understanding of the relationship between gender and technology. As Simona De Iulio and Marion Dalibert show in their chapter comparing German and French children's magazines, these magazines assign artefacts and uses of different ICTs to illustrate the relationship to information and communication of preteen boys and girls, from listening to music to phone conversations. This relationship does not relate to a single technology but is located at the convergence of multiple sectors, including the mobile phone and the MP3 player.

Connecting the telegraph, the telephone and low-status labour in the computing field does not seem like such a stretch if we cross-analyse the primarily female-held occupations within those sectors, like telephone switchboard operators, punchcard operators and other repetitive functions that are considered menial. Women's position in communication tool production seems to be characterised by a placement on the periphery of power and decision-making, with few notable exceptions. Women hold a more central role in consumption. Dominique Pinsolle's description of the conflict between a famous actress and the *demoiselles du téléphone* illustrates the ambiguity of feminine subordination within networking and communications: the female early adopter versus the unskilled female labourer and the wealthy female consumer versus the young woman of modest background. Social roles diagonalise gender relationships without ever truly questioning them.

Of course, not all information and communication technologies are represented in this collection. It would certainly have been interesting to include an analysis of women's place in television's landscape and its construction. Their role in television's entry into the domestic space, particularly in France, as Claire Blandin highlighted for our conference, and the production of programmes 'specifically catering to female viewers', resulting in the soap genre first developed on the radio, would certainly have provided additional paths of analysis. That being said, television is widely studied (see, e.g. the work of the Centre for the Study of Women in Television and Film at San Diego State University), and it gave us a useful theoretical framework and set of 'confirmation data' for our working hypotheses on some less developed fields explored here.

In the same vein, video games might also have had a place in this reflection, especially since they are strongly represented in gender studies (see, e.g. *From Barbie to Mortal Kombat*[20]; and the works of Fanny Lignon, Jessica Soler-Benonie and many others), and gendered boundaries are sometimes pushed to the edge, nourishing fierce controversies like #gamergate, as noted by Karen Lee Ashcraft and Catherine Ashcraft.

Resolutely programmatic and conceived as an invitation to dialogue, this book intends to open spaces for discussion around the fields of communication and the spaces occupied by women, the feminine and gender, without pretence of exhaust-

---

[20] Cassell, Justine, and Henry Jenkins. 1998. *From Barbie to Mortal Kombat: gender and computer games*. Cambridge, MA: MIT Press.

ing the topic. It seeks less to set boundaries than to map out new areas for collective exploration. Thus, the role of gender and women in early online exchanges, beyond women's participation in the Internet and Web history, suggests promising material for historical study. In effect, entire sections of contemporary communications culture regarding women's relationship with technology, with communities of users, uses and popular culture, remain in the shadows and are almost virgin territory for historians.

To mention only one, consider the role of gender and women in telematics, which has not yet received extensive historical study despite the systematic use of women in sales strategies over the 1980s and 1990s. One must only recall the naked women plastered on every wall in France promoting the famous 'messageries roses' like Ulla and Aline – chat rooms that sometimes employed behind the screen men pretending to be women so as to keep their male clients online and paying for the connection time as long as possible.[21] On the Minitel already, 'nobody knows you're a dog'! Here was 'gender trouble' in the era of the first public networks.

The Minitel became a catalyst for the expression of multiple identities and desires and deeply influenced popular culture. Pop songs featured female protagonists that one could hope to encounter there. From Jean Ferrat's *Les petites filles Modèles* (Good Little Girls) to Noë Willer and to Michel Polnareff's *Goodbye Marylou* in 1990, they were the widely sung objects of desire:

'Et j'ai branché mon minitel J'ai choisi le bon code d'accès Style rendez-vous très personnel J'ai commencé à dialoguer {Refrain:} Et je t'appelle sur minitel Mais où est-elle sur minitel ?' Noë Willer, *SurMinitel*, 1986	'And I plugged in my minitel I chose the correct access code Like I had a personal rendezvous I started to speak {Refrain:} And I call you on the minitel But where is she on the minitel?' Noë Willer, *OnMinitel*, 1986
'Quand l'écran s'allume, je tape sur mon clavier Tous les mots sans voix qu'on se dit avec les doigts Et j'envoie dans la nuit Un message pour celle qui Me répondra OK pour un rendez-vous […]'. Michel Polnareff, *Goodbye Marylou*, 1990	'When the screen lights up, I type on my keyboard All the voiceless words that one says with fingers And I send in the night A message for she who Will respond OK for a rendezvous […]'. Michel Polnareff, *Goodbye Marylou*, 1990

These examples invite deepened reflection on female representations in popular culture, for example, in comic strips, as Sylvie Allouche examined during our 2014 symposium in her study of Yoko Tsuno, a character that holds her own alongside

---

[21] Like the French journalist Jean-Marc Manach, who revealed in June 2012: 'I was a host on the Minitel rose. […] I was even paid to do it' http://owni.fr/2012/06/28/jai-ete-animatrice-de-minitel-rose/. Accessed 2 February 2015.

television characters like Abby Sciuto (*NCIS*), Angela (*Bones*), Penelope Garcia (*Criminal Minds*), the multitalented investigator Kalinda Sharma (*The Good Wife*) or the fascinating Lisbeth Salander in the thriller trilogy *Millennium*.

Considering the case of the Minitel also encourages us to revisit domestic uses of this technology. As Jacques Perriault recalled during a workshop held on 28 June 2012 (the day before Transpac and the Télétel services closed) at the Institut des Sciences de la Communication (CNRS, Paris-Sorbonne, UPMC), women knitted decorative doilies to protect the device or place beneath that little beige box in 1980s design that was a symbol of modernity[22] and perhaps to ensure the positive introduction of this new technology into the home.

Of course, the early explosion of online services also raises questions about the female use of the Minitel. Josianne Jouët, a French sociologist who studied the use of telematics and early 'family microcomputers', recalls that from the first Minitel experiments of the early 1980s, it took ten years for the gap between male and female use rates to disappear.[23]

> [...] Overall, women began to distance themselves from Télétel, saying they got little or no use from it at first, then less and less. [...] In a competitive environment where correctly using Télétel is considered a demonstration of knowledge and competence, and the relationship to the machine can be a way of judging others, many women tend to devalue their own use by stating that others use it better than they do.[24]

In terms of female use, chat rooms dedicated to erotic encounters and exchanges have also been analysed by Josianne Jouët, who emphasised not only the ways in which some women have been able to turn them into tools of liberation, but also the point that women's relationship to technology cannot ignore in parallel the question of masculinity:

> In the post-68 era where some men felt a little destabilised by the advances in women's equality in society and by an ambient critique of machismo, they could, in many chat rooms, behave 'male', as 'guys'. And it became even more important for them that they greatly outnumbered women: in the *messageries roses*, the woman then became a rare and high-value figure who was courted by several men, who in turn were to confirm themselves as 'pouvant assurer' (able to perform well). For women, the *Minitelrose* was liberating because in contrast to a traditional romantic encounter, where the woman had to wait for the man to take the lead and the opposite would have been unseemly, on chat they could flirt with impunity. But in parallel, many women, including those flirting, presented themselves as sex objects on the Minitel: they took on all the traditional attributes of femininity, playing on their charm and calling for "viril" men. In short, we returned to the traditional canon of feminine and masculine seduction.[25]

[22] Schafer, Valérie, and Benjamin G. Thierry. 2012. *Le Minitel. L'enfance numérique de la France*. Paris: Nuvis.

[23] Jouët, Josianne. 2003. Technologies de communication et genre. Des relations en construction. *Réseaux* 120: 53–86.

[24] Mallein, P., Y. Toussaint, and M. Bydlowski. 1984. Teletel 3V, Les Adolescents et leur Famille. In *Rapport CPE, Centre d'Etude Prospective et d'Evaluation*. Paris: Ministère de la Recherche et de l'Industrie.

[25] Dakhlia, Jamil, and Géraldine Poels. 2012. Le minitel rose: du flirt électronique... et plus, si affinités. Entretien avec Josiane Jouët. *Le Temps des médias* 19: 221–228. doi: 10.3917/tdm.019.0221.

1.1.2 Entwining Temporalities

The long stretch of time covered in this book allows for the linkage of major technical systems over more than a century, e.g. the telegraph and the Web, which nevertheless share in common the attributes of immediacy and ubiquity while also manifesting the different stages of trade globalisation despite various technical, political, cultural, economic and social contexts.

In effect, these temporalities should also be entwined with societal rhythms, and it is not useful to spend too long here discussing the point to which women's access to employment, their return to work after marriage or childbirth, notions of youth developed by Simona De Iulio and Marion Dalibert, gendered relationships, consumption and purchasing power, communication practices, etc., have evolved.

Comparing in Chap. 4 the readers of *MarieClaire* in the 1940s to today's bloggers, Alexie Geers lays out dramatic changes in women's relationship to media and ICT, as well as to their body, sexuality and motherhood. She shows how women on the Web express themselves publicly about gynaecological and other intimate aspects of life, thereby allowing topics that had little exposure just a few decades ago, although women already discussed them in small private circles.

Dominique Pinsolle's study of telephony in the beginning of the twentieth century allows us to take stock of the changes that occurred over its course. Comtesse de Pange's vivid description in her memoir *Comment j'ai vu 1900* (How I saw 1900) puts our current hyperconnected state in striking contrast:

> It's hard to say what year we installed the phone at the house. I believe it was around 1896 or 1898. My parents made this sacrifice in the spirit of modernity in large part to remedy the remoteness and solitude of my sister who since her marriage to the Marquis de Luppé had lived in a beautiful mansion between a courtyard and a garden, solemn and sad at the end of the Rue Barbet de Jouy. We pitied her [...]. The device was placed in our home in a sitting room. It was made of rosewood and nailed to the wall. Its shape somewhat resembled the little toilet paper dispensers in the bathroom. Two speakers hung from hooks on each side and in the centre was a button you could press to connect with the central station. The ringing was shrill and could be heard throughout the house. But we did not run to the telephone. A servant was assigned to this task, picked up the earpiece, inquired what was wanted and went off to find the requested person.[26]

These technical, societal, political and economic temporalities should be considered when discussing a specific context. As noted by Simone Müller, starting out as a relatively gender-neutral form of employment, the position of telegraph clerk became gendered over the course of the late nineteenth century. The gendering of clerical positions changed yet again with the First World War and the shortage of male labour. The importance of the temporalities and contexts is also obvious in José Emilio Pérez Martínez's study on the free radio in the post-Franco period. Another is the diverse histories of computerisation across European countries, as described in *HackingEurope*[27] or in Chantal Morley and Martina Mc Donnell's

---

[26] de Pange, Pauline (comtesse). 2013. *Comment j'ai vu 1900*. Paris: Grasset.

[27] Alberts, Gerard, and Ruth Oldenziel (eds.). 2014. *Hacking Europe: from computer cultures to demoscenes*. London/Heidelberg/New York/Dordrecht: Springer.

chapter. Such diversity makes a comprehensive, unified European analysis challenging.

Relations between European countries have also evolved. Certainly, universalising goals, idea transfers and circulation and cross-border information sharing were initiated early, for example, with documentation sharing technology. Women's contributions to the Mundaneum initiative developed by Paul Otlet and Henri Lafontaine are particularly relevant here.[28] Alec Badenoch's work and the Women's Radio in Europe Network (WREN) researches tell of female (and sometimes feminist) radionetworks, as well as early transnational ICT cooperation, which has become transnational networks.[29] More generally, research on European technology by Ruth Oldenziel and Mikael Hård (2013),[30] Fickers et al. (2008),[31] Gerard Alberts et al. (2008)[32] and Frank Schipper and Johan Schot (2011),[33] while not all dealing with gender and women, illustrates beyond national specificities the importance of transnational issues, calling for European cross-analysis.

1.1.3 Mapping Europe

There is no more unity in the rate of ICT adoption across Europe than there exists a single political or organisational rule across the continent for addressing technological challenges. Diversity seems to be the rule. Thus, if we examine only the speed of technology penetration in companies and market rates, Europe proves to be a land of contrasts.[34]

---

[28] Levie, Françoise, and Benoît Peeters. 2006. L'homme qui voulait classer le monde: Paul Otlet et le Mundaneum. Bruxelles: Impressions Nouvelles. Rayward, Boyd W. 2010. Paul, Otlet, encyclopédiste, internationaliste belge. In Paul Otlet. Fondateur du Mundaneum (1868–1944). Architecte du savoir, artisan de paix. Liège: Les impressions Nouvelles.

[29] Ferree, Myra Marx, and Barbara Risman. 2001. Constructing global feminism: transnational advocacy networks and Russian women's activism. Signs: Journal of Women in Culture and Society 26(4): 1155–1186. Dufour, Pascale, Dominique Masson, and Dominique Caouette (eds.). 2010. Solidarities beyond borders: transnationalizing women's movements. Vancouver-Toronto: UBC Press.

[30] Oldenziel, R., and M. Hård. 2013. Consumers, tinkerers, rebels the people who shaped Europe. Basingstoke: Palgrave Macmillan.

[31] Fickers, Andreas et al. (2008). Transmitting and receiving Europe. The tensions of Europe/inventing Europe working papers series. http://www.tensionsofeurope.eu/www/en/publications/working-papers. Accessed 15 Mar 2015.

[32] Gerard Alberts et al. 2008. Software for Europe: constructing Europe through software. Tensions of Europe/inventing Europe working paper no. 2008_03. http://www.tensionsofeurope.eu/www/en/files/get/publications/2008_3.pdf. Accessed 15 Mar 2015.

[33] Schipper, Frank, and Johan Schot. 2011. Infrastructural Europeanism, or the project of building Europe on infrastructures: an introduction. History and Technology 27(3): 245–264.

[34] Bussière, Eric, Michel Dumoulin, and Sylvain Schirmann. 2008. Milieux économiques et intégration européenne au XXe siècle: La relance des années quatre-vingt (1979–1992). Paris: Comité pour l'Histoire économique et financière. Aubourg, Valérie, Gérard Bossuat, Eric Bussière, Lucia Coppolaro, et al. 2006. L'Europe et la mondialisation. Paris: Editions Soleb.

Corinna Schlombs notes that unlike the United States, where punchcard operator was a female profession, one thing in common with some European countries, in Germany this was not the case:

> In Germany, for example, Hollerith machines were located in separate rooms that were extremely noisy and dominated by heavy industry [...]. In such an environment, tabulating rooms became male-dominated technical dungeons, and punch-card operations turned into a male-only profession. A German insurance manager noted with evident surprise during a visit to the United States in the 1950s that women operated punch-card machines there.[35]

Nor is there uniformity in the media, as Simona De Iulio and Marion Dalibert show in their comparison of French and Germanpreteenmagazines.

We must therefore think of Europe as lacking generalisability. Eastern Europe during the Soviet era encountered different challenges than its Western neighbours in computer science,[36] even if the exchanges between the two regions are not to be underestimated, as Larissa Zakarova has shown (2010, 2012).[37] Some questions remain specific. At the LabEx EHNE 'Women, Gender and ICT' (WGICT) symposium, Ioana Cîrstocea described the Network of East-West Women (NEWW) created by a group of New York feminist activists to meet their 'Eastern European sisters' at the end of the Cold War and their 1994 launch of the 'On-Line Project' to supply them with equipment and Internet training. Karine Bergès evoked contemporary feminist uses of ICT by Spain's pro-choice movement's efforts to impact policy in 2013. However, beyond the societal and religious characteristics of the Spanish context, Karine Bergès described how the movement transcended borders with the #Alertafeminista hashtag, posting photos posing with hangers or knitting needles, symbols of illegal abortions, alongside the message 'Nunca Mas' or 'Never Again'.

Despite these challenges from Spain to Scandinavia, across France and various socio-technical fields, the authors present a first mapping of gendered relations that

---

[35] Schlombs, C. 2010. A gendered job carousel. In *Gender codes: why women are leaving computing?* ed. Thomas J. Misa, 75–94. Hoboken: Wiley/IEEE Computer Society.

[36] Durnova, Helena. 2009. Computers as messengers of freedom in Soviet bloc countries. *The Tensions of Europe/Inventing Europe working papers series.* http://www.tensionsofeurope.eu/www/en/publications/working-papers. Accessed 4 Apr 2015. Gerovich, Slava. 2008. InterNyet: why the Soviet Union did not build a nationwide computer network. *History and Technology* 24(4): 335–350. Jakić, Bruno. 2014. Galaxy and the new wave: Yugoslav computer culture in the 1980s. In *Hacking Europe. From computer cultures to demoscenes,* ed. Gerard Alberts and Ruth Oldenziel, 107–128. London/Heidelberg/New York/Dordrecht: Springer. Wasiak, Patryk. 2014. Playing and copying: social practices of home computer users in Poland during the 1980s. In *Hacking Europe. From computer cultures to demoscenes,* ed. Gerard Alberts and Ruth Oldenziel, 129–150. London/Heidelberg/New York/Dordrecht: Springer.

[37] Zakharova, Larissa. 2010. Competition or cooperation? Transfers of telephone and telegraph technologies from Europe to the USSR, 1918–1960s. *The tensions of Europe/inventing Europe working papers series.* http://www.tensionsofeurope.eu/www/en/publications/working-papers. Accessed 15 Mar 2015. Zakharova, Larissa. 2012. Téléphones et télégraphes au pays des Soviets. Vecteurs et procédés de circulation des techniques de communication en URSS (1918–1939). *Histoire Economie, Sociétés* 4: 75–90.

open new perspectives to consider the relationships between Europeans and technology.

1.1.4   Crossing Issues

To Europe's complexity is added that of gender and women. As Janet Abbate articulates in her introduction to *Recoding Gender*, 'The second pitfall is to equate studying gender with studying women, as if men and masculine culture were gender neutral'.[38]

Some of the chapters here focus on ICT female actors as collective figures. Certainly some individual historical figures emerge, like Hedy Lamarr, an Austrian actress and inventor who succeeded to invent an early technique for spread spectrum communications and frequency hopping presented by Nicola Hille at the WGICT conference, or Mary Agnes Hamilton, a distinguished intellectual and British radio personality who hosted the BBC's *The Week in Westminster* starting in 1929, a political programme intended for a female audience, as Audrey Vedel Bonnéry discussed at the LabEx EHNE symposium. But our authors focus primarily on the collective group. Groups include the women workers at the Rothamsted Statistics Department, women using, investing in or working for the telegraph network, the 'computer girls' and others. These groups' collective stories are cross-analysed with individual examples, like that of Brenda Watler and Vera Wiltsher in Giuditta Parolini's chapter, or with remarkable life stories like that of Dina Vaughan and Stephanie Shirley,[39] as Chantal Morley and Martina McDonnell remind us. The feminine trumps the female in this historical framework that, without laying claim to completeness, strives to achieve a comprehensive and thus a collective approach.

The second axis of the book is a reflection on gendered representations of ICT actors and audiences and their evolutions. Through preteenmagazines Simona De Iulio and Marion Dalibert show how these media can either be vectors of gender construction[40] or subvert representations through the use of fiction. It's a reminder that while the media can be a purveyor of stereotypes, it can also project a discourse of empowerment, and that it contains interstitial spaces where minority representation finds expression. Still, empowering discourse may also contain a certain amount of ambiguity, as demonstrated in the case of the ladybirds: 'As Corn (1979)[41] masterfully shows, ladybirds were deliberately used by airplane manufacturers, salesmen, and flight schools to shame men into flying with the explicit message: If *she*

---

[38] Abbate 2012: 5.

[39] Abbate 2012.

[40] Julliard, Virginie, and Nelly Quemener. 2014. Le genre dans la communication et les médias: enjeux et perspectives. *Revue française des sciences de l'information et de la communication*. 4. http://rfsic.revues.org/693. Accessed 12 Mar 2015.

[41] Corn, J.J. 1979. Making flying unthinkable: women pilots and the selling of aviation, 1927–1940. *American Quarterly* 31: 556–571.

can do it, flying must be easy and safe; these ships are so durable, almost any pilot (even the flightiest!) will do', Karen Lee Ashcraft and Catherine Ashcraft remind us in their chapter.

Our sensitivity to the issue of 'technological democracy' and stakeholders born in the Resendem project directed by Pascal Griset[42] led us to bring a close gaze to the groups involved in ICT that are traversed by questions of gender. While this axis and the others could each merit their own book, they do inform several papers. Dominique Pinsolle's work shows how, in the conflict between Ms. Sylviac and the *demoiselles du téléphone*, each party is exploited by consumers' and labourers' associations. Simone Müller reminds us that the Society of Civil Engineers applied strict gender directives at the end of the nineteenth century. Karen Lee Ashcraft and Catherine Ashcraft's research on the role of professional associations for ICT Practitioners and Commercial Aviators and Martina McDonnell and Chantal Morley's exploration of the phenomenon of old boys' clubs in Finland as taken up by Vehviläinen (1997, 1999)[43] shed light on the ambiguous role of professional associations and mediating groups that can negatively impact women's ambition. But these associations' role is not always discriminatory: Janet Abbate (2012)[44] recalls the 1974 election of Jean E. Sammet as the first female president of ACM, the 1984 election of Adele Goldberg as the first woman in the IEEE Computer Society, Martha Sloan as its first woman president and so on. Karen Lee Ashcraft and Catherine Ashcraft in their chapter also draw our attention to other forms of associations: 'The social identities of occupations can stem from their demographic alignment with certain groups of people, known as *physical* or *nominal* association, and/or from their ideational or emblematic alignment with particular embodied identities, known as *symbolic* or *ideological* association.[45] Physical association involves actual or usual practitioners, whereas symbolic association entails figurative practitioners'.

Finally, this book addresses how ICTs produce new spaces for gender expression, e.g. the *Hellocoton* platform studied by Alexie Geers, and the way feminist movements find a platform in the Spanish free radio that aspires towards 'giving voice to those who haven't had the opportunity to appear in the media' in José Emilio Pérez Martínez's chapter.

---

[42] The Resendem project's 'Les grands réseaux techniques en démocratie: innovation, usages et groupes impliqués dans la longue durée (fin du 19e – début du 21e siècle)' (Large technical networks in democracy: long-term implications for innovation, uses and groups, late nineteenth to early twenty-first century) was funded by the Agence Nationale de la Recherche (National Research Agency) (ANR-09-SSOC- 036-01) until 2014 (http://www.msha.fr/resendem/).

[43] Vehviläinen, Marja. 1997. Gender and expertise in retrospect: pioneers in computing in Finland. In *Women, work and computerisation: spinning a web from past To futur*, ed. Anna Frances Grundy et al., 435–448. Proceedings of the 6th international IFIP conference. London: Springer. Vehviläinen, Marja. 1999. Gender and computing in retrospect: the case of Finland. *IEEE Annals of the History of Computing* 21(2): 44–51.

[44] Abbate 2012.

[45] Britton, D.M. 2000. The epistemology of the gendered organization. *Gender and Society* 14: 418–434.

1.1.5 Diversifying Approaches, Sources and Scales

Distinct approaches and methodologies respond to these various if intermixed problems, depending on where they fall in social, economic, technical or cultural history, or if the subject falls within the rubrics of professionalisation, representations, media or/and computing.

Giuditta Parolini uses an approach based on the history of sciences and computing to address her topic, whereas Dominique Pinsolle anchors her approach in the history of media but also in the history of the telecommunications administration and the implicated groups. For their part, Karen Lee Ashcraft and Catherine Ashcraft work within the history of occupational identities, while Simone Müller uses a global approach to elucidate women's role in the telegraph (2014) at the intersection of the history of technology, innovation, business and gender. Simona De Iulio and Marion Dalibert cross an analysis of gender and age imagery with ICT uses as a way of examining media-on-media discourse, in this case the discourse of 'technologies of gender' on other 'technologies of gender'.

This diversity of approaches can also be seen in the sources, attesting to the wealth of possibilities that a historian has for examining the themes of gender and women: newspaper archives, archives of scientific research, institutional policies of national governments, oral histories, digital archives in the case of blogs or audio archives in the case of radio, etc.

This variety of sources and approaches also promotes diversity in the scale of research. We move from a British research centre specialising in agricultural research analysed by Giuditta Parolini to the national scale with Chantal Morley and Martina McDonnell, to some communities studied by Alexie Geers and José Emilio Pérez Martínez, to producers of information and representations in the work of Simona De Iulio and Marion Dalibert and to that of employees with Dominique Pinsolle and of female clerks and investors with Simone Müller. The figure of the receiver/consumer whose significance is discussed in the work of Margolis and Fisher (2001)[46] is also present, though not as acute. Finally, the approaches are at times national (Pinsolle), at others comparative (De Iulio and Dalibert, Morley and McDonnell). They reflect a diversity of historiographical approaches when it comes to thinking the European space. The potential remains to add wide transnational approaches and to work on an international approach that could include, for example, the study of international groups like the ACM-W and the Ad Hoc Committee for Women within Global Knowledge 97.

1.2 ConneXXions

The diverse contributions gathered for this book intersect several historiographical and epistemological fields and multiple methodologies. Those chapters nevertheless address the common question of the relationship between gender, women and

---

[46] Margolis and Fisher 2001.

technology and more broadly the theme of communications and the 'revolutions' it enables.[47] The chapters gradually connect, and multiple points of commonality can be identified.

1.2.1 'The Invisible Women'

The history of computing is marked by extraordinary women like Ada Lovelace, Grace Hooper, Margaret Hamilton, Frances Allen, Elizabeth Jake Feinler and Barbara Liskov. Beyond their exceptional careers and our society's fascination with the trajectories of great innovators, it is also important to recognise the trajectories of less famous men and women in the field.

Anglo-Saxon research provided valuable insights on the relative and progressive invisibility of women in computing, a topic that weaves through this collection. Certainly, this phenomenon reaches across the Atlantic and into research institutions, as in the British case that Giuditta Parolini analyses here, focusing on the Rothamsted Statistics Department while drawing on Steven Shapin's idea of 'invisible technicians', when she writes: 'Gender was not the main element that contributed to the invisibility of the female assistants in the Rothamsted statistics department. It was the lack of authority[48] to preside over scientific work that relegated these women to invisibility'. Giuditta Parolini also applies Janet Abbate's categories of labour and expertise and more broadly that of assistants and technicians in science.

We can connect her chapter and that of Chantal Morley and Martina McDonnell to Nathan Ensmenger's observation about the ENIACGirls, which pointed out that the 'hierarchical distinctions and gender connotations it embodies – between 'hard' technical mastery and the 'softer', more social (and implicitly, of secondary importance) aspects of computer work – are applicable even in the earliest of electronic computing development projects'.[49]

The way in which women are confined to tasks considered secondary and how they are seen as 'low-cost, high-turnover, relatively unskilled workers'[50] is found in Simone Müller's discussion of the telegraph analysing the female clerks. She notes that while women were used in domestic routes, female operators were not employed until the First World War on the 'much more complicated' ocean lines.

It is evident that a reflection on women's invisibility must relate back to the framework of subaltern studies, as well as that of occupational identities, as in the

---

[47] Griset, Pascal. 1991. *Les révolutions de la communication XIXe-XXe siècle*. Paris: Hachette Supérieur.

[48] Shapin, Steven. 1989. The invisible technician. *American Scientist* 77(6): 554–563.

[49] Ensmenger 2010a: 14.

[50] Hicks, Mary. 2010b. Only the clothes changed: women operators in British computing and advertising, 1950–1970. *IEEE Annals of the History of Computing* 32(4): 5–17.

research of Karen Lee Ashcraft (2013)[51] and her chapter with Catherine Ashcraft in this book, not to mention the works on gender division in labour.[52]

This invisibility constitutes a transversal link across many of our studies, especially since its counterpart, visibility, cannot be ignored, in the same way that a study of women's role cannot be separated from that of men. In Dominique Pinsolle's chapter, for example, Ms. Sylviac uses visibility to give weight to her position in her conflict with the French administration. Her supporters, for their part, immediately understand the value of media coverage of the conflict. Visibility also plays a role in the motivation of actors on the Spanish free radio to change the portrayal of women, as José Emilio Pérez Martínez notes:

> Its clear objective was to denounce the "frustrations produced by the monotonous voice sounding every evening [referring to the pre-existing female oriented radio programmes]". All the media have exploited women turning them into "a minor voice, a sweet and sensual sound", presenting them as "a sexual icon, stimulating male desires and always ready to serve them". These are the reasons why free radios are important as they allow to "listen to another kind of voice, non monotonous, non ritual, a voice that does not advertise, gives advice or talks about chastity".

1.2.2   The Question of Collectives and Empowerment

Another theme explored in this book is that of the collective group. Some collectives, like the *demoiselles du téléphone*, are already well documented.[53] Others, like the ENIACgirls,[54] typists and office workers[55] and gender patterns in the computerisation of the British civil service,[56] have been subject to extensive study. Several chapters explore professional groups and collective associations. Giuditta Parolini analyses the Rothamsted Statistics Department's human computers and keypunch

---

[51] Ashcraft, Karen Lee. 2013. The glass slipper: "incorporating" occupational identity in management studies. *Academy of Management Review* 38(1): 6–31.

[52] Downs, Laura Lee. 2002. *L'inégalité à la chaîne: La Division sexuée du travail dans l'industrie métallurgique en France et en Angleterre, 1914–1939*. Paris: Albin Michel.

[53] Delarue, Bernard. 1997. *Histoire d'une mutation: Des demoiselles du téléphone à la mondialisation des telecommunications*. Paris: Le Cherche Midi. Schwartz, Colette, Yveline Jacquet, and Pierre Lhomme. 2009. *Des demoiselles du téléphone aux opérateurs des centres d'appel*. Paris: Le Temps des Cerises.

[54] Light, Jennifer S. 2003. Programming. In *Gender and technology: a reader*, ed. Nina Lerman, Ruth Oldenziel Nina, and Arwen P. Mohun, 295–327. Baltimore: John Hopkins University Press. Ensmenger 2010a.

[55] Gardey, Delphine. 1999. The standardization of a technical practice: typing (1883–1930). *His Technol* 15: 313–343. Gardey, Delphine. 2004. *La Dactylographe et l'expéditionnaire: histoire des employés de bureau (1890–1930)*. Paris: Belin and Gardey, Delphine. 2008. *Écrire, calculer, classer. Comment une révolution de papier a transformé les sociétés contemporaines (1800–1940)*. Paris: La Découverte.

[56] Hicks, Mary. 2010a. Meritocracy and feminization in conflict: computerization in the British Government. In *Gender codes: why women are leaving computing?* ed. Thomas J. Misa, 95–114. Hoboken: Wiley/IEEE Computer Society.

operators; Chantal Morley and Martina McDonnell discuss IT associations, the French 'engineering corps' and the student groups studied by Isabelle Collet (2005)[57]; Catherine Ashcraft and Karen Lee Ashcraft's essay 'Breaking the "Glass Slipper": What Diversity Interventions Can Learn From the Historical Evolution of Occupational Identity in ICT and Commercial Aviation' focuses on a diachronic construction and gendered perception of two sectors (commercial aviation and ICT) from ladybirds to airline pilots and from computer girls to computer boys. Simona De Iulio and Marion Dalibert examine representations of preadolescence, a category with its foundations in marketing as much as in culture. Beyond their significance to this study, all these cases show a historiographical tendency towards working around collectives, corresponding to the end of an internalist historiography centred on the machine or the lonely innovator, accounting instead for surrounding social dimensions. We are also far from a compensatory history, engaging fully in the idea that to understand the relationship between gender, women and ICT, we must go beyond studying the major figures and truly face the part of the iceberg that has been submerged by the 'victors'.

The notion of empowerment also cuts across the contributions in this collection. It is made explicit in the work of José Emilio Pérez Martínez, since free radio became a tool for participation and struggle, and women's emancipation and action was explicitly radio based. We find a less spectacular form of gender identity and vocabulary appropriation in the work of Alexie Geers, which describes the process of moving from a prescribed to an assumed gender identity in women's blogs. We observe a desire to act economically, politically and socially in reading about female cable company's shareholders and women entrepreneurs like Dina Vaughan and Stephanie Shirley, who opened their own businesses in the UK. Janet Abbate, on the other hand, showed how the motivations can vary among actors and must be analysed individually. She pointed out that Stephanie Shirley runs her entrepreneurial adventure 'as a charity', while on the contrary, Dina Vaughan leads hers as a businesswoman.[58]

1.2.3 The 'Hidden History' of Women in Technology and the 'Hidden History' of Technology Through Women

In 'Making Programming Masculine', Nathan Ensmenger notes:

> The focus of most of this literature has been, understandably enough, on what Judy Wajcman, among others, has called the "hidden history" of women in technology. The goal was to explore what the history of women in computing had to say about women- about their contributions, experiences and abilities.
>
> This essay will address instead the flip side of this question: namely, what has the history of women in computing had to say about *computing*.[59]

---

[57] Collet, Isabelle. 2005. *La masculinisation des études d'informatique. Savoir, pouvoir et genre.* Thèse de doctorat en Sciences de l'Education, Université Paris X.

[58] Abbate 2012: 129.

[59] Ensmenger, N. 2010b. Making programming masculine. In *Gender codes: why women are leaving computing?* ed. Thomas J. Misa, 115–142. Hoboken: Wiley/IEEE Computer Society.

This approach is shared by several of our authors. As Giuditta Parolini notes in her conclusion: 'To the historian's gaze the female assistants in the Rothamsted statistics department cannot and should not remain invisible, unless we accept to perpetuate partial histories of the scientific enterprise that neglect the development of scientific practices in favour of theoretical achievements'. Dominique Pinsolle similarly uses the conflict between Miss Sylviac and the *demoiselles du téléphone* as much to show the history of women and their professionalisation as that of the telephone, since the case brings together questions of the telephone network management and the role of the phone user, who increasingly came to parallel a consumer.

By becoming a backdoor for allowing the exploration of socio-technological issues without using the usual routes, the figure of the woman becomes a new hermeneutics for objects that we may have presumed to know, revealing new facets.

This book's different contributions also show how the media is at once a tool, vector and vehicle for the expression and construction of gender identity. Whether it regards the magazines studied by Dominique Pinsolle, Alexie Geers, Simona De Iulio and Marion Dalibert or the uses of the radio, the relationship to media, its function and role is ambiguous and ever changing.

Of course, other media could have been called upon as well. Isabelle Collet's work (2006, 2011)[60] in particular provides an analysis on the construction of the figure of the geek and its impact. At the LabEx EHNE WGICT conference, Justine Marillonet presented a corpus of ISP advertisements, applying a semiotic analysis of representations and stereotypes of male–female relationships to the online world and noting that 'For women, the time to make hours of calls at a reduced price and the ease of a visit from a qualified technician to install their modem; for men, finding their wives in a compromised position with that technician, or surfing almost naturally on every screen in the house without limit'. But she also demonstrated the subversion of some of these stereotypes through humour.

The role of advertising was highlighted by Mary Hicks (2010b)[61] and Aristotle Tympas et al. in the case of Greece, based on a large corpus of 1500 advertisements, depicting women's and men's attitudes to computers and the relationship to computing those representations generated.[62] We find a similar approach in Simona De Iulio and Marion Dalibert's study, even if the target audience and technological objects differ. The point remains that, as William Vogel demonstrates in his paper 'Shifting Attitudes: Women in Computing, 1965–1985', media discourse evolves over time, but also with business trends: images, like politics, with regard to women's recruitment that were generated by Burroughs differed profoundly from that of control data in the 1960s.

---

[60] Collet 2006, 2011.

[61] Hicks 2010b.

[62] In Misa 2010: 187 and ss. See also Vogel, Wiliam F. 2014. Shifting attitudes: women in computing, 1965–1985. *SIGCIS workshop*. http://www.sigcis.org/files/Vogel.pdf. Accessed 16 Mar 2015.

1.2.4 The Role of Professionalisation and Occupational Identities

As Wendy Gagen's article 'The Manly Telegrapher: The fashioning of a Gendered Company Culture in the Eastern and Associated Telegraph Companies' (2013)[63] and Simone Müller's chapter attest, the question of women's role in ICT arises just as the first major telecommunications networks appear and runs along the course of the twentieth century.

Furthermore, the parallel in occupational identities that Catherine Ashcraft and Karen Lee Ashcraft show in the fields of aviation and ICT leads us to reflect more broadly on the relationships between women, technology and professionalism. While at first glance the two fields may appear unrelated, upon fuller inspection their diachronic cases are shown to be mutually relevant. We find the phenomenon of a profession's masculinisation parallel to its institutionalisation, as Nathan Ensmenger also wrote:

> Perhaps most significantly, professionalization requires segmentation and stratification. In order to elevate the overall status of their discipline, aspiring professionals had to distance themselves from those aspects of their work that were seen as low-status and routine. This work did not just disappear – it was just done by other people.[64]

We also find in the Finnish case a tendency that Tom Haigh noted in 'Masculinity and the Machine Man' of professional associations like the Data Processing Management Association to voluntarily disassociate with the female professional world to enhance their professional status: '[…] the push to position business computing as men's work occurred because of, not despite, the presence of women in the field'.[65] The phenomena of the glass ceiling and shrinking pipeline are common to many countries. But complete generalisation is impossible, as already shown by the seminal work edited by Canel et al. (2005).[66] For example, Janet Abbate has described how Stephanie Shirley's company tried to solve the problem of motherhood and the social status of mothers of young children in Britain by employing part-time mothers as work-from-home freelancers.[67] But this model was not as easily exported to Denmark, where childcare was more developed.

---

[63] Gagen, Wendy. 2013. The manly telegrapher: the fashioning of a gendered company culture in the eastern and associated telegraph companies. In *Global communication electric: actors of a globalizing world*, ed. Michaela Hampf and Simone Müller-Pohl, 170–195. Frankfurt: Campus Verlag. Hampf, Michaela, and Simone Müller-Pohl (eds.). 2013. *Global communication electric. Business, news and politics in the world of telegraphy*. Frankfort: Campus Verlag.

[64] Ensmenger 2010a: 135.

[65] Haigh in Misa 2010: 52.

[66] Canel, Annie, Ruth Oldenziel, and Karin Zachmann (eds.). 2005. *Crossing boundaries, building bridges. Comparing the history of women engineers 1870s–1990s*. London: Routledge.

[67] Abbate 2012: 135.

1.2.5 Gender/Technologies Co-construction and Intersectionality

Finally, we would like to emphasise that the approaches in this book are based on the idea of a co-construction of gender and ICT. Technology and gender are constantly conceived in interrelation, so as to understand how they form one another through language, cultural and historical processes, representations and discursive constructs,[68] as evidenced, for example, in Marion Dalibert and Simona De Iulio's cross-analysis of ICTs, gender and youth. Karen Lee Ashcraft and Catherine Ashcraft remind us that occupational identity is defined as "an evolving, co-constructed answer to two questions revolved in relation to one another: 'What is this line of work (e.g., accoun*ting*), and who does it (e.g., accoun*tants*)?'".[69]

This interest in understanding the co-construction of gender and ICTs that runs through this book also leads us to consider forms of intersectionality and particularly questions of low-status jobs, 'class conflict' and social status. These are present, for example, in the conflict between Ms. Sylviac and the *demoiselles du telephone* and in Simone Müller's chapter, analysing telegraphy at the intersection of gender and class. The status of science, of age, of power relationships and of expertise that pass through the scientific world are as much a presence here as gender.

It remains to be said that politics receives little explicit mention: it would be appropriate to understand why it is so little represented with regard to the economic, social, cultural and technological aspects under discussion. A few mentions of the telecommunications administration, of equal pay policies and of strategic investment in computer industry reflect the fact that the state is not completely absent from the regulation of gendered relations, but little analysis refers to it explicitly. Is this a sign of its peripheral and marginal action, of its indifference or its laissez-faire approach? Or more likely, does this reflect its tenuous but real presence, which occurs not only through 'politics' but also specific 'policies', like the diversity interventions in ICT professions evoked by Karen Lee Ashcraft and Catherine Ashcraft?

Delphine Gardey, to whom this work's conclusion returns, underlines by referring to Hoskyns (2005)[70]

> the importance of wondering "how politically active is a space." These are elements for analysis when the transition is made, for example, from the socio-technical infrastructure of the "pool" to that of the "open-plan office" to the more recent "cybertariat". Such issues as control, power, agency, empowerment and domination, seem to remain underrepresented in the investigation of the more contemporary forms of organization of the technical and cognitive space of information processing. However, one can hardly study these transforma-

---

[68] Jouët 2003; Ashcraft, Karen Lee. 2007. Appreciating the "work" of discourse: occupational identity and difference as organizing mechanisms in the case of commercial airline pilots. *Discourse & Communication* 1: 9–36.

[69] Ashcraft 2013: 15, original emphasis.

[70] Hoskyns, Teresa. 2005. Designing the Agon: questions on architecture, space, democracy and "the political". In *Making things public: atmospheres of democracy*, ed. Bruno Latour and Peter Weibel, 798–803. Cambridge/Karlsruhe: MIT Press/ZKM Center for Art and Media.

tions without considering the distribution of agency and control among humans and non-humans, among social groups, among men and women, and local and outsourced workers

Such questions are further incentive to pursue cross-analytical research on gender, women and ICT on both sides of the Atlantic.

References

Abbate, J. 2012. *Recoding gender: women's changing participation in computing.* Cambridge, MA: The MIT Press.

Alberts, Gerard, and Ruth Oldenziel (eds.). 2014. *Hacking Europe: from computer cultures to demoscenes.* London/Heidelberg/New York/Dordrecht: Springer.

Alberts, Gerard et al. 2008. Software for Europe: constructing Europe through software. *Tensions of Europe/inventing Europe working paper no. 2008_03.* http://www.tensionsofeurope.eu/www/en/files/get/publications/2008_3.pdf. Accessed 15 Mar 2015.

Ashcraft, Karen Lee. 2007. Appreciating the "work" of discourse: occupational identity and difference as organizing mechanisms in the case of commercial airline pilots. *Discourse & Communication* 1: 9–36.

Ashcraft, Karen Lee. 2013. The glass slipper: "incorporating" occupational identity in management studies. *Academy of Management Review* 38(1): 6–31.

Ashcraft, Catherine. 2014. *Increasing the participation of women and underrepresented minorities in computing: missing perspectives and new directions.* Orlando: National Science Foundation Computer Science Education Summit.

Aubourg, Valérie, Gérard Bossuat, Eric Bussière, Lucia Coppolaro, et al. 2006. *L'Europe et la mondialisation.* Paris: Editions Soleb.

Blandin, Claire. 2014. Les discours sur la sexualité dans la presse féminine: le tournant des années 1968. In *Sexualités*, ed. Etienne Armand Amato, Fred Pailler, and Valérie Schafer, 82–87. *Hermès* 69.

Bourdeloie, Hélène, and Virginie Julliard. 2013. La question du genre et des TNIC au prisme du dialogue de la sociologie et de la sémiotique. *Episteme* 9: 243–270.

Britton, D.M. 2000. The epistemology of the gendered organization. *Gender and Society* 14: 418–434.

Burman, Annie. 2013. *Gendering decryption – decrypting gender: the gender discourse of labour at Bletchley Park 1939–1945.* MA thesis, Uppsala University.

Bussière, Eric, Michel Dumoulin, and Sylvain Schirmann. 2008. *Milieux économiques et intégration européenne au XXe siècle: La relance des années quatre-vingt (1979–1992).* Paris: Comité pour l'Histoire économique et financière.

Canel, Annie, Ruth Oldenziel, and Karin Zachmann (eds.). 2005. *Crossing boundaries, building bridges. Comparing the history of women engineers 1870s–1990s.* London: Routledge.

Cassell, Justine, and Henry Jenkins. 1998. *From Barbie to Mortal Kombat: gender and computer games.* Cambridge, MA: MIT Press.

Cavallo, Gugliemo, and Roger Chartier. 2001. *Histoire de la lecture dans le monde occidental.* Paris: Editions du Seuil.

Chartier, Roger. 2003. *Pratiques de la lecture.* Paris: Payot.

Cohoon, Joanne, and William Aspray (eds.). 2006. *Women and information technology: research on under-representation.* Cambridge, MA: MIT Press.

Collet, Isabelle. 2005. *La masculinisation des études d'informatique. Savoir, pouvoir et genre.* Thèse de doctorat en Sciences de l'Education, Université Paris X.

Collet, Isabelle. 2006. *L'informatique a-t-elle un sexe? Hackers, mythes et réalités.* Paris: L'Harmattan.

Collet, Isabelle. 2011. Effet de genre: le paradoxe des études d'informatique. *tic&société* 5: 1. http://ticetsociete.revues.org/955. Accessed 14 Mar 2015.

Corn, J.J. 1979. Making flying unthinkable: women pilots and the selling of aviation, 1927–1940. *American Quarterly* 31: 556–571.

Dakhlia, Jamil, and Géraldine Poels. 2012. Le minitel rose: du flirt électronique… et plus, si affinités. Entretien avec Josiane Jouët. *Le Temps des médias* 19: 221–228. doi:10.3917/tdm.019.0221.

de Pange, Pauline (comtesse). 2013. *Comment j'ai vu 1900*. Paris: Grasset.

Delarue, Bernard. 1997. *Histoire d'une mutation: Des demoiselles du téléphone à la mondialisation des telecommunications*. Paris: Le Cherche Midi.

Downs, Laura Lee. 2002. *L'inégalité à la chaîne: La Division sexuée du travail dans l'industrie métallurgique en France et en Angleterre, 1914–1939*. Paris: Albin Michel.

Dufour, Pascale, Dominique Masson, and Dominique Caouette (eds.). 2010. *Solidarities beyond borders: transnationalizing women's movements*. Vancouver-Toronto: UBC Press.

Durnova, Helena. 2009. Computers as messengers of freedom in Soviet bloc countries. *The Tensions of Europe/Inventing Europe working papers series*. http://www.tensionsofeurope.eu/www/en/publications/working-papers. Accessed 4 Apr 2015.

Ensmenger, Nathan. 2010a. *The computer boys take over: computers, programmers and the politics of technical expertise*. Cambridge, MA: MIT Press.

Ensmenger, N. 2010b. Making programming masculine. In *Gender codes: why women are leaving computing?* ed. Thomas J. Misa, 115–142. Hoboken: Wiley/IEEE Computer Society.

Ferree, Myra Marx, and Barbara Risman. 2001. Constructing global feminism: transnational advocacy networks and Russian women's activism. *Signs: Journal of Women in Culture and Society* 26(4): 1155–1186.

Fickers, Andreas et al. 2008. Transmitting and receiving Europe. The tensions of Europe/inventing Europe working papers series. http://www.tensionsofeurope.eu/www/en/publications/working-papers. Accessed 15 Mar 2015.

Gagen, Wendy. 2013. The manly telegrapher: the fashioning of a gendered company culture in the eastern and associated telegraph companies. In *Global communication electric: actors of a globalizing world*, ed. Michaela Hampf and Simone Müller-Pohl, 170–195. Frankfurt: Campus Verlag.

Gardey, Delphine. 1999. The standardization of a technical practice: typing (1883–1930). *His Technol* 15: 313–343.

Gardey, Delphine. 2004. *La Dactylographe et l'expéditionnaire: histoire des employés de bureau (1890–1930)*. Paris: Belin.

Gardey, Delphine. 2008. *Écrire, calculer, classer. Comment une révolution de papier a transformé les sociétés contemporaines (1800–1940)*. Paris: La Découverte.

Gerovich, Slava. 2008. InterNyet: why the Soviet Union did not build a nationwide computer network. *History and Technology* 24(4): 335–350.

Griset, Pascal. 1991. *Les révolutions de la communication XIXe-XXe siècle*. Paris: Hachette Supérieur.

Gürer, Denise, and Tracy Camp. 2002. An ACM-W literature review on women in computing. *SIGCSE Bulletin* 34(2): 121–127.

Haigh, T. 2010. Masculinity and the machine man. In *Gender codes: why women are leaving computing?* ed. Thomas J. Misa, 51–71. Hoboken: Wiley/IEEE Computer Society.

Hampf, Michaela, and Simone Müller-Pohl (eds.). 2013. *Global communication electric. Business, news and politics in the world of telegraphy*. Frankfort: Campus Verlag.

Haralanova, Kristina. 2010. *L'apport des femmes dans le développement du logiciel libre*. Master en communication. Montréal: Université du Québec. http://www.archipel.uqam.ca/3873/. Accessed 20 Mar 2015.

Hicks, Mary. 2010a. Meritocracy and feminization in conflict: computerization in the British Government. In *Gender codes: why women are leaving computing?* ed. Thomas J. Misa, 95–114. Hoboken: Wiley/IEEE Computer Society.

Hicks, Mary. 2010b. Only the clothes changed: women operators in British computing and advertising, 1950–1970. *IEEE Annals of the History of Computing* 32(4): 5–17.

Hoskyns, Teresa. 2005. Designing the Agon: questions on architecture, space, democracy and "the political". In *Making things public: atmospheres of democracy*, ed. Bruno Latour and Peter Weibel, 798–803. Cambridge/Karlsruhe: MIT Press/ZKM Center for Art and Media.

Jakić, Bruno. 2014. Galaxy and the new wave: Yugoslav computer culture in the 1980s. In *Hacking Europe. From computer cultures to demoscenes*, ed. Gerard Alberts and Ruth Oldenziel, 107–128. London/Heidelberg/New York/Dordrecht: Springer.

Jouët, Josianne. 2003. Technologies de communication et genre. Des relations en construction. *Réseaux* 120: 53–86.

Julliard, Virginie, and Nelly Quemener. 2014. Le genre dans la communication et les médias: enjeux et perspectives. *Revue française des sciences de l'information et de la communication.* 4. http://rfsic.revues.org/693. Accessed 12 Mar 2015.

Lerman, N., R.O. Nina, and A.P. Mohun (eds.). 2003. *Gender and technology: a reader.* Baltimore: John Hopkins University Press.

Levie, Françoise, and Benoît Peeters. 2006. *L'homme qui voulait classer le monde: Paul Otlet et le Mundaneum.* Bruxelles: Impressions Nouvelles.

Light, Jennifer S. 1999. When computers were women. *Technology and Culture* 40(3): 455–483.

Light, Jennifer S. 2003. Programming. In *Gender and technology: a reader*, ed. Nina Lerman, Ruth Oldenziel Nina, and Arwen P. Mohun, 295–327. Baltimore: John Hopkins University Press.

Mallein, P., Y. Toussaint, and M. Bydlowski. 1984. Teletel 3V, Les Adolescents et leur Famille. In *Rapport CPE, Centre d'Etude Prospective et d'Evaluation.* Paris: Ministère de la Recherche et de l'Industrie.

Margolis, Jane, and Allan Fisher. 2001. *Unlocking the clubhouse.* Cambridge, MA: MIT Press.

McMillan, R. 2014. *Feminist Hacker Barbie is just what our little girls need.* Wired. 21 Nov 2014.

Misa, Thomas J. (ed.). 2010. *Gender codes: why women are leaving computing?* Hoboken: Wiley/IEEE Computer Society.

Oldenziel, R., and M. Hård. 2013. *Consumers, tinkerers, rebels the people who shaped Europe.* Basingstoke: Palgrave Macmillan.

Rayward, Boyd W. 2010. Paul, Otlet, encyclopédiste, internationaliste belge. In *Paul Otlet. Fondateur du Mundaneum (1868–1944). Architecte du savoir, artisan de paix.* Liège: Les impressions Nouvelles.

Schafer, Valérie, and Benjamin G. Thierry. 2012. *Le Minitel. L'enfance numérique de la France.* Paris: Nuvis.

Schipper, Frank, and Johan Schot. 2011. Infrastructural Europeanism, or the project of building Europe on infrastructures: an introduction. *History and Technology* 27(3): 245–264.

Schlombs, C. 2010. A gendered job carousel. In *Gender codes: why women are leaving computing?* ed. Thomas J. Misa, 75–94. Hoboken: Wiley/IEEE Computer Society.

Schwartz, Colette, Yveline Jacquet, and Pierre Lhomme. 2009. *Des demoiselles du téléphone aux opérateurs des centres d'appel.* Paris: Le Temps des Cerises.

Shapin, Steven. 1989. The invisible technician. *American Scientist* 77(6): 554–563.

Vehviläinen, Marja. 1997. Gender and expertise in retrospect: pioneers in computing in Finland. In *Women, work and computerisation: spinning a web from past To futur*, ed. Anna Frances Grundy et al., 435–448. Proceedings of the 6th international IFIP conference. London: Springer.

Vehviläinen, Marja. 1999. Gender and computing in retrospect: the case of Finland. *IEEE Annals of the History of Computing* 21(2): 44–51.

Vogel, Wiliam F. 2014. Shifting attitudes: women in computing, 1965–1985. *SIGCIS workshop.* http://www.sigcis.org/files/Vogel.pdf. Accessed 16 Mar 2015.

Wasiak, Patryk. 2014. Playing and copying: social practices of home computer users in Poland during the 1980s. In *Hacking Europe. From computer cultures to demoscenes*, ed. Gerard Alberts and Ruth Oldenziel, 129–150. London/Heidelberg/New York/Dordrecht: Springer.

Zakharova, Larissa. 2010. Competition or cooperation? Transfers of telephone and telegraph technologies from Europe to the USSR, 1918–1960s. *The tensions of Europe/inventing Europe working papers series.* http://www.tensionsofeurope.eu/www/en/publications/working-papers. Accessed 15 Mar 2015.

Zakharova, Larissa. 2012. Téléphones et télégraphes au pays des Soviets. Vecteurs et procédés de circulation des techniques de communication en URSS (1918–1939). *Histoire Economie, Sociétés* 4: 75–90.

Part I
Networks and Empowerment. Introductory Remarks

Delphine Diaz and Régis Schlagdenhauffen

The first part of the book shows how networks were gendered and how gendered networks were formed around information and communication technology since the late nineteenth century, focusing on three media: the telegraph, the press and the radio. The contributions by Simone Müller, José Emilio Pérez Martínez and Alexie Geers address how women appropriated certain forms of media and communications, and how the telegraph, the press and the radio allowed women to strengthen their demands for equality and emancipation. This wide-ranging and long-term discussion on the evolution of women's societal position allows us to see how, contrary to the common belief, women played a significant role in the development of the telegraph as a modern means of communication at the end of the nineteenth century. This can be understood in the light of the emerging figure of the 'New Woman' and of the strategic choices that some women made to financially support the development of the telegraph (including its transatlantic iteration) as a new form of communication. On the other hand, women's press is analysed, particularly the French magazine *Marie-Claire*, along with the feminine exchange networks they engendered with their manifold uses. An analysis of women's networking allows the discussion to transcend the superficiality that often enshrouds perceptions of such magazines. The readers' networks that they formed – whose different modalities we observe up until the emergence of 'readers blogs' – thereby contributed to creating and transforming a positive feminine identity based on the transmission and sharing of models. The contributions highlight the gendered norms that were also

D. Diaz (✉)
Laboratoire CERHiC EA 2616, Université de Reims Champagne-Ardenne,
57 rue Pierre Taittinger, 51096 Reims, France
e-mail: delphinediaz@gmail.com

R. Schlagdenhauffen
Université de Lorraine, Nancy, France
e-mail: regis.schlag@gmail.com

transcended through women's free radio programmes created in European countries, in particular in Spain. In countries where there was resistance against forms of oppression (including authoritarian regimes in Southern Europe), these free radio programmes contributed to the creation of feminine and feminist European networks whose continuations are discussed in the second and third part of the book.

Chapter 2
Telegraphy and the "New Woman" in Late-Nineteenth-Century Europe

Simone M. Müller

Abstract This article explores the history of telegraphy in the late nineteenth century at the intersection of class and gender. It brings together approaches from social history and the history of finance with communication studies. The article demonstrates that our understanding of telegraphy as a *masculine* undertaking in terms of science, technology, and technology-in-use needs to be expanded. Contemporary discourses of telegraphy included practices of exclusion for the woman engineer and the female telegraph user based on constructions of *femininity* as "the other." Yet, telegraphy also afforded women new avenues of independence, which resulted in an expansion of the domestic sphere. Middle-class women in particular used the opportunities telegraphy offered as a means for employment as a female telegraph clerk or investment in telegraph shares. At the end of the nineteenth century, telegraphy thus helped the "new woman" carve out a new social geography for herself.

In 1877, a story of a British lieutenant in India and his "telegraphic wedding" was making the rounds in newspapers across the British Empire. Mocking both the new technology of the telegraph and women's inability to deal with it, the story was "too good to be lost," according to the *Belfast News-Letter*.[1] The young lieutenant was on sick leave and had taken up residence at a hotel not far from Poonah where he was stationed. There he was "immediately smitten" by a young lady to whom he proposed within merely a couple of days after first meeting. The lieutenant's colonel, who also happened to be a friend of the young man's father, was eager to halt the imminent marriage. He sent a telegram with the wording "join at once." While the young soldier was devastated upon the receipt of the telegram, as he understood it to mean that he was to return at once to his regiment and halt his wedding plans, his young fiancée interpreted the telegraphic message differently. "With a blush of maiden simplicity and virgin innocence," she saw the telegram as a sign of the

---

[1] The Lady and the Telegraph, *Belfast News-Letter*, November 30, 1877.

S.M. Müller (✉)
Department of History, University of Freiburg, Freiburg, Germany

Albert-Ludwigs-University, Rempartstraße 15, KG IV, 79085 Freiburg, Germany
e-mail: simone.mueller@geschichte.uni-freiburg.de

V. Schafer, B.G. Thierry (eds.), *Connecting Women*, History of Computing,
DOI 10.1007/978-3-319-20837-4_2

colonel's approval of their match. According to the young lady, the colonel's telegram could only mean that they should get married immediately. Joyfully, also the lieutenant jumped upon this interpretation of the telegraphic conundrum. Within 48 h, the colonel received the reply: "Your orders are obeyed. We were joined at once" (The Lady and the Telegraph, *Belfast News-Letter*, November 30, 1877).

This anecdote, which newspapers passed on to each other from India to England to Ireland in late 1877, perfectly illustrates contemporaries' gendered view on telegraphy. Not only did this story invoke the well-known warning of women luring suitable young men into marriage for the newspaper's primarily male readers. It also entailed a story of successful male and dysfunctional female conversation via telegraph. While both male protagonists in this story immediately understand the telegram's phrasing, it is the female in the story that distorts its content. Moreover, it is her intellectual ineptitude, her mental "simplicity" and female "innocence" which lead her to misunderstand the telegraphic message typical for short, instructional, and *masculine* modes of conversation.[2] Within the dichotomy of feminine nature and masculine science, the article's author not only aligned successful telegraphic conversation with inalienable masculine traits but also applied biological determinism to this communications technology. By mere existence as woman, the lady in the story could simply not relate to telegraphy in any other, *understanding* or *mastering* or *knowledgeable* way.

Contemporaries viewed – and scholars today still view – telegraphy, and in particular submarine telegraphy, as an inherently masculine communications technology: invention, technology, and technology-in-use were primarily shaped by and through men. Men, such as Charles Bright, Cyrus Field, and John Pender, feature as the "heroic" inventor or telegraph entrepreneur, and primarily male characters populate the narratives on telegraph engineering as well as telegraph cable management.[3] Throughout telegraphic history, women, in turn, are more often than not merely objectified. They are cast as the muse and inspiration in an entangled story between invention and inventor, as in the case of Samuel Morse and the telegraph or Alexander Graham Bell and the telephone.[4] Alternatively, they are the objects of ridicule in contemporary male narratives of telegraphy as technology-in-use when women fail to master masculine modes of business conversation, as illustrated by the above anecdote.

Such constructions of telegraphy as a primarily masculine technology did, however, not necessarily reflect reality – in particular when we look at telegraphic history through an intersectional lens of gender *and class*.[5] In fact, the relationship

[2] Idem.

[3] Latham, Jean L., and Victor Mays. 1958. *Young man in a hurry: the story of Cyrus W. Field*. New York: Harper; Bright, Charles. 1908. *The life story of sir Charles Tilston Bright civil engineer: with which is incorporated the story of the Atlantic cable, and the first telegraph to India and the colonies*. London: Archibald Constable; Cookson, Gillian. 2003. *The cable: the wire that changed the world*. Strout: Tempus publishing; Appleyard, Rollo. 1939. *The history of the institution of electrical engineers (1871–1931)*. London: The Institution of Electrical Engineers.

[4] Staiti, Paul J., and S.F.B. Morse. 1989. *Samuel F.B. Morse*. Cambridge, NY: Cambridge University Press; Mackay, James A. 1997. *Alexander Graham Bell: a life*. New York: J. Wiley.

[5] On intersectionality, see Berger, Michelle T., and Kathleen Guidroz. 2010. *The intersectional approach: transforming the academy through race, class, and gender*. Chapel Hill: University of North Carolina Press and Chow, E.N., M.T. Segal, T. Lin, and V.P. Demos. 2011. *Analyzing gender, intersectionality, and multiple inequalities: global, transnational and local contexts*. Bingley: Emerald.

between telegraphy and gender was performed differently in various sections of the nineteenth-century Victorian society.[6] The female in the introductory story, for instance, is identified as "a lady" enjoying the company of a "lieutenant." Hereby, contemporary readers could place her – despite the fact that the colonel deemed her not quite suitable – in a particular Victorian social setting of at least upper-middle class. Gendered dimensions of telegraphy, and with it the narrative of female estrangement, change, however, if we expand our view further into the middle class. For educated middle-class women, in particular, telegraphy offered new venues of emancipatory selfhood as it was put forward by the "new woman" of the late nineteenth century. At the *fin de siècle*, women, such as George Eliot, sought to break with traditional gender stereotypes restricting them solely to inhabit the domestic sphere. Feminists of the early twentieth century later considered the new woman as a form of proto-feminism.[7] Seeking female independence from their male counterparts in economic matters, telegraphy represented a means of employment as a female telegraph clerk as well as of investment in the form of telegraph shares for women. Both secured them with a reliable income of their own. As Thomas Jepsen points out for the USA, women played an important role in the telegraph industry from the 1840s onward.[8] In contrast to their male counterparts, however, there exist few corresponding stories about women. Although women telegraphers were commonplace in the nineteenth century, there is little history to them. Rather, they were consequently written out of telegraphic history.[9]

The strictly gender-separated narrative further changes when we look at telegraphy as a means of finance and investment within the emerging modern capitalist economy. Only recently, scholars have increasingly recognized women's economic influence and in particular their investment activities during the first age of globalization. Female capital played an important role in financing global capitalism, and women were active as investors in utility and transport companies such as gasworks, waterworks, railroads, and tramways.[10] The analysis of telegraph companies' shareholder lists reveals that almost half of the companies' stocks were typically owned by women. Since stocks were considered a risky investment, this gives lie to the widespread assumption that female investors were generally risk averse. For middle-class women who chose to or had to support themselves, telegraphy provided an avenue for financial independence and was therefore part of their living experience.

---

[6] On gender as performance, see Jagger, Gill. 2008. *Judith Butler: sexual politics, social change and the power of the performative*. London: Routledge.

[7] Ledger, Sally. 1997. *The new woman: fiction and feminism at the fin de siècle*. Manchester: Manchester University Press; Richardson, Angelique, and Chris Willis. 2002. *The new woman in fiction and fact: Fin-de-siècle feminisms*. Basingstoke/Hampshire/New York: Palgrave.

[8] Jepsen, Thomas C. 2000. *My sisters telegraphic: women in the telegraph office, 1846–1950*. Athens: Ohio University Press.

[9] Jepsen 2000: 2.

[10] Beachy, Robert, Béatrice Craig, and Alastair Owens (eds.). 2006. *Women, business, and finance in nineteenth-century Europe: rethinking separate spheres*. Oxford: Berg Publishers; Deere, Carmen D., and Cheryl R. Doss. 2006. A special issue on women and wealth. *Feminist Economics* 12: 1–2.

This chapter aims at restoring female agency to the history of telegraphy by bringing together social history and economic history with a history of communications. By applying the concept of intersectionality in terms of gender and class, this article will shed light on the engagement of primarily educated middle-class women with telegraphy as a means of investment as well as employment. In terms of a social history of telegraphy, this paper will show differences in discourse and lived experience with telegraphy regarding the social status of women in the late nineteenth century. With respect to a financial history of telegraphy, this article builds on recent economic scholarship, which challenges the separate spheres model, that is the ideology dictating a separation of a female domestic and a male public sphere based on "natural" gender roles. This paper further adds to the emerging picture of the active female investor, who was, moreover, not necessarily risk averse.[11]

In the first part, this paper looks at gendered views on telegraphy and contemporaries' construction of telegraphy as a masculine undertaking in terms of science, technology, and technology-in-use. It shows how in contemporary discourse women are merely objectified as the inventor's muse or object of male ridicule in terms of ill-functioning telegraphic communication. In the second part, the paper moves on to analyze telegraphy at the intersection of gender and class, focusing first on the female telegraph clerk and second on the female investor. Contrasting as well as coalescing existing biological deterministic constructions of telegraphy as distinctly *masculine*, this section adds another layer, namely, class, to this highly gendered narrative. It reveals that as the new (middle-class) women were carving out spaces of their own in the late nineteenth century, telegraphy played an important role in that process.

2.1 From the Telegrapher's Muse to Female Telegraphic "Bow Wow"

The emergence of telegraphy, submarine as well as terrestrial, as a means of communication brought about pervasive changes in the mid-nineteenth century. This new possibility to converse at "telegraphic speed" throughout a network with worldwide reach allowed for the development of globalization processes which scholars generally subsume under the emergence of world commerce, world politics, and a "global" public.[12] After Samuel Morse in the USA and Charles Wheatstone and William Cooke in Great Britain conducted successful experiments with transmitting

---

[11] Doe, Helen. 2010. Waiting for her ship to come in? The female investor in nineteenth-century sailing vessels. *The Economic History Review* 63(1): 85–106.

[12] North, Michael (ed.). 1995. *Kommunikationsrevolutionen: Die neuen Medien des 16. und 19. Jahrhunderts*. Köln: Böhlau; Osterhammel, Jürgen, and Niels P. Petersson. 2007. *Geschichte der Globalisierung: Dimensionen, Prozesse, Epochen*. München: C. H. Beck Wissen; Müller-Pohl, Simone. 2010. 'By Atlantic Telegraph': a study on Weltcommunication in the 19th century. *Medien & Zeit* 4: 40–54.

electrical signals over wire in the 1830s, the first terrestrial telegraph lines were laid throughout the world in the 1840s and 1850s. While in many countries, these cables were initially linked to facilitate primarily military and political communication, soon after their installation, they were opened to the public for communications. In 1849 in Austria, 1850 in Prussia, and 1851 in France, telegraphic communication was available for a paying, primarily commercial public.[13] In 1866, the successful completion of a durable transatlantic submarine cable inaugurated a new era by offering "instantaneous communication" across the ocean. In the following years, cables were laid from Europe to India, Southeast Asia, Australia, Latin America, and Africa. Simultaneously, landline systems became denser and stretched into tiny towns in places as disparate as the Habsburg Empire, British India, and the Western USA. By the late 1870s, almost any commercial center could be reached from Europe via telegraph through a network spanning between 70,000 and 100,000 miles of ocean cables.[14] In the 1880s and 1890s, popular connections were duplicated and even triplicated. The ocean network became ever more densely linked with landline connections that were themselves also expanding. In addition, technological developments, such as duplex telegraphy, enabled the passage of two or even four messages from both ends of the wire simultaneously. By 1903, roughly 400,000 miles of submarine cables spanned the world's oceans. The highly important North Atlantic connection alone processed about 10,000 messages daily.[15] By 1900, the world had become a connected place, with the telegraph providing the essential tool for these connections.[16]

While the emergence of the telegraph in combination with a network of railways and ships set in motion globalization processes allowing for world commerce, world politics, and a "global" public, it also cocreated a particular social geography of the modern world. Actors within these new global settings based on worldwide communication were predominantly white, male, and Euro-American, as the setup of the telegraph facilitated the exclusion of vast groups of the globe's population. Based on the communications system's tariff structure and operational setup in addition to Euro-American contemporaries' supremacist approach to technological progress, telegraphy disadvantaged many people based on conceptualizations of race, class, and gender. In the context of gender, the underlying narratives usually placed women at the margins of the development of global communications and

---

[13] Winseck, Dwayne R., and Robert M. Pike. 2007. *Communication and empire: media, markets, and globalization, 1860–1930*. Durham: Duke University Press; Telegraph Construction and Maintenance Company. 1950. *The Telcon story 1850–1950*. London.

[14] Field, Cyrus W. 1879. Ocean telegraphy: the twenty-fifth anniversary of the organization of the first company ever formed to lay an ocean cable. See http://searchworks.stanford.edu/view/617519

[15] Bright, Charles. 1898. *Submarine telegraphs: their history, construction and working*. London: C. Lockwood; Wenzlhuemer, Roland. 2013. *Connecting the nineteenth-century world: the telegraph and globalization*. Cambridge: Cambridge University Press.

[16] Rosenberg, E.S. (ed.). 2012. *A world connecting: 1870–1945*. Cambridge, MA: Belknap Press of Harvard University Press.

processes of globalization, which were understood to be "a fundamentally masculine activity".[17]

The general absence of women as subjects in the history of telegraphy is strongly connected to the long tradition of a focus on inventions within the history of science. Moreover, following the narratives of telegraphic invention, women are not necessarily willfully written out of history, rather they are almost nonexistent in contemporary contexts based on discrimination against women in scientific contexts. Contemporary accounts as well as today's scholarship focus on Samuel Morse, William Cooke, and Charles Wheatstone. Several books center on a great men thesis of scientific inventions.[18] In these narratives, women occur only at the side of their male partners, who appear as the ingenious investors, entrepreneurs, or inventors. Narratives place women as beautiful adjuncts to the male undertaking, there only to fill out representative roles. No story on the invention of the telegraph, for instance, is complete, so it seems, without the famous episode when Morse's "muse" and object of attraction, "Annie" Ellsworth, chooses the first words to be sent via telegraph from Washington, DC, to Baltimore. Many stories conceal that Anne Ellsworth was not only the object of Morse' courtship but also the daughter of his friend and US patent commissioner Henry L. Ellsworth, who helped Morse get his telegraph patented.[19] Rather she is portrayed as the inspiration for Morse as the inventor. According to legend, it was Anne Ellsworth who brought Morse news on the passage of his patent bill for the telegraph in March 1843. On this occasion, Morse supposedly told Anne, "You have been the first to bring me this happy news. Accordingly you shall have the honor of composing the first message to be transmitted over the new line." Anne chose "What hath God wrought?" from the bible.[20] Similarly, the female influence in the background of a famous inventor's story is also tangible in the narratives of the telephone only some decades later. Alexander Graham Bell's mother and wife were both deaf. This supposedly influenced his work on the telephone in profound ways. In fact, according to historian Richard John, it was primarily to achieve favor with his future father-in-law, Gardiner Greene Hubbard, that Alexander Bell accepted Hubbard's offer to research multiplex telegraphy, which in the end led to his invention of the telephone. Along the same lines, the Italian inventor of the telephone, Antonio Meucci, is also claimed to have "invented" the telephone to communicate with his wife across the two floors of his house – she was an invalid and so confined to the domestic sphere of one of the two

---

[17] Bright 1898: 144; Wenzlhuemer 2013: 119.

[18] Coe, Lewis. 1993. *The telegraph: a history of Morse's invention and its predecessors in the United States*. Jefferson: McFarland; Bunch, Bryan H., and Alexander Hellemans. 2004. *The history of science and technology: a browser's guide to the great discoveries, inventions, and the people who made them, from the dawn of time to today*. Boston: Houghton Mifflin; or contemporary see Cooke, William F. 1857. *The electric telegraph: was it invented by professor Wheatstone? or by William Fothergill Cooke*. London: W.H. Smith and Son.

[19] Silverman, K. 2003. *Lightning man, the accursed life of Samuel F.B. Morse*. New York: Knopf; John, Richard R. 2010. *Network nation: inventing American telecommunications*. Cambridge, MA: Belknap Press of Harvard University Press.

[20] John 2010: 59; Coe 1993: 32.

floors.[21] In all three cases, women have an important personal influence on the inventor. They are objects of desire and sources of inspiration. While patent commissioner Henry Ellsworth may or may not have considered Morse's telegraph patent rights as a dowry for his daughter Anne in a potential match with his old friend Morse, Hubbard "unquestionably conceived of Bell's telephone patent rights as a wedding gift for his daughter Mabel".[22] Both women were social capital in a story of economic capital connected to patent rights and inventions. Similar to the plot of ancient fairy tales, the princely inventor first had to conquer the dragon of science before he was eligible to marry the princess. In an inventor-focused framing of the history of the telegraph, women had little individual subjectivity in their relationship with science or technology.

Positioning women solely as the muse of the inventor is not necessarily ill will on the side of the authors of such narratives. Rather, the absence of female subjects in the field of electrical science is based on the fact that there were no women engineers in electrical science at the time of telegraphic inventions. At that time, the field of electric science and technology was entirely male dominated. This had three reasons. First, science generally became highly gendered in the nineteenth century, making it "unattractive" or even "inappropriate" for a woman to do science. Constructing and performing gender in oppositions, contemporaries saw nature as "feminine" and science as "masculine".[23] In such a setting, engineering was "part of a larger system attributing essential characteristics to men and women alike".[24] Although constructions of masculinity and femininity were not simple or uncontested, in such a system, women had to be essentially different as there was no other way of knowing for men "that they were, in fact, manly".[25] A female engineer in consequence had to be and has been "almost by definition, a non-conformist, an iconoclast, *the other*".[26] Few women chose that path. Second, women's engagement in science was strongly dependent upon their personal and familial situations. Almost exclusively as daughters or wives of amateur scientists, could women engage with science in the domestic sphere throughout the eighteenth and early nineteenth centuries.[27] When in the nineteenth century, science increasingly moved out of the domestic, amateur sphere and became institutionalized, this affected

---

[21] Meucci, S. 2010. *Antonio and the electric scream: the man who invented the telephone.* Wellesley: Branden Books.

[22] John 2010: 164.

[23] Abir-Am, Pnina G., and Dorinda Outram. 1987. *Uneasy careers and intimate lives: women in science, 1789–1979.* New Brunswick: Rutgers University Press; Schwartz Cowan, R. 2005. Foreword: musings about the woman engineer as muse. In *Crossing boundaries, building bridges. Comparing the history of women engineers 1870s–1990s,* ed. Annie Canel, Ruth Oldenziel, and Karin Zachmann, xii–xv. London: Routledge.

[24] Pursell, C.W. 2005. 'Am I a Lady or an engineer?': the origins of the women's engineering society in Britain, 1918–1940. In *Crossing boundaries, building bridges,* ed. Annie Canel, Ruth Oldenziel, and Karin Zachmann, 51–73. London: Routledge.

[25] Pursell 2005: 51.

[26] Schwartz Cowan 2005: xv.

[27] Abir-Am and Outram 1987: 3.

women's positions in science far more than men's. With the move of science away from the domestic realm, women were increasingly excluded from scientific discourse.[28] Finally, in the institutionalizing setting of nineteenth-century science, three institutions further blocked women's access to careers in engineering: universities, industries, and professional societies (on the history of women engineers see Canel, Oldenziel, Zachmann 2005). Paying tribute to the stellar rise of (submarine) telegraphy, the Society of Telegraph Engineers, for instance, was set up in 1872. Women, however, were exempt from membership and despite a relatively large number of female telegraph operators, this did not change until the turn of the century. Although among the engineering societies in Great Britain, the Society of Telegraph Engineers was the first to consider admitting women to its meetings as early as the 1880s, it followed the strict gender directives of its mother institution, the Society of Civil Engineers. The Civils had deemed it inappropriate to consider admitting women to their meetings. Only in 1899 did the Society of Telegraph Engineers, now renamed as Institute of Electrical Engineers, admit its first female member, Hertha Ayrton.[29] Scientific institutions, universities, and industry consequently participated in gender constructions that powerfully supported male privilege in British society.[30] In the context of telegraphic science, this resulted in a noticeable absence of women for today's historians to report upon.

The second dominant strand of the telegraphs' masculinity narrative follows contemporaries' gendering of the style and purpose of telegraphic communication; the result of which was the strengthening of a separation between a female domestic and a male economic sphere of action. Soon after the adoption of the short and abbreviated telegram style for communications via telegraph for economic reasons, contemporaries also identified this form of communication as genuinely male.[31] They thus set telegraphic communication apart from the supposedly chitchatty and lengthy nature of female conversation. Most prominently, newspapers all over Great Britain mocked Countess of Mayo's conversation via telegraph in June 1870 when the Eastern and Associated Telegraph Companies had just opened a submarine cable connection to India. To entertain guests during the celebration of the opening of the cable to India, a telegraph station was put up at the location. Everybody present could telegraph all around the world free of charge. Lady Mayo made use of the opportunity and sent an extensive, letter-like telegram to her husband in India.[32] As, according to Lady Mayo, the telegraph was not only fulfilling its purpose of "serving political interests" but also assisting "domestic relations," she used the cable connection to India to send "almost instantaneously an affectionate greeting" to her

---

[28] Abir-Am and Outram 1987: 3.

[29] Buchanan, Robert A. 1989. *The engineers: a history of the engineering profession in Britain, 1750–1914*. London: Kingsley; Institute of Electrical Science, "Hertha Ayrton. Online Biographies," http://www.theiet.org/resources/library/archives/biographies/ayrtonh.cfm (last accessed March 11, 2015).

[30] Pursell 2005: 51.

[31] Occasional notes, *Pall Mall Gazette*, June 25, 1870.

[32] A telegraphic evening party, *Illustrated London News*, July 2, 1870.

husband and two sons. The *Pall Mall Gazette* further jeered that had Lady Mayo had "the wires all to herself for five minutes she would have forgotten 'the obligation science owes to the world' and applied them to *purely* domestic purposes."[33] Lord Mayo's telegraphic answer in turn was in absolute obedience with the law of brevity, containing only a couple of words in the sense of "all well."[34] Certainly, so the *Pall Mall Gazette*, Lord Mayo's reply "must have been refreshing to the wires after all they had endured in the shape of what is called 'bow wow'," senseless female chatter.[35] The international submarine cables were too precious, so the media consensus went, to be abused for domestic, and that meant female, conversation.

Contemporaries based Lady Mayo's inability to master the telegraphic style of communication on the fact that telegraphs were not made for the domestic sphere and its conversations. Following the separate spheres model, that is, the distinct ideology which dictated that according to "natural" gender roles, men inhabited the "public sphere" of politics, economy, commerce, and law and women the private realm of domestic life, child-rearing, housekeeping, and religious education, contemporaries prescribed telegraphy a distinct, *masculine* space of action in Victorian life. The decision to keep the telegraph out of the *feminine* domestic sphere seems also to have been made to "save" men from such "bursts" of the "natural feeling of the wife and mother," as the one prominently displayed by Lady Mayo in June 1870.[36] As early as 1859, however, the British satire magazine *Punch* discusses the proposal to lay telegraph wires within 100 yards of "every man's door." While the author accepts the benefits of being "within five minutes" of pleasant invitations and news, he also deplores the consequences "of being within five minutes of every noodle who wants to ask a question." *Punch* rather favored the then present arrangement of a telegraph office which would spare any men "Mrs. P.'s anxieties and other questions." A house telegraph would only bring him in a "perpetual *tête-a-tête* with her" – and that was a state to be avoided at any cost.[37]

But it was not only men who saw the telegraph squarely located within the masculine sphere of action, women did, too. This shows the wide acceptance, which the idea of separate spheres had found in some sections of Victorian society. In 1860, for instance, an unidentified "lady" complained in a letter to *Punch* that men were "only studying and scheming to promote [their] *creature* comforts." To her, the invention of the London District Telegraph Company was consequently only a means for "sending messages to *[themselves]*." Men's promises that the wires would be open to the ladies were only a "paltry excuse." By its mere location, the London district telegraph was clearly not "meant for women." Its stations were located where men congregated, not in places where they were accessible to women.[38]

---

[33] Occasional notes, *Pall Mall Gazette*, June 25, 1870.

[34] A telegraphic evening party, *Illustrated London News*, July 2, 1870.

[35] Occasional notes, *Pall Mall Gazette*, June 25, 1870.

[36] Idem.

[37] *Punch* 35, 1858: 244.

[38] *Punch* 38, 1860: 181; on electricity and the domestic sphere, see Gooday, Graeme. 2008. *Domesticating electricity: technology, uncertainty and gender, 1880–1914*. London: Pickering & Chatto.

Following the social geography of separate gender spheres in Victorian society, telegraph companies located the nodes to their worldwide network in distinctly masculine spaces of political and economic interaction, purposely excluding the female sphere of interaction. Telegraph offices were set up in financial institutions rather than in shops.

Combining contemporaries' exclusion of women from telegraphic science as well as telegraphic communication, we receive a highly gendered perspective of a predominantly masculine sphere of telegraphic interaction, which is duly reproduced in telegraph history. On the one hand, women are feminized – in the sense that they are reduced to their bodily and biological markers. Their emotions, or their beauty, serve as adornment and inspiration for the male inventor. A female engineer, on the other hand, represents the unwanted, non-conventional *other*. Women were also geographically separated from the telegraph – in the sense that their sphere of action, the domestic realm, remained unconnected to the global telegraphic network. Women are ill represented in telegraph history not because they were deliberately written out of it, but because they were kept out of its (narrative) space in the first place.

2.2   Telegraphic History at the Intersection of Gender and Class: The Female Clerk

This masculine narrative changes when we combine aspects of gender with aspects of class, enlarging the established perspective with that of a social history from "below" or rather a lower social spectrum than high-class Victorian Britain. For middle-class women in particular, the new technology of telegraphy offered not only new means of employment but also investment. Not only in the USA, as Jepsen points out, but all over Europe, the female telegraph clerk was no uncommon phenomenon. For educated unmarried women, it was a respectable and prudent way to support oneself. Additionally, as my analysis of the telegraph company's shareholder lists show, women were keen investors in ocean cable companies. As the "new women" were carving out spaces of their own in the fields of politics and economy, middle-class women in particular were also populating the *masculine* telegraphic sphere. Paralleling the intersectional hybridity of gender and class, telegraphic space in the late nineteenth century also became a hybrid of masculine *and* feminine spaces of action and interaction.

While female engineers were absent from the highly gendered realm of electrical telegraphic *science*, female clerks became a common sight in telegraph offices. In fact, the young and initially relatively "gender-neutral" field of telegraph *technology* offered new venues for women to seek employment outside of their domestic sphere. Unlike many of the occupations women entered for the first time in the mid-nineteenth century, landline telegraphy admitted women to its ranks before its gender roles had solidified. Throughout much of the nineteenth century, men and women performed the same tasks using the same equipment, working cooperatively and often anonymously at either end of the wire.[39] According to the *Pall Mall Gazette* (June 23, 1883), in Europe, the "experiment" of employing women as telegraph clerks was begun in Finland in the early days of the telegraph before the practice then spread to other European countries. Starting in the 1850s in Europe (and the 1840s in the USA), telegraph companies employed female operators on the domestic lines. In 1859, the chairman of the London District Telegraph Company announced that its telegraph offices were staffed entirely by women (*Punch* 37, 1859: 100). In 1860, the Telegraph School for Women was established in London and in 1862 the Queen's Institute for the Training and Employment of Educated Women began running classes in telegraphy in Dublin.[40] In 1870, British telegraph companies employed about 2030 men and roughly 470 women, the number going up to around 700 in 1883.[41] Generally, newspapers agreed that the services of women as telegraphers were "of great value" and that women were "not excelled by men in the swiftness and accuracy of their manipulation of the type-writer."[42] It was women's very feminine qualities that made the job of telegraph operator seemingly perfect for them. As the London District Telegraph Company's chairman pointed out, women in telegraphy were particularly apt, since "young ladies [were] noted for their readiness in always giving a quick and happy answer [and were] much more expert and industrious than a man […] in working the *needle*" (*Punch* 37, 1859: 100). By *feminizing* the job of telegraphist in such a way, however, contemporaries also made the separate spheres model fit changes in the job market. The domestic sphere was expanded to now also cover work outside the home.[43]

Still, at a time when the labor market was generally widening for single women, telegraphy offered yet another opportunity for middle-class women to achieve independence and financial security. Over the course of the second half of the nineteenth century, employment rates of unmarried (not counting widowed) women rose extensively as well as did the types of employment available to them. In 1851 almost the only work available to single women was as a teacher or dressmaker. This range expanded in the last quarter of the century, when jobs as shop assistants or in clerical positions started featuring prominently. Skilled positions, such as telegraphist, telephonist, and typist,[44] became more and more common among women who worked. Middle-class spinsters were "no longer restricted to needlework or

[39] Jepsen 2000: 3.

[40] Porthcurno Telegraph Museum, "Women telegraphers in the First World War," 19. August 2012.

[41] Reader, William J. 1987. *A history of the institution of electrical engineers, 1981–1971*. London: P. Peregrinus.

[42] *Trewman's Exeter Flying Post or Plymouth and Cornish Advertiser*, December 11, 1889.

[43] Scott, Alison M. (ed.). 1994. *Gender segregation and social change: men and women in changing labour markets*. Oxford: Oxford University Press.

[44] Gardey, D. 1999. The standardization of a technical practice: typing (1883–1930). *History and Technology* 364(15): 313–343.

governessing."[45] Moreover, employment as a telegraph clerk represented a respectable position for single middle-class women who either chose to or were forced to work to support themselves. Characterized as the period's "whizz kids," telegraph operators were among the first technological elites of the nineteenth century and illustrative of the new upward mobility of the "middle classes." Their role was similar to that of today's softwareprogrammer. A rapidly growing industry had a sudden need for people with technical skills. A good telegraph clerk had to be extremely literate and a good speller, capable of learning Morse code, and to have some knowledge of electricity and telegraphy.[46] Telegraphy created opportunities for ambitious men *as well as* women.

Yet even the initially gender-neutral telegraphic technology grew increasingly "gendered" over time, hierarchizing male clerks over female. As early as 1879, a writer for the London paper *The Graphic* lamented that the British government was gradually shaping the telegraphic staff "into a purely masculine mould" (*The Graphic*, May 24, 1879). Simultaneously, the labor-specific discourse increasingly centered on biological determinism, rendering women less fit for telegraphic work in the eyes of their would-be employers. According to *The Graphic*, the masculinization of the telegraph happened because the Central Telegraph Office found women "not equal to the strain of the work." An 8-hour day may not have seemed long to many contemporaries, but as the nervous system of a woman was "more delicately strung than that of a man," 8 hours of "continuous bustle and noise" were "enough to try the strength of the strongest" (*The Graphic*, May 24, 1879). Some publications even claimed that despite the advantages of fine female bodily features, i.e., their small hands which made them particularly well suited to work the key switch, it was women's brains that proved ill suited for the job. The technical magazine*The Telegraphist*, for example, argued that "the majority of the text-books [were] too technical" for women and that "the very sight of a page of mathematical formulae [was] enough to strike terror into the heart of any inquisitive young lady who opens a manual of electricity of telegraphy."[47]

It remains unclear whether such discourse caused or reflected an increasing gendering of the telegraphtechnology in favor of the male. In any case, in 1874, the British Government decided to limit the number of female clerks working its domestic lines to 30 percent (*Pall Mall Gazette*, June 23, 1883); by that time, France and Russia, for instance, had already dismissed women all together.[48] The wages for female telegraphists had also gone down considerably, probably due to the "run" of

---

[45] Freeman, Ruth, and Patricia Klaus. 1984. 'Blessed or Not?': the new spinster in England and the United States in the late nineteenth century and early twentieth centuries. *Journal of Family History* 9: 394–414. On the railway, see Dorré, Gina M. 2006. *Victorian fiction and the cult of the horse*. Aldershot: Ashgate. On the telephone, see Martin, Michèle. 1991. *"Hello, Central?": gender, technology, and culture in the formation of telephone systems*. Montreal: McGill Queen's University Press.

[46] Jepsen 2000: 2.

[47] Electron, telegraph instruments, and how to understand them, in *The Telegraphist. A Monthly Journal for Postal, Telephone, and Railway Telegraph Clerks*, December 1, 1883: 3.

[48] Women who work, *Liverpool Mercury*, June 23, 1868; *The Examiner*, June 21, 1873.

women on these jobs. When telegraph companies had first been formed in the 1840s and 1850s, a female clerk's pay was 8 shillings a week, to be increased by 1 shilling a year until it reached 14 shillings. By 1868, female competition had allowed companies to lower payment to 5 shillings a week – a sum on which women could "scarcely live unassisted."[49] Even greater gender distinctions were found on the submarine cable lines. In contrast to the landlines, the telegraph girl remained an unknown phenomenon on the more "complex" and better paid ocean lines. Only during the First World War, when companies faced a shortage of labor as young men rather wanted (and had) to join the "real" war effort than the telegraphers' office, women also started to be employed on the ocean lines.[50]

2.3 Telegraphic History at the Intersectionality of Gender and Class: The Woman Investor

Telegraphy not only provided middle-class women with a new source of employment but also of investment. The last quarter of the nineteenth century generally witnessed profound changes in the financial structure of Great Britain. Contemporaries increasingly measured "income in dividends and wealth in the quotation of the Stock Exchange".[51] The telegraphs with their provision for swift communication were largely responsible for enabling a new form of capitalist economy with the stock exchange at its heart.[52] In particular, toward the end of the nineteenth century, striking changes took place in Britain's shareholding population. A growing number of individuals from a widening social spectrum, including those less affluent, began to own stocks.[53] Recent scholarship on gender and investment in the nineteenth century has put a spotlight on the female investor, thereby further contesting the separate spheres model. Women were not restricted to the domestic sphere and its typically noneconomic activities. Rather, women's capital made up a substantial part of the financial resources backing the capitalist industrial economy of the nineteenth century.[54]

---

[49] Idem.

[50] Tarrant, Donald R. 1999. *Atlantic sentinel: Newfoundland's role in transatlantic cable communications.* St. John's Nfld: Flanker Press.

[51] Rutterford, J., G. David, M. Josephine, and O. Alastar. 2011. Who comprised the nation of shareholders? Gender and investment in Great Britain, c. 1870–1935. *The Economic History Review* 64(1): 157–187.

[52] Müller, Simone M., and Heidi Tworek. 2015. 'The telegraph and the bank': on the interdependence of global communications and capitalism, 1866–1914. J. Glob. Hist. **2**: forthcoming.

[53] Rutterford et al. 2011: 157.

[54] On the Victorian shareholder, see Maltby, A., and J. Rutterford (eds.). 2006. She possessed her own fortune: women investors from the late nineteenth century to the early twentieth century. *Business History* 48(2):220–253 or Davis, Lance E., and Robert A. Huttenback. 2010. *Mammon and the pursuit of Empire: the political economy of British imperialism, 1860–1912.* Cambridge: Cambridge University Press.

Within investment portfolios owned by women, telegraph companies also played an important role. An article from 1886, commenting on the visitors to the Atlantic cable stations, remarked, for instance, that "[e]lderly ladies" who came to visit not only "display[ed] an evident degree of common sense" concerning the working of the telegraph but were also "frequently [...] pecuniarily interested."[55] Drawing from the Direct United States Cable Company (DUSC) shareholder lists, we find that women constituted a significant number of shareholders invested in the generally risky business of submarine telegraphy.[56] Together with a small group of primarily continental European investors, the Siemens brothers had set up DUSC in London in 1873. Its purpose was to break the established monopoly on the Atlantic submarine cable market by means of an independent cable provider.[57] Ownership lists of DUSC shares show that women were almost as active in the financial market as their male counterparts, paralleling the general emergence of a broader and less affluent shareholding base toward the turn of the century.

Upon its establishment in 1873, DUSC shares started out with only seven entries marked as female: three widows, three spinsters, and one married woman. These seven made up 3.7 percent of all shareholders and represent 1852 shares or about 2.8 percent of the total capital. Thereafter, female investment grew quickly; until by the beginning of the twentieth century, women made up almost half of the company's shareholders. In 1887, for instance, we find that 443 out of 1795 shareholders total were women. In total, roughly 25 percent of all shareholders that year were women; 227 of them marked as spinsters, 114 as widows, 100 as married women, in addition to one lady and one princess. They represented 10,748 stocks with a nominal value of £20 each, which was about 16 percent of the company's capital. Shares from 1909 underline this steady increase. By the beginning of the twentieth century, 784 shareholders were female, or 44 percent of the total. Yet they only represented 17,264 shares at £20, worth £345,280 in total, which translated to about 26 percent of the company's capital.[58]

Female shareholders' relatively modest capital investment made them the typical small investor that became increasingly common for Britain as a nation of investors at the turn of the century. In 1887, for instance, only 68 women owned more than 30 DUSC shares; more than half of those women owned ten shares or less. Still, over the years, there were some exceptions – usually wealthy widows – such as Elise Louise Adlegonde Cromlery from Belgium or Isidora Collier de la Martiere from Paris, who held exceptionally large numbers of shares. In 1909, only 164 women

---

[55] "Visitors by Old Electric," *The telegraphist. A monthly journal for postal, telephone and railway-telegraph clerks*, January (1886), 14.

[56] Direct United States Cable Company Ltd., *Annual list of members and summary of capital and shares of the Direct United States Cable Company Limited*, Public Record Office, National Archives Kew. The analysis is based on samples from the years 1873, 1877, 1887, and 1909.

[57] Müller, Simone M. 2015. *Wiring the world: the social and cultural creation of global telegraph networks*. New York: Columbia University Press.

[58] Of those 784 female shareholders, we find 395 spinsters = 50.4 %, 225 married women = 28.7 %, 158 widows = 20.2 %, 4 ladies, and 2 misses = 0.7 %.

held 30 shares or more and only 24 held 100 shares or more. Yet Comtesse Isabelle Gontran de la Baume-Pluvinel, who came from an old noble family, represented the largest individual shareholder, man or woman. The analysis of DUSC shares shows that nineteenth-century women were not necessarily forced into the restricted roles of wives, mothers, or helpmeets and thus excluded from active participation in economic and social life. Rather, they could also take on roles of active financial agents providing for the financial and communication infrastructure of the modern world.

Telegraphy, as well as other stock market companies, allowed women who had to or chose to support themselves an important outlet for individual economic freedom. Originally, bourgeois respectability required that women live in a state of social and economic dependence on men – either by marriage or through the protection of a male relative, containing them "within the safe haven of a family unit".[59] This setting was increasingly challenged over the course of the late nineteenth century, most importantly by the legal changes concerning female property ownership. The considerable rise of female investment between 1873 and 1887 was closely connected with the Women's Property Act of 1882. The English Married Women's Property Act of 1870 had already recognized a woman's right to maintain property separate from her husband's control. In 1882 these rights were considerably expanded.[60] These changes manifested themselves in the cable company's shareholder lists, as we see in the case of Isidora Collier de la Martiere. Among the seven women visibly investing in cable shares in 1873, Isidora Collier de la Martiere alone held 1763 shares – making her one of the leading investors in the company. Yet, following British law, this widow is listed together with a Sigismond Picard, her financial warden. This practice of listing female investors together with a male warden changed with the passage of the women's property acts. Until the 1880s, married women's shares usually had to be listed under their husband's name. Thereafter, they appeared as fully independent entities in the shareholder lists. Only an insignificant number of women among the DUSC's members are listed together with their husbands or some sort of male guardian.

Women flocked to investment in telegraphy for a variety of reasons. Stock brokerage represented a new means for female freedom as secured in the Women's Property Acts. Stock investments had a special appeal for middle-class women, who were generally denied access to the professions and excluded from entrepreneurial activities, but who still needed to make money. This was the case in particular when they were unmarried.[61] Throughout the years, the group classified as "spinsters" generally made up the majority among women investors. In 1909, for example, of those 784 female shareholders, 395 or roughly 50 percent were spinsters as compared to 29 percent married women and 20 percent widows.

[59] Gordon, E., and G. Nair. 2003. *Public lives: women, family, and society in Victorian Britain*. New Haven: Yale University Press.

[60] Robb, G. 2009. Ladies of the ticker: women, investment, and fraud in England and America 1850–1930. In *Victorian investments: new perspectives on finance and culture*, ed. Nancy Henry and Cannon Schmitt, 120–142. Bloomington: Indiana University Press.

[61] Robb 2009.

Typical female investments seem to have been safe and low risk, such as government bonds, banks, railways, utilities, or debentures. Similar to Helen Doe's findings on investment in shipping, DUSC shares expand and challenge this picture of women as the risk-averse investor. The ocean cables with their likelihood to break, fierce competition, and ultimately great ups and downs on the stock market should not have ranked high among female investors.[62] Still, female investment in ocean cables was as high as 25 percent in 1887 and 44 percent in 1909. Women might have been attracted to submarine telegraphy by the relatively high revenues, the fact that the cables were not as risky as thus far perceived, and the accessibility of the companies' product. From the very beginning, ocean cables had been a very public project, highly visible in the media. Women were usually kept out of traditional circles and places of information, such as clubs or fraternal lodges, where relevant business and stock market information was being traded.[63] Also, investment manuals excluded women from financial debates, "on the explicit grounds that [women could not] understand investment".[64] In contrast to such male secrecy about stock market information, the progress as well as failures of the cables could be easily followed in the daily papers. In 1876, a charge was even filed against DUSC when it had allegedly not immediately reported on its cable's breakage.[65] Women could gather relevant stock market information from home. Thus, they could act relatively independently without having to leave "their sphere." There are hardly any primary accounts of women discussing their financial strategies to allow a conclusive statement on female investment strategies. Nevertheless, DUSC shareholder lists underline how stock investment in general, and telegraph stocks in particular, offered women opportunities to expand and cross existing gender stereotypes. Femininity could exercise an alternative performance mode targeted at women's economic independence from male patronage.

2.4 Conclusion

Telegraphy was a highly gendered communications technology. At first glance, telegraphy appears to serve in the forms of invention, technology, and technology-in-use for a primarily male sphere of global electric communication agency. Within stories of male entrepreneurship displaying genius, women appear as objects that are purposely brought into the male public sphere: either as electricity's muse or electricity's ridicule, that is, women's misunderstanding of proper telegraphic

---

[62] Robb 2009: 122.

[63] Robb 2009: 121.

[64] Preda, Alex. 2001. The rise of the popular investor: financial knowledge and investing in England and France, 1840–1880. *The Sociological Quarterly* 42(2): 205–232.

[65] Summary of this morning's news, *Pall Mall Gazette*, January 27, 1876.

usage. By conceptualizing male and female in opposition, contemporaries did not allow women to perform telegraphy successfully, based solely on the fact that they were women.

This interpretation broadens the picture when we look at telegraphy through the lenses of a combined approach of social history, economic history, and communications studies. Intersecting gender and class, for instance, reveals a complex assemblage of telegraphic femininities. In particular for middle-class women, telegraphy offered new spaces for performing their gender. They could find respectable employment as telegraph clerks and make use of telegraph stocks as a means of securing further income. Both offered tools to achieve the freedoms, which the new women strove for at the end of the nineteenth century. In fact, telegraphy played an important role in providing these new freedoms. While women were excluded from a predominantly male sphere of global communication, they regained agency by entering another male sphere of agency – labor, finance, and stock investment – by means of telegraphy.

Variant constructions of female gender, finally, were not only based on class but also saw change over time. Starting out as a relatively gender-neutral form of employment, the position of telegraph clerk became gendered or rather hierarchized over the course of the late nineteenth century. The number of female clerks became limited to 30 percent and wages decreased. Male clerks received priority treatment on the landlines and exclusivity on the submarine lines. The gendering of clerical positions changed yet again with the First World War and a shortage of male labor and over the course of the twentieth century when the position of the telephonist, for instance, became entirely female dominated.

In fact, telegraphy was a highly gendered communications technology – but one that allowed for fluent gender constructions, as well as hybrid gender spaces of performing masculinity and femininity "by telegraph" alongside each other. Additionally, telegraphy offered variants of femininity dependent on women's social status. Indeed, the relationship between telegraphy and gender cannot be understood without the relationship between telegraphy and class. It remains to point out that all femininities in this article were those of white European women. Telegraphy's constructions of social geographies within the modern world can also not be fully understood without taking into account its intersection with race. In the end, this article set forth to not only overcome telegraphic histories' biological determinism but also its technical determinism. Just as the colonel's telegram "join at once" had allowed several interpretations, telegraphy allowed for myriad performances of gender as well.

Acknowledgment I would like to thank Valérie Schafer, Benjamin Thierry, and Torsten Kathke for their invaluable support and feedback.

References

Abir-Am, Pnina G., and Dorinda Outram. 1987. *Uneasy careers and intimate lives: women in science, 1789–1979*. New Brunswick: Rutgers University Press.

Ahvenainen, Jorma. 1995. The role of telegraphs in the 19th century revolution of communication. In *Kommunikationsrevolutionen: Die neuen Medien des 16. und 19. Jahrhunderts*, ed. Michael North, 73–80. Köln: Böhlau.

Appleyard, Rollo. 1939. *The history of the institution of electrical engineers (1871–1931)*. London: The Institution of Electrical Engineers.

Beachy, Robert, Béatrice Craig, and Alastair Owens (eds.). 2006. *Women, business, and finance in nineteenth-century Europe: rethinking separate spheres*. Oxford: Berg Publishers.

Berger, Michelle T., and Kathleen Guidroz. 2010. *The intersectional approach: transforming the academy through race, class, and gender*. Chapel Hill: University of North Carolina Press.

Bright, Charles. 1898. *Submarine telegraphs: their history, construction and working*. London: C. Lockwood.

Bright, Charles. 1908. *The life story of sir Charles Tilston Bright civil engineer: with which is incorporated the story of the Atlantic cable, and the first telegraph to India and the colonies*. London: Archibald Constable.

Buchanan, Robert A. 1989. *The engineers: a history of the engineering profession in Britain, 1750–1914*. London: Kingsley.

Bunch, Bryan H., and Alexander Hellemans. 2004. *The history of science and technology: a browser's guide to the great discoveries, inventions, and the people who made them, from the dawn of time to today*. Boston: Houghton Mifflin.

Canel, Annie, Ruth Oldenziel, and Karin Zachmann (eds.). 2005. *Crossing boundaries, building bridges. Comparing the history of women engineers 1870s–1990s*. London: Routledge.

Chow, E.N., M.T. Segal, T. Lin, and V.P. Demos. 2011. *Analyzing gender, intersectionality, and multiple inequalities: global, transnational and local contexts*. Bingley: Emerald.

Coe, Lewis. 1993. *The telegraph: a history of Morse's invention and its predecessors in the United States*. Jefferson: McFarland.

Cooke, William F. 1857. *The electric telegraph: was it invented by professor Wheatstone? or by William Fothergill Cooke*. London: W.H. Smith and Son.

Cookson, Gillian. 2003. *The cable: the wire that changed the world*. Strout: Tempus publishing.

Davis, Lance E., and Robert A. Huttenback. 2010. *Mammon and the pursuit of Empire: the political economy of British imperialism, 1860–1912*. Cambridge: Cambridge University Press.

Deere, Carmen D., and Cheryl R. Doss. 2006. A special issue on women and wealth. *Feminist Economics* 12: 1–2.

Doe, Helen. 2010. Waiting for her ship to come in? The female investor in nineteenth-century sailing vessels. *The Economic History Review* 63(1): 85–106.

Dorré, Gina M. 2006. *Victorian fiction and the cult of the horse*. Aldershot: Ashgate.

Field, Cyrus W. 1879. Ocean telegraphy: The twenty-fifth anniversary of the organization of the first company ever formed to lay an ocean cable. See http://searchworks.stanford.edu/view/617519

Freeman, Ruth, and Patricia Klaus. 1984. 'Blessed or Not?': the new spinster in England and the United States in the late nineteenth century and early twentieth centuries. *Journal of Family History* 9: 394–414.

Gardey, D. 1999. The standardization of a technical practice: typing (1883–1930). *History and Technology* 364(15): 313–343.

Gooday, Graeme. 2008. *Domesticating electricity: technology, uncertainty and gender, 1880–1914*. London: Pickering & Chatto.

Gordon, E., and G. Nair. 2003. *Public lives: women, family, and society in Victorian Britain*. New Haven: Yale University Press.

Henry, Nancy, and Cannon Schmitt (eds.). 2009. *Victorian investments: new perspectives on finance and culture*. Bloomington: Indiana University Press.

Jagger, Gill. 2008. *Judith Butler: sexual politics, social change and the power of the performative*. London: Routledge.

Jepsen, Thomas C. 2000. *My sisters telegraphic: women in the telegraph office, 1846–1950*. Athens: Ohio University Press.

John, Richard R. 2010. *Network nation: inventing American telecommunications*. Cambridge, MA: Belknap Press of Harvard University Press.

Latham, Jean L., and Victor Mays. 1958. *Young man in a hurry: the story of Cyrus W. Field*. New York: Harper.

Ledger, Sally. 1997. *The new woman: fiction and feminism at the fin de siècle*. Manchester: Manchester University Press.

MacEwen, Alison. 1994. Gender segregation and the SCELI research. In *Gender segregation and social change: men and women in changing labour markets*, ed. Alison M. Scott, 1–38. Oxford: Oxford University Press.

Mackay, James A. 1997. *Alexander Graham Bell: a life*. New York: J. Wiley.

Maltby, A., and J. Rutterford (eds.). 2006. She possessed her own fortune: women investors from the late nineteenth century to the early twentieth century. *Business History* 48(2):220–253.

Martin, Michèle. 1991. *"Hello, Central?": gender, technology, and culture in the formation of telephone systems*. Montreal: McGill Queen's University Press.

Meucci, S. 2010. *Antonio and the electric scream: the man who invented the telephone*. Wellesley: Branden Books.

Müller, Simone M. 2015. *Wiring the world: the social and cultural creation of global telegraph networks*. New York: Columbia University Press.

Müller, Simone M., and Heidi Tworek. 2015. 'The telegraph and the bank': on the interdependence of global communications and capitalism, 1866–1914. J. Glob. Hist. **2**: forthcoming.

Müller-Pohl, Simone. 2010. 'By Atlantic Telegraph': a study on Weltcommunication in the 19th century. *Medien & Zeit* 4: 40–54.

North, Michael (ed.). 1995. *Kommunikationsrevolutionen: Die neuen Medien des 16. und 19. Jahrhunderts*. Köln: Böhlau.

Osterhammel, Jürgen, and Niels P. Petersson. 2007. *Geschichte der Globalisierung: Dimensionen, Prozesse, Epochen*. München: C. H. Beck Wissen.

Preda, Alex. 2001. The rise of the popular investor: financial knowledge and investing in England and France, 1840–1880. *The Sociological Quarterly* 42(2): 205–232.

Pursell, C.W. 2005. 'Am I a Lady or an engineer?': the origins of the women's engineering society in Britain, 1918–1940. In *Crossing boundaries, building bridges*, ed. Annie Canel, Ruth Oldenziel, and Karin Zachmann, 51–73. London: Routledge.

Reader, William J. 1987. *A history of the institution of electrical engineers, 1981–1971*. London: P. Peregrinus.

Richardson, Angelique, and Chris Willis. 2002. *The new woman in fiction and fact: Fin-de-siècle feminisms*. Basingstoke/Hampshire/New York: Palgrave.

Robb, G. 2009. Ladies of the ticker: women, investment, and fraud in England and America 1850–1930. In *Victorian investments: new perspectives on finance and culture*, ed. Nancy Henry and Cannon Schmitt, 120–142. Bloomington: Indiana University Press.

Rosenberg, E.S. (ed.). 2012. *A world connecting: 1870–1945*. Cambridge, MA: Belknap Press of Harvard University Press.

Rutterford, J., G. David, M. Josephine, and O. Alastar. 2011. Who comprised the nation of shareholders? Gender and investment in Great Britain, c. 1870–1935. *The Economic History Review* 64(1): 157–187.

Schwartz Cowan, R. 2005. Foreword: musings about the woman engineer as muse. In *Crossing boundaries, building bridges. Comparing the history of women engineers 1870s–1990s*, ed. Annie Canel, Ruth Oldenziel, and Karin Zachmann, xii–xv. London: Routledge.

Scott, Alison M. (ed.). 1994. *Gender segregation and social change: men and women in changing labour markets*. Oxford: Oxford University Press.

Silverman, K. 2003. *Lightning man, the accursed life of Samuel F.B. Morse*. New York: Knopf.

Staiti, Paul J., and S.F.B. Morse. 1989. *Samuel F.B. Morse*. Cambridge, NY: Cambridge University Press.

Tarrant, Donald R. 1999. *Atlantic sentinel: Newfoundland's role in transatlantic cable communications*. St. John's Nfld: Flanker Press.

Telegraph Construction and Maintenance Company. 1950. *The Telcon story 1850–1950*. London.

Wenzlhuemer, Roland. 2013. *Connecting the nineteenth-century world: the telegraph and globalization*. Cambridge: Cambridge University Press.

Winseck, Dwayne R., and Robert M. Pike. 2007. *Communication and empire: media, markets, and globalization, 1860–1930*. Durham: Duke University Press.

Chapter 3
Airing the Differences: An Approach to the Role of Women in the Spanish Free Radio Movement (1976–2014)

José Emilio Pérez Martínez

Abstract The free radio movement appeared in Spain in the late 1970s, right after Franco's death, claiming for a new model of doing and understanding communication. Taking advantage of the new sociopolitical situation and with clear references in both French and Italian movements, hundreds of small, alternative, free radio stations appeared all over the country, making the 1980s their golden decade. This article explores the ways this movement established a series of relationships with feminism and women attending to its two main representations: women-related programmes and women's groups. The article deploys, mainly, a diachronic perspective, analyzing the development of this relationship from the late 1970s until today (as the movement is still alive and struggling), although it also attends to address its transnational features, as free radios have been an international phenomenon since their inception and these women's groups have very often established international networks.

Conducting research on the Spanish free radio movement from 1976 to 1989 – the dates correspond to the appearance of the first station in Madrid and the passing of the LOT (Ley de Ordenación de las Telecomunicaciones) – I was surprised by the continuous references to women and feminism that appeared both in the documentation and the oral testimonies. According to this amount of references, the relationship between free radios and women was obvious; it was only a matter of measuring its significance.

Therefore, this article aims to present this relationship by analyzing how this phenomenon has dealt with Spanish women's struggles during the last decades and by checking how since its inception, the free radio movement has understood the

This work is part of the researching activity developed by the Project HAR2011-26344 "Mujer, liberalismo y espacio público en perspectiva comparada" led by Prof. Rosa Mª Capel and funded by the Ministerio de Economía y Competitividad (MINECO).

J.E. Pérez Martínez (✉)
Department of Contemporary History, Universidad Complutense de Madrid,
Avda. de Séneca, 2 Ciudad Universitaria, 28040 Madrid, Spain
e-mail: joseempe@ucm.es

specificity of women and their subaltern condition, giving voice to those who did not have the chance of appearing in the media.

Consequently, this chapter will focus on the different manners deployed by these radio stations to support feminism and women's struggles: women dedicated programmes (1976–1989) and the appearance of women's groups within some of these radios.

3.1   An Introduction to the Spanish Free Radio Movement

Although the Spanish movement was highly influenced by the Italian and French experiences, it is necessary to do a brief introduction, as the particular context – both geographical and chronological – gives these radios particular features.

The first free radios appeared in Spain in 1976, right after Franco's death and while the Francoist regime was starting to move towards democracy. Those first radios were *Radio La Voz del Pobre* in Madrid[1] and *Radio Maduixa* in Granollers (Catalonia),[2] and can be seen as the "prehistory" of the movement.

In 1978, during the celebration of an Anti-Repression Meeting at Vic (Catalonia), some experimental broadcasts were held. Historically, these precarious experiments have been considered the starting point of free radios in Spain.[3]

Right after, in April 1979, a new project was set up in Barcelona by a collective of "autonomous, gays, feminists, pacifists, anti-militarists, and communication students and teachers".[4] This radio, *Ona Lliure*, became the milestone of the movement in Spain. Its short life due to a government closure was broadcasted live and was turned into a legend within the free radios collective imaginary

After these primary experiences, the phenomenon spread from Catalonia, Valencia, Madrid and the Basque Country to the rest of Spain, becoming a nationwide movement. Its development went through different phases: after the first radios appeared, the movement started some self-organization dynamics through "Coordinadoras" – these are coordinating groups – both local and national. Some national meetings were held, the first manifestos written and problems with authorities followed, as well as the first administrative closures. Because of its growth, the movement faced some internal debates,[5] and finally in 1989, the Socialist Party government passed the Ley de Ordenación de las Telecomunicaciones – a law to reorganize the media – which meant the first general closure of free radios. Some of

---

[1] Aguilera, Miguel. 1985. *Radios libres y radios piratas*. Madrid: Editorial Forja.

[2] Aisa, Manel. 2013. *Las jornadas libertarias de 1977 y la transición libertaria 1974–1979*. http://manelaisa.com/articulo/articulo-1-las-jornadas-libertarias-de-1977-y-la-transicion-libertaria-1974–1979-version-2/. Accessed 17 Oct 2011.

[3] Colectivo de Radios Libres. 1981. *Alicia es el diablo*. Barcelona: Hacer.

[4] Translations by the author.

[5] Within these internal debates, we should mention those related with financial aspects and the ones about the relationship between some stations and political organizations such as the MC (Movimiento Comunista) or the LCR (Liga Comunista Revolucionaria).

them reopened during the beginning of 1990s, and others disappeared forever. The last 30 years were full of twists and turns, but the movement has kept on struggling for democratic communication.

A free radio is, according to its essential features, an autonomous station, independent, secular, pluralistic, promoted and managed by non-profit organizations with a democratic functioning – usually based on an open assembly – that pursues the rights of information and communication, a participatory, pluralistic and protest way of broadcasting, and an improvement of social conditions. This is a general definition,[6] since free radios are a changing reality depending on geographical, ideological and economic elements.

When defining Spanish free radio stations, it is also important to bear in mind that they shared the waves with other kinds of radios. First of all, we have to differentiate free radios from public or private ones. The first difference is that free radios broadcast without licence, this is illegally, while public and private radios have licence. The second different feature is their approach to communication: free radios promote, as seen before, a horizontal participatory way of making radio (e.g. open telephone lines during the programmes allow direct feedback and participation; anyone could lead a programme as membership was open; etc.), while public and commercial stations operate in the traditional vertical exclusive manner.

Secondly, we have to take into account that free radios are not the only ones broadcasting without licence in Spain since the late 1970s. We have to differentiate free radios from pirate ones. The point here is that free radios have never included ads in their broadcast due to their non-profit ethos. However, pirate radios do, so they clearly get profits from their activities.

We should also exclude municipal radios, that is, radio stations that existed during the 1980s, belonging to and promoted by some city councils. Although they did not have licences, they were close to different political powers; in fact, they usually worked as loudspeakers for political propaganda, which obviously excludes them from the free radio category.[7]

Concerning the origins of the Spanish free radio stations, there are some clear precedents in the French and Italian experiences, which got high repercussions in the Spanish press, both mainstream and alternative. Thus, we are facing a transnational phenomenon; so if we want to trace its origins, we should look for a common layer to all the known cases: France, Italy, Spain, Belgium, Germany, etc.

Without pretending to minimize the impact of individual agency, it seems that the origins of free radio have to be found in the superstructure of Western democratic societies and the importance given to the right of free speech and the right to communicate within these societies. France and Italy's constitutions – direct models for the Spanish radios – include articles which are devoted to these rights. The Italian Constitution in its 21st article affirms that "anyone has the right to freely

---

[6] Pérez Martínez, and José Emilio. 2012. Libertad en las ondas: la radio libre madrileña (1976–1986). In *Coetánea. Actas del III Congreso Internacional de Historia de Nuestro Tiempo*, 333–342. Logroño: Universidad de La Rioja.

[7] Aguilera 1985: 66; Santos Díez, Maria Teresa. 1999. *La radio vasca (1978–1998)*. Bilbao: Servicio Editorial de la Universidad del País Vasco: 30–38.

express their thoughts in speech, writing, or any other form of communication", always according to the law.[8] In France, the Constitution proclaims the country's attachment to "the Rights of Man and the principles of national sovereignty as defined by the Declaration of 1789" (1958),[9] which expressed in its 11th article that "the free communication of ideas and of opinions is one of the most precious rights of man"; thus, any citizen may "speak, write and publish freely" except "what is tantamount to the abuse of this liberty in the cases determined by Law".[10]

The Spanish Constitution carries on with this legacy, and in its 20th section, it recognizes and protects the right to "freely express and spread thoughts, ideas and opinions through words, in writing or by any other means of reproduction" and to "freely communicate or receive truthful information by any means of dissemination whatsoever", eliminating "prior censorship". It also guarantees the access to media by the significant social and political groups, "respecting the pluralism of society".[11]

As these ideas become part of the dominant ideology in Western democratic societies, we have to bear in mind how the organization of the media in these countries prevented the complete and satisfactory observance of these rights. The development of media networks through state monopolies and private oligopolies depending on economic and political interests prevented citizens to become active agents in the media. Any hope of establishing bidirectional means of communication vanished, and the idea of a more democratic communication, which is a requirement to accomplish a full development of the rights exposed above, remained as an unfulfilled dream.

This context leads to a situation of "communicational anomy", using Robert K. Merton's redefinition of Émile Durkheim's idea of anomy. We are facing a situation in which some specific targets gather high importance, without a proportional importance of the institutional procedures available to reach those specific targets. Thus, there is a tension between the "culturally defined objectives, purposes and interests supported by the whole society or by individuals in different positions within this society" and "acceptable means to reach these objectives".[12]

Translating Merton's ideas into the Spanish context, we find a situation in which the groups involved in the construction of the newborn democratic regime's identity took the rights to free communication and free speech and introduced them into the new dominant ideology. Once these rights are part of the dominant ideology, they are projected to and assimilated by the subaltern groups as something natural and given – through the dynamics of social hegemony. However, as it is not possible to

---

[8] Senato della Reppublica. 1947. Constitution of the Italian Republic.

[9] Assemblée Nationale. 1958. Constitution of October 4, 1958. http://www.assemblee-nationale.fr/english/. Accessed 25 Oct 2014.

[10] Assemblée Nationale. 1789. Declaration of Human and Civic Rights of 26 August 1789. http://www.conseil-constitutionnel.fr/conseil-constitutionnel/root/bank_mm/anglais/cst2.pdf. Accessed 25 Oct 2014.

[11] Cortes Generales. 1978. Constitution. http://www.congreso.es/portal/page/portal/Congreso/Congreso/Hist_Normas/Norm/const_espa_texto_ingles_0.pdf. Accessed 25 Oct 2014.

[12] Merton, Robert K. 1964. *Teoría y estructura sociales*. Mexico: Fondo de Cultura Económica.

fulfil them legally, individuals and groups within the subaltern try to reach them using nonnormative/deviant means.

Within all the modes of adaptation given by Merton to solve the anomy, the one that comes closer to the origins of the free radio movement is probably the "innovation".[13] The groups and individuals that set up the free radios accepted that those rights were clearly desirable and considered that the normative ways to reach them (the mass media) were not enough, so they started their own illegal media. One more factor motivated the appearance of the free radio stations: the democratization of both the technological and the cognitive means needed to establish a small radio station. During the late 1970s and the 1980s, some low-cost do-it-yourself kits were widely commercialized to build a radio broadcaster. It was also possible to introduce illegal broadcasters in Spain from other countries such as Italy.[14] This made the appearance of these projects possible, together with the increase of new telecommunications engineers – who had the knowledge to establish and maintain this machinery. Finally, we can also underline the fact that this phenomenon was born within a youth subculture existing in Spain during those years. This "alternative subculture" was a hybrid form, mixing influences from the New Left, the Counterculture and the opposition to Francoist dictatorship. It can be identified with the groups from the extreme left wing and the social movements (ecologists, feminists, Trotskyites, Maoists, anarchists, etc.). As any subculture, it had its own representations and cultural practices – listening to these radio stations was, in fact, one of these practices. Therefore, the free radios could be considered "subcultural institutions" as they took an important part in the reproduction of the subcultural ideology.

Amongst the subjects that were part of these radios' contents (antimilitarism, ecologism, municipal and local issues, pacifism, etc.), feminism and women-related issues had a constant presence since the inception.

3.2   Women and Free Radio

The relationship between women – especially those involved in the feminist struggle – and free radios can be traced back to the movement's first steps. References about this relationship appeared in the movement's first documents; however, this link between women and free radio in Spain was never as deep as it was in France or Italy, where feminist collectives established free radios such as the French *Radioteuses* or the Italian *Radio Lilith*.[15]

As mentioned above, there was a feminist group in the collective that established *Ona Lliure*. Its role appeared in the radio's founding manifesto: "When we talk about the Movement [referring to the different social movements], we consider that

---

[13] Merton 1964: 149.

[14] Gas, Julia and Pérez, Javier. 2010. Hay que seguir luchando por la FM, ya que es accesible a todo el mundo. *Diagonal*, 120. Accessed 16 Jan 2011.

[15] Anonymous. 1981. Radios Libres, FM-92 Mc, el aire es de todos. *Bicicleta* 39, May.

the radio should not be just a resource to make these movements public (feminists, gays, conscientious objectors, ecologists, etc.), it should be a radio in which these movements take part to give a global sense to the audience's life".[16] Feminism and its struggle would not be just a mere topic in *Ona Lliure*'s programmes; it had to become a central point of its agenda to become a central part of its audience's life.

Little by little feminist programmes appeared in almost every free radio, as shown by different sources such as personal interviews, pamphlets, underground magazines, scripts, etc. Due to their alternative nature, it is difficult to find recordings of these programmes. Consequently, we don't know how the programmes exactly dealt with women issues. Nevertheless, they were a really outstanding part of these radios' agendas, although women usually constituted about 24 % of the people involved in these radio stations.[17]

In *Radio Cero* (Madrid), a radio connected to the Comisión Anti-OTAN, there was a programme led "by the **feministmovement**" – which is not surprising considering that the radio was close to the "alternative movements".[18] Amongst other guests, they interviewed people like Empar Pineda, a well-known feminist activist[19]: this clearly represents the significance given to feminism by *Radio Cero* and expressed in the radio's founding manifesto, which affirmed that one of its objectives was to "become a means of expression and communication for […] the **feminist movement** and its fight for women's rights and freedom against familiar, individual and social discriminations".[20]

One of the main aims of *Onda Sur Villaverde* (Villaverde, Madrid) was to become a "way of expressing the problems and ideals" of groups such as "youngsters, **women**, workers, unemployed and marginal people… as well as cultural, musical, sportive associations, etc.".[21] In the radio's founding document, called *A la desesperada*, the group behind the project clearly expressed its intention of dealing with "some subjects considered interesting and contrast obsessions [sic.] (ecology, labor movement, antimilitarism, **feminism**, etc.)".[22] A script from "A por todas", a *Onda Sur*'s feminist programme, that was broadcasted in 1985, shows some fixed sections such as female health (contraception, motherhood, information about the body, etc.), cultural criticism and women (books, magazines, films and theatre reviews), women and education, women and leisure time and legends about women (myths and witches). It would also pay attention to female hot news, addressing women-related problems, ideas or projects. This programme talked about women from a small village in southern Spain called Ubrique. Its case was interesting because there were not enough single young men in the village and women were organizing a "men parade" to solve that. This programme also mentioned a female-

---

[16] Anonymous 1985a. Propuesta para una radio libre. *Germinal* 3: 12.

[17] Anonymous. 1989. Censo de Radios Libres. Private Archive.

[18] Portuondo, Ernesto. 2008. Personal interview with the author. Madrid.

[19] Calero, Juan Pablo. 2011. Personal interview with the author. Madrid.

[20] Radio Cero. No date. *Declaración Fundacional (extracto)*. Madrid: Radio Cero.

[21] Anonymous. 1985b. Onda Sur. *Germinal* 3: 34.

[22] Colectivo Ecologista de Villaverde. 1982. *A la desesperada*. Private Archive.

managed textile workshop in Prádena (Segovia), a clear example of an empowering initiative that could become an example for the listeners.[23]

Radio Piel Roja (Leganés) was established by a group of "belligerent squaws" which decided to build a "wireless telegraph" because "there was nothing to do with white people".[24] Through this comparison with the American Indian struggle, they tried to inform on the restrictive access to the media in Spain during the 1980s.

Eguzki Irratia (Pamplona), in spite of its ecologist calling, decided to open its schedule to "collectives such as **feminists**, antimilitarists, etc."[25] Unfortunately, the experience lasted only 10 days. The radio was closed by the authorities and became a referent for the rest of the projects in Navarra.

In Albacete, there were some free radios, one of them *Radio Karacol* was born after a proposal done by "a local left-wing organization to other political, union related and civic organizations as well as individuals", and, in spite of their preference for musical programmes, they homed to "**women**, workers, antimilitarists, ecologists, etc."[26]

Onda Verde (Madrid) was the continuation of a previous project named *Onda Verde Vallekana*. This last radio defined itself as "ecologist [...], free, alternative and civic" with a clear preference, as for other projects, for subjects like antimilitarism and feminism.[27] *Onda Verde* kept on with this agenda, and both women and feminism became a capital part of its schedule.[28]

In Coslada, a small town near Madrid, *Radio Jabato* used to have a feminist programme called "Nosotras".[29] At this stage, nothing but its name remains.

In Bilbao (Basque Country), *Irola Irala Irratia* saw the appearance of a feminist space called "Arrímate" in 1986.[30] In the same town, *Illuna Irratia* (one of the pioneers in the area) had since its inception a feminist programme, which is symptomatic of the importance of women in this radio.[31]

Continuing with the Basque Country, *Hala Bedi Irratia* (Vitoria) had, as it appears in one of its fanzines, a programme called "El General mola" that apparently had a "marxists-leninist-maoist-pacifist-**feminist**-occupacionist [sic.]-religious-abertzale-marginal and naff point of view".[32] That fanzine also contained a manifesto entitled "Y nosotras de qué vamos...?" which exposed the opinion of the members of "Adiós Penélope, adiós" – a feminist programme – on a really

[23] A por todas. 1985. *Programa: A por todas*. Private archive.

[24] Anonymous. 1985c. Radio Piel Roja. *Germinal* 3: 36.

[25] Anonymous. 1985d. Eguzki Irratia. *Germinal* 3: 38.

[26] Anonymous 1985d: 39.

[27] Beaumont, J.F. 1983. Onda Verde Vallekana, una emisora laternativa para grupos ciudadanos del barrio madrileño. *El País*, 9 May.

[28] Onda Verde. 1988. *Onda Verde*. Madrid.

[29] Anonymous. 1985e. Radio Jabato. *J.A.B.A.T.O.* 6: 32.

[30] Irola Irratia. 2000. Irola Irala Irratia 107.5 FM. In *Radios libres utopía comunicativa*, ed. Irola Irrativa, 21. Bilbao: Autoedited.

[31] Anonymous. 1984. Los años de crecimiento. *Irratia* 1: 4.

[32] Anonymous. No date a. Use las orejas. *Halabedidatzita*. 1: 2.

polemic topic: abuses. The manifesto also expresses the relations between the radio and the feminist struggle against patriarchal society:

> We are in a free radio like Hala Bedi, with a bunch of girls and boys that apparently have something in common with us: we all reject this imposed shitty society, we all hate it and we want to change it. In this process it is essential to reverse all the chauvinist ideas and attitudes because they are both really present in our daily lives and very deep inside our brains. Most of you ignore this struggle.
>   Maybe this page could open a debate about the subject. Our programme, every Thursday from 2 to 4 pm is also opened for this. We encourage you to phone or write us to make this debate useful.[33]

We find in this paragraph the idea of how the feminist struggle, in spite of being part of the social movements and the free radios, needs its own spaces, due to its specific features and demands as well as its own dynamics to generate both discourse and consciousness.

In *Txapa Irratia*'s first fanzine (Bergara, Basque Country), one can find a text written by a friend radio, *Radio Pottoka*, from Eibar (Basque Country) explaining the problems between the radio's feminist group and the local authorities, when the last ones did not allow the use of a public facility to hold a talk entitled: "Women and NATO".[34]

There were certainly thousands of radio experiences related with women and feminism during those years; however, the lack of documents prevents a wider list of examples. We have verified that feminism was a constant presence in free radios' lives, and it is time now to focus on the "women's groups" existing since the 1980s in some of these stations. There were sections created, obviously, by women whose main aim was to analyze the role of women in communication and how these radios could be used to deal with the problems derived from women's situation in contemporary societies. These groups have usually generated international networks, which is a clear example of these radios' emancipatory potential.

The first existing group in Spain was the *Grup de dones de Radio Venus* (*Radio Venus*' women's group in Barcelona, Catalonia). This group expressed in a document called "Mujer y radio libre"[35] the importance of women in the free radio movement, and it had its origins in a previous feminist programme in *Radio Gavina*: "El programa de la dona". Its clear objective was to denounce the "frustrations produced by the monotonous voice sounding every evening [referring to the pre-existing female oriented radio programmes]". All the media have exploited women, turning them into "a minor voice, a sweet and sensual sound", presenting them as "a sexual icon, stimulating male desires and always ready to serve them". These are the reasons why free radios are important as they allow to "listen to another kind of voice, non monotonous, non ritual, a voice that does not advertise, gives advice or talks about chastity".

---

[33] Anonymous. No date b. Y nosotras, de qué vamos.... *Halabedidatzita* 1: 11.
[34] Anonymous. 1986. Akaidada II eibarko radixo libria. *Txapa Radio Almorrana* 1: 17.
[35] Grup de Dones de Rádio Venus. 1985. Mujer y radio libre. *Germinal* 3: 17.

For this group, the women working in free radios "don't need to talk with that sensual voice or explain the life of any evil bastard who forces his wife to wash his house with Ajax". Quite the opposite, free radios' female-oriented programmes:

are for women in general, they try not to convert them into a marginal myth, they want to represent femininity as an active movement fighting to get a series of rights that society denied them a long time ago.[36]

The group aimed at opening people's eyes, while being more than "just a voice and a microphone". During the time the group lasted, they organized programmes dedicated to topics such as women and the army, natural childbirth or abortion, with the clear intention of "communicating the truth without hats, moustaches or beards that could dull the programme".

As women's role within the Spanish free radio movement evolved, in 1986, Valencia held an "Encuentro Internacional de Mujeres de las Radios Libres" ("International Meeting of Women from Free Radios").[37] A few years later, in 1992, during the Oaxtepec Assembly (Mexico), the *Women's International Network* was established within AMARC (Asociación Mundial de Radios Comunitarias) – World Association of Community Radio Broadcasters – the organization that has been representing the free and community radios since 1983. This network is a "mixture of good communicator women who work to secure women's right to communicate and be part of the community radio movement".[38] Amongst its principles, we find "supporting women's empowerment, gender equity and a general improvement of women's position in the world", promoting "women's access to every level in community radios, including the decision making ones", supporting "women's effort to express themselves both inside and outside their communities" and trying to change "negative representations of men and women in the media and challenge the stereotypes reproduced by them around the world".[39]

In parallel, within the *Network Interknonnexiones*, promoted by *Radio Dreyckland* (Germany) in 1989, the first working group composed exclusively of women appeared in 1993. This group concluded that "women had plenty of specific subjects to deal with, and that they are underrepresented in the media (including the alternative ones)". In 1995 this group that had become an international network had a second encounter in Freiburg and a third the next year held by *Radio Klara* in Valencia. In 1997 the network held a meeting dedicated to immigrant women's role in alternative communication in Freiburg and its fourth network meeting under the title: "Women, racism and media". In 1998 they celebrated the second encounter

---

[36] Grup de dones 1985: 3.

[37] García, Javier and Sáez, Chiara. 2011. *¿Algo nuevo bajo el sol? El rapto de frecuencias de radio en el estado español y la discriminación hacia las radios comunitarias (1979–2011)*. Unpublished paper given up by the authors.

[38] AMARC-WIN. No date. ¿Qué es la Red Internacional de Mujeres – RIM de AMARC? AMARC-WIN. http://win.amarc.org. Accessed 4 Aug 2011.

[39] AMARC-WIN no date.

dedicated to immigrant women and communication, showing that there was a lot of work to do as of yet.[40]

Women's groups have kept on with their activities both at national and international levels. In Spain we can find examples such as *Mujeres Conv-boca*[41] from a radio called *Desencadena Usera* (Madrid). This group started a programme with the intention of "spreading the progress and the challenges of the feminist movement and contribute to women empowerment and gender equity".[42]

There is also an interesting project that started as a women's group with local intentions and ended up as an international network. The *Área de la mujer* (Women's Area) in *Radio Vallekas* (Madrid) was created in the year 2000. The establishment of this group meant the integration of all the women-related projects that the radio had been developing for almost 20 years. Its main aim is to reinforce radio's role as a way of connecting women with society: they support women organizations by becoming their mean of expression and try to deal with information from a gendered perspective. Their objectives are clear: promoting equity through "information, dialogue, debate and opinion", as well as providing women access to "the resources, activities and announcements that increase their welfare, educational, labour, cultural and leisure chances" and promoting and supporting the work done by women's groups and associations.[43] In 2004 this group became an international network called *Nosotras en el mundo* (*Us* [referring to women] *in the world*).[44] The inclusion of an Argentinian woman in this group was the starting point for a network that nowadays includes three working centres: Argentina (Southern Cone), Spain (Europe) and El Salvador (Central America). This network claims to put women at the centre of communication and clarify that "a feminist pedagogy is of vital importance to raise awareness about the less obvious ways of chauvinism [...]" because, still today, "chauvinism is reproduced amongst the youth and the media play a disastrous role that has to be contested". That opposition would be the network's *raison d'être*.[45]

---

[40] Anonymous. 2000. Mujeres creando espacios de comunicación. Red internaciona feminista de mujeres de las radios libres y comunitarias. In *Radios libres utopía comunicativa*, ed. Irola Irrativa, 51–52. Bilbao: Autoedited.

[41] Translating the group's name is a little bit complicated, as it is a pun. It means something close to *Women with mouth*, consequently, women who can talk.

[42] Grupo de Mujeres Conv-Boca. No date. Grupo de mujeres Conv-Boca. http://www.cornisa.org/orientación_aymutua/grupomujeres.html. Accessed 4 Aug 2011.

[43] Radio Vallekas no date Nosotras en el mundo. http://radiovallekas.org/spip/spip.php?artocleI. Accessed 4 Aug 2011.

[44] Nosotras en el Mundo 2014.

[45] Oliveras, Lucía R. 2012. No nos representan. Mujeres en los medios. La experiencia de la Red.

3.3 Becoming Women's Voice?

Is it possible to measure the influence of these radios in the results of feminist struggles? As having statistics about the audiences is clearly difficult and prevents a quantitative approach, the only way is to read the phenomenon from a qualitative point of view, to understand it in a double perspective: one is to consider these programmes as a site of resistance, and the other is to read this relationship as a chance.

The free radio stations, and all their women-related programmes, constitute a site of resistance against the dominant ideology and its gender representations. Their amateurism and their alternative way of doing radio made it easier to break up with the pre-existing communicative models and the stereotypes that they produced and reproduced. Stereotyping is a cultural practice that "tends to occur where there are gross inequalities of power", so through these stereotypes, "power is usually directed against the subordinate or excluded group".[46] Therefore, the female stereotypes developed by the general-interest radios, which depend on the dominant groups, constitute a clear example of symbolic violence against women, a subaltern group victim of contemporary societies' patriarchal oppression.

The way free radios deal with these issues clearly contests the dominant female representation, as we have seen in examples like the *Grup de dones de Ràdio Venus*. The abolishing of that image of women as mere "sensual voices" and their transformation into the centre, the subject and the object of the communicative processes turn the free radios into a site of resistance against dominant ideology. They replace the dominant paternalistic discourse with a new one in which women become conscious transmitter, activist and questioning receivers, and women themselves are the important part of the message. Through this new discourse, free radios contest dominant ideology, and their daily praxis can be understood as a subversion of that ideological order.

Free radios also constitute a chance for women, a chance to take part in public opinion, generate ideology, project it and finally be an active part in the processes of negotiating social hegemony. These radio stations are also a way of leaving the private sphere, where women have been historically set aside, and gain the public one through a media. They also strengthen, through the establishment of networks, female associationism. Free radio's role both as subcultural practice and institution and its close relationship with the rest of social movement allow a first access to the public and to a wider social network. Being part of these radios means for the feminist collectives a chance for making new contacts and creating solidarity networks with other social movements and other feminist collectives at both national and international levels. For women coming from social movements different from feminism, it would mean the possibility of discovering the feminist struggle and becom-

---

[46] Hall, Stuart. 2009. The spectacle of the 'other'. In *Representation: cultural representations and signifying practices*, ed. Stuart Hall, 223–290. London: Sage.

ing an active part of it. Finally, for all the anonymous listeners, it means the access to a new way of doing and understanding communication, a chance to be an active part of it and be finally represented in the media. It is also possible to think that due to their ideological role, free radios could have been an active agent in the establishment of social hegemony, so they could be, through the generation of a counterhegemonic discourse, a tool for introducing new elements into the dominant ideology.

3.4   Conclusion

This chapter addresses a marginal phenomenon. It is marginal for three reasons: it comes from society's margins, it is part of popular culture and it has not been taken seriously by the academic world. Thus, the relationship between women/feminism and these radios constitutes a clear example of how subaltern exclusion can be fought from the margins. Going in depth, this relationship incorporates free radio to the feminist catalogue of means of resistance and is also a way to discover a relatively unknown feature of alternative radio. Although the first radio stations appeared 28 years ago, their struggle is still ongoing, enduring almost the same problems. So, have they finally been able to change communicative practices? Do women take a non-subordinated part in communication? Have female stereotypes disappeared from the media? Are women-related issues well represented in general-interest media? Unless we can answer in the affirmative to all these questions, subaltern groups will need a loudspeaker to spread their words, and free radios would probably remain a major part of it as they constitute a well-organized nationwide network collaborating with other community media such as televisions, digital platforms and medias, news agencies and media producers, e.g. the Red Estatal de Medios Comunitarios that counts 27 associated and 13 collaborator members.[47] The expansion of the access to the Internet has somehow altered the media landscape allowing for the development of different means of overtaking the communicational anomy, such as personal blogs or websites. However, they will not outpace free and community radios, as the latter play a community-based role that is not done by the firsts, which are usually individualistic initiatives. The Internet also had a positive impact on free radios. Firstly, it allows establishing "only Internet" radio stations, which means a lower economic investment, while secondly, it has increased radio's audiences. Listening "through the Internet" permits getting worldwide listeners, also giving the chance of re-listening and archiving programmes thanks to podcasting platforms. These facts have facilitated the contact between women's groups as well as turned local women-related programmes into global or national experiences. Although the legal context has not specially changed within these 30 years – most

[47] REMC. 2014. Anexo: Proyectos que integran la Red de Medios Comunitarios. http://es.wikipedia.org/wiki/Anexo:Proyectos_que_integran_la_Red_de_Medios_Comunitarios. Accessed 15 Jan 2015.

of these radios still broadcast without licence (illegally) – we are now living good times for free radios as some of these projects are winning some awards and public recognition.[48]

References

Aguilera, Miguel. 1985. *Radios libres y radios piratas*. Madrid: Editorial Forja.
Colectivo de Radios Libres. 1981. *Alicia es el diablo*. Barcelona: Hacer.
Hall, Stuart. 2009. The spectacle of the 'other'. In *Representation: cultural representations and signifying practices*, ed. Stuart Hall, 223–290. London: Sage.
Merton, Robert K. 1964. *Teoría y estructura sociales*. Mexico: Fondo de Cultura Económica.
Nosotras en el Mundo. 2014. In *Comunicación para el cambio social. Universidad, sociedad civil y medios,* ed. Iñaki Chavel Gil, 133–141. Madrid: Los Libros de la Catarata.
Oliveras, Lucía R. 2012. No nos representan. Mujeres en los medios. La experiencia de la Red.
Pérez Martínez, and José Emilio. 2012. Libertad en las ondas: la radio libre madrileña (1976–1986). In *Coetánea. Actas del III Congreso Internacional de Historia de Nuestro Tiempo*, 333–342. Logroño: Universidad de La Rioja.
Santos Díez, Maria Teresa. 1999. *La radio vasca (1978–1998)*. Bilbao: Servicio Editorial de la Universidad del País Vasco.

Sources

A por todas. 1985. *Programa: A por todas*. Private archive.
Agencias. 2006. Aguirre entrega los Premios de Periodismo 8 de Marzo. *El País*. 8 March.
Aisa, Manel. 2013. Las jornadas libertarias de 1977 y la transición libertaria 1974–1979. http://manelaisa.com/articulo/articulo-1-las-jornadas-libertarias-de-1977-y-la-transicion-libertaria-1974–1979-version-2/. Accessed 17 Oct 2011.
AMARC-WIN. No date. ¿Qué es la Red Internacional de Mujeres – RIM de AMARC? AMARC-WIN. http://win.amarc.org. Accessed 4 Aug 2011.
Anonymous. 1981. Radios Libres, FM-92 Mc, el aire es de todos. *Bicicleta* 39, May.
Anonymous. 1984. Los años de crecimiento. *Irratia* 1: 4.
Anonymous. 1985a. Propuesta para una radio libre. *Germinal* 3: 12.
Anonymous. 1985b. Onda Sur. *Germinal* 3: 34.
Anonymous. 1985c. Radio Piel Roja. *Germinal* 3: 36.
Anonymous. 1985d. Eguzki Irratia. *Germinal* 3: 38.
Anonymous. 1985e. Radio Jabato. *J.A.B.A.T.O.* 6: 32.
Anonymous. 1986. Akaidada II eibarko radixo libria. *Txapa Radio Almorrana* 1: 17.
Anonymous. 1989. Censo de Radios Libres. Private Archive.

---

[48]Agencias. 2006. Aguirre entrega los Premios de Periodismo 8 de Marzo. *El País*. 8 March; Europa Press. 2009. Pepa Bueno (La 1), Cruz Morcillo (ABC) y Lucía Ruiz (Radio Vallekas) serán galardonadas hoy con los premios 'AMECO'. Europa Press. http://www.europapress.es/epsocial/fundaciones/noticia-pepa-bueno-cruz-morcillo-abc-lucia-ruiz-radio-vallekas-seran-galardonadas-hoy-premios-ameco-20090226073627.html. Accessed 15 Jan 2015; Onda Color. 2014. Onda Color es la radio más rentable socialmente de Andalucía. *Onda Color*. http://www.ondacolor.org/index.php/noticias-y-actividades/159-onda-color-es-la-radio-masrentable-socialmente-de-andalucia. Accessed 14 Jan 2015.

Anonymous. 2000. Mujeres creando espacios de comunicación. Red internaciona feminista de mujeres de las radios libres y comunitarias. In *Radios libres utopía comunicativa*, ed. Irola Irrativa, 51–52. Bilbao: Autoedited.

Anonymous. No date a. Use las orejas. *Halabedidatzita*. 1: 2.

Anonymous. No date b. Y nosotras, de qué vamos.... *Halabedidatzita* 1: 11.

Assemblée Nationale. 1789. Declaration of Human and Civic Rights of 26 August 1789. http://www.conseil-constitutionnel.fr/conseil-constitutionnel/root/bank_mm/anglais/cst2.pdf. Accessed 25 Oct 2014.

Assemblée Nationale. 1958. Constitution of October 4, 1958. http://www.assemblee-nationale.fr/english/. Accessed 25 Oct 2014.

Beaumont, J.F. 1983. Onda Verde Vallekana, una emisora laternativa para grupos ciudadanos del barrio madrileño. *El País*, 9 May.

Calero, Juan Pablo. 2011. Personal interview with the author. Madrid.

Colectivo Ecologista de Villaverde. 1982. *A la desesperada*. Private Archive.

Cortes Generales. 1978. Constitution. http://www.congreso.es/portal/page/portal/Congreso/Congreso/Hist_Normas/Norm/const_espa_texto_ingles_0.pdf. Accessed 25 Oct 2014.

Europa Press. 2009. Pepa Bueno (La 1), Cruz Morcillo (ABC) y Lucía Ruiz (Radio Vallekas) serán galardonadas hoy con los premios 'AMECO'. Europa Press. http://www.europapress.es/epsocial/fundaciones/noticia-pepa-bueno-cruz-morcillo-abc-lucia-ruiz-radio-vallekas-seran-galardonadas-hoy-premios-ameco-20090226073627.html. Accessed 15 Jan 2015.

García, Javier and Sáez, Chiara. 2011. *¿Algo nuevo bajo el sol? El rapto de frecuencias de radio en el estado español y la discriminación hacia las radios comunitarias (1979–2011)*. Unpublished paper given up by the authors.

Gas, Julia and Pérez, Javier. 2010. Hay que seguir luchando por la FM, ya que es accesible a todo el mundo. *Diagonal*, 120. Accessed 16 Jan 2011.

Grup de Dones de Rádio Venus. 1985. Mujer y radio libre. *Germinal* 3: 17.

Grupo de Mujeres Conv-Boca. No date. Grupo de mujeres Conv-Boca. http://www.cornisa.org/orientación_aymutua/grupomujeres.html. Accessed 4 Aug 2011.

Irola Irratia. 2000. Irola Irala Irratia 107.5 FM. In *Radios libres utopía comunicativa*, ed. Irola Irrativa, 21. Bilbao: Autoedited.

Onda Color. 2014. Onda Color es la radio más rentable socialmente de Andalucía. *Onda Color*. http://www.ondacolor.org/index.php/noticias-y-actividades/159-onda-color-es-la-radio-mas-rentable-socialmente-de-andalucia. Accessed 14 Jan 2015.

Onda Verde. 1988. *Onda Verde*. Madrid.

Portuondo, Ernesto. 2008. Personal interview with the author. Madrid.

Radio Cero. No date. *Declaración Fundacional (extracto)*. Madrid: Radio Cero.

Radio Vallekas. No date. Nosotras en el mundo. http://radiovallekas.org/spip/spip.php?artocleI. Accessed 4 Aug 2011.

REMC. 2014. Anexo: Proyectos que integran la Red de Medios Comunitarios. http://es.wikipedia.org/wiki/Anexo:Proyectos_que_integran_la_Red_de_Medios_Comunitarios. Accessed 15 Jan 2015.

Senato della Reppublica. 1947. Constitution of the Italian Republic.

Chapter 4
From *Marie-Claire* Magazine's Authoritative Pedagogy to the *Hellocoton* Blog Platform's Knowledge Sharing: Between Gender Construction and Gender Appropriation

Alexie Geers

Abstract When *Marie-Claire* magazine was first published in 1937 in France, it broke new journalistic ground as the first written format directed at women. Despite its favourable reception, this type of publication, now commonly referred to as a *women's magazine*, is regularly decried as a vehicle for transmitting stereotyped models of a femininity that is confined to domestic life and superficial appearances. From a diachronic perspective, the participative web – 'women's' blogs in particular – offers key areas of observation of what women do when they self-express directly to other women. Do they fall along the continuum of women's magazines' editorial style, or rather, do they break with those magazines' gender codes and conceptions?

When *Marie-Claire* magazine was first published in March 1937 in France, it broke new journalistic ground as the first written format directed at women. Building on the progress in women's literacy,[1] the editorial team created a magazine to unite a readership not around social affiliation but sexual identity: 'You are all *Marie-Claire*, and this magazine has been designed for you'.[2] The magazine's success was so immediate that it became a model for subsequent publications for women.

Despite the favourable reception, this type of publication, now commonly referred to as a *women's magazine*, is regularly decried as a vehicle for transmitting stereotyped models of a femininity that is confined to domestic life and superficial appearances.[3] This paradox complicates our observation of the relationship between women and the cultural objects that are made for them and the gender preconceptions

---

[1] Mayeur, Françoise. 2008. *L'éducation des filles en France au XIXe siècle*. Paris: Perrin (1st edn: Hachette 1979).

[2] Marie-Claire. 1937a. *Editorial*.

[3] Dardigna, Anne-Marie. 1978. *La presse féminine, fonction idéologique*. Paris: Maspero; Chollet, Mona. 2012. *Beauté fatale, les nouveaux visages de l'aliénation féminine*. Paris: Zones.

A. Geers (✉)
Livic, EHESS, Paris, and Espe, Université Reims Champagne Ardenne, Reims, France
e-mail: alexie.geers@gmail.com

© Springer International Publishing Switzerland 2015

V. Schafer, B.G. Thierry (eds.), *Connecting Women*, History of Computing,
DOI 10.1007/978-3-319-20837-4_4

associated with those cultural objects. From a diachronic perspective, the participative web – 'women's' blogs in particular – offers key areas of observation of what women do when they self-express directly to other women. Do they fall along the continuum of women's magazines' editorial style, or rather, do they break with those magazines' gender codes and conceptions?

The online platform *Hellocoton.fr* offers centralised access to a 'selection of the best women's blogs', according to its home page. The site was chosen as a field of observation because it offers bloggers visibility subject to membership. This means that in choosing to register with *Hellocoton*, bloggers subscribe to the concept of 'women's blogs' and acknowledge that their own production of writing may be characterised as 'feminine', recognising themselves within the site's provided categories. By choosing to observe this platform, we are not claiming to faithfully reflect women's online production in general – a goal made difficult by the inability to ascertain sexual identity and a complex delimitation of the corpus – but it allows us to access a sample of production qualified by its authors as 'feminine'. The array of subjects, styles and profiles gives us the possibility to observe how these bloggers appropriate or contest the media messaging that is created for them.

4.1 Conceptions of Femininity

Marie-Claire was founded in 1937 by journalist Marcelle Auclair and newspaper publisher Jean Prouvost, who had owned the popular daily *Paris-Soir* since 1930. The concept of providing a magazine for women was validated by its immediate success upon publication.[4] At the time, upper-class women consumed fashion magazines, but others had no regular publication at their disposal aside from the 'magazine pages' inserted into the daily paper.[5] Since its origins, written media had been principally aimed at men, who were more literate and were culturally viewed as the primary consumers of information. *Marie-Claire*'s editorial mission was stated in its title:

> To give the French woman, in a single newspaper, every week, all she may find to be of interest or of use.[6]

The magazine's topics ranged well beyond fashion and style tips, the likes of which had been previously published. A study of *Marie-Claire* issues from 1937 to the present allows a typology of subjects. They can be grouped broadly into three categories that define the feminine along three facets: mother, guardian of the home and seductress.

These themes are not addressed equally over time. From its first publication in 1937 until it stopped publishing in 1944, personal care dominates, showcasing a

---

[4] Sullerot, Evelyne. 1963. *La presse féminine*. Paris: Armand Colin.
[5] Chermette, Myriam. 2009. *"Donner à voir", La photographie dans Le Journal: discours, pratiques, usages (1892–1944)*. Ph.D. Université de Saint Quentin en Yvelines.
[6] Marie-Claire 1937a.

femininity based on seduction and expressed in beauty treatments and fashion. Beginning in 1954, when publication resumed, and until around 1970, the predominant themes are interior decoration, home management, cooking and childcare, emphasising a femininity centred on the home. From 1970 to 1995, sexual satisfaction becomes central, equating femininity with sexual liberation. From 1995 until the early 2000s, sexuality remains a major topic but moves beyond affirming feminine sexuality and into managing couple relationships.

While the approach changes over time, no theme ever truly disappears and these three pillars persist. This continuity reinforces an essentialist conception of the feminine around concerns described as shared. This formula, based on sexual commonality, has been repeated in other women's publications like *Elle* and *Marie-France* and until recently in magazines like *Femme Actuelle*, *Biba* and *Cosmopolitan*.

The *Hellocoton* platform, for its part, provides a 'selection of the best women's blogs' and showcases an assortment of articles categorised by theme on its home page. The site was created in 2008 by Hubert Michaux and Victor Cerutti, alums of the customisable French web portal *Netvibes*. From the outset, showcased blogs were not selected by the editorial team alone, but also by readers' votes. By January 2010, the platform was receiving two million unique visits each month.[7] In July 2012, it was purchased by the Prisma Media publishing group, which also owns *Voici*, *Gala*, *Télé Loisirs*, *Prima* and *Femme Actuelle*, the best-selling women's magazine in France, with approximately 752,000 copies sold annually.

According to its *Publicité* page, *Hellocoton* now receives nearly three million unique visitors each month and hosts 30,000 blogs, not all of them active. Although a publishing group owns the site, it neither organises nor controls the bloggers' writing. Bloggers are independent and free to choose whether to register on the platform. Blog posts are selected via an algorithm that calculates the frequency of shares, number of votes and reader comments, which are seen as positive signs of interaction.

In 2008, the home page was organised into the following categories: *people*, *fashion*, *gardening*, *cooking*, *culture*, *beauty*, *family*, *creation*, *decoration*, *technology* and *chatterbox*, each one allowing access to selected posts on member blogs. Six years later in 2014, *gardening*, *people*, *technology* and *chatterbox* disappeared; *creation* and *decoration* merged into the single category called *créa déco*; three new categories called *moods*, *lifestyle* and *buzz* (for viral videos) emerged, while *fashion*, *beauty*, *cooking*, *culture* and *family* all remained unaltered. The editorial team modified its classifications to better match its member blog content and blogger interests. In *beauty*, for example, the subcategory *nail art* was created. *Nail art*, a practice connecting nail cosmetics to design creativity,[8] now widely adopted by manufacturers of nail polish, wildly varied rhinestones and other nail equipment, was in part catalysed by bloggers who wrote about this theme, which pushed *Hellocoton* to create a dedicated subcategory for it.

---

[7] Menneveux, Richard. 2010. Be.com le nouveau féminin en ligne de Lagardère, *FrenchWeb.fr*. http://frenchweb.fr/be-com-le-nouveau-feminin-de-lagardere. Accessed 17 Feb 2015.

[8] L'am0ureuse. 2014. #*La Reine des Neiges version 2*. http://am0ureuse.wordpress.com/2014/05/13/la-reine-des-neiges-version-2/.

Several days of observation show that the categories still in place since 2008 – *fashion, beauty, cooking* and *family* – are those that have been the most amended by bloggers. They are also the same themes taken up by *Marie-Claire* throughout its existence, but here, bloggers have appropriated them to the point of devoting entire blogs to them and sharing their own specialised topics.

Since *Hellocoton*'s classification is theme based, readers can navigate directly to topics of interest. The editorial team creates 'thematic folders' that each include several articles from different blogs that treat transversal topics, for example, 'Parfumée pour le printemps-été', '50 manucures de fête', '20 fonds de teint pour un maquillage parfait', 'Réussir son smockey eye', etc. (Perfumed From Spring to Summer, 50 Festive Manicures, 20 Foundations for the Perfect Makeup, Successful Smokey Eyes[9]).

Hellocoton's style of reading is also generated from the way that authors conceptualise writing on their blogs, in ways that are often specialised. Unlike *Marie-Claire*'s 'generalist' conception, which asserts a homogenised femininity, most bloggers write on only one or two topics. A blog's title indicates its content, as with cooking blogs like *Gastronoome, Cuisinez comme Céline, Papilles et Pupilles, La cuisine à quatre mains* and *La ligne gourmande* ('The Gourmet Within', 'Cook like Celine', 'Taste Buds and Eye Pupils', 'Cooking for Four Hands', 'Foodie's Figure'); fashion blogs like *Les tribulations d'Anaïs: blog mode* Montpellier, *La souris coquette* and *Modeuse* timbrée (Anais's Tribulations: a Montpellier Fashion Blog, The Coquette Mouse, The Crazy Fashionista); or beauty blogs like *Blackbeauty bag, Chicissime beauté* (Majestic Beauty) and *Destination beauté: mon petit monde girly* (Destination Beauty: My Little Girly World).

Bloggers also discuss topics that interest them without speaking generally of *femininity*. Readers meanwhile don't come from a single essentialised source but from centres of interest. This specialisation does not represent a fundamental transgression against the elements composing the female gender as magazines like *Marie-Claire* propose it, but more of a shift produced by the fact of women managing their own material and freeing themselves from women's magazines' homogeneity.

4.2 Towards More Symmetrical Communication and Exchanges

4.2.1 *Marie-Claire: Vertical Transmission*

In order to transmit to readers the information the magazine considered necessary to fulfil their social role, successive *Marie-Claire* columnists mainly used the journalistic form, writing articles and reports. The themes of motherhood, appearance and

---

[9] All translations by L. Kraftowitz.

the home were discussed like any current event or political topic, meaning they were explained in an objective narrative tone.

For example, in the article entitled 'La mode sculpturale' (Sculptural fashion), published on 3 September 1937,[10] the columnist informs readers that:

> Fashion has become a sculptor this coming season. Years ago, learning to dress required a painter's palette and a draftsman's drawer. Now what counts is a sense of volume, a taste for contours, and a pure and perfect knowledge of anatomy.

The information is written in the present tense, with a declarative and objective mood, leaving no room for doubt or the conditional tone. Columnists also use this approach for dispensing advice:

> A truly womanly woman, neither thin nor fat: this is how you should look in these new dresses.

The prescription draws merit from its presentation: journalistic flourish naturalises the assertion into truth. It is followed by a procedure to achieve this desired result:

> The most important is to have a shapely waist.

This description is illustrated by a photograph of an antique sculpture accompanied by a legend indicating the parts of the body – neck, shoulders, chest, etc. – to which the directions relate. This metaphorical use of imagery gives the text a visual translation.

The visual formula can also be more explicit, taking the form of a manual. In the article 'Mettez votre visage en valeur' ('Enhance your face'), dated 14 January 1938,[11] four photographs show two before-and-after examples of faces. Arrows positioned around the images indicate the areas of the face requiring work and lead to paragraphs explaining what actions to take.

The directive nature of this writing recalls the nineteenth-century instruction manuals. The guides, made available to teachers as they were facing the progressive and unprecedented growth of the number of girls in their classrooms[12]; to mothers responsible for their children's, especially their daughters', upbringing[13]; and to young girls themselves,[14] provided a set of knowledge and information deemed useful to women's daily lives at the time. Activities or behaviours attributed to women were described in great detail in the formulas of a user's manual. Laundry, cooking, personal care, etc., were explained step by step, indicating that they required specific technical knowledge. The transmission of this knowledge occurred through a

---

[10] Marie-Claire. 1937b. *La mode sculpturale.*

[11] *Marie-Claire* 1938a. *Mettez votre visage en valeur*, 8–9.

[12] Mayeur 2008.

[13] Fonssagrives, Jean-Baptiste. 1869. *L'éducation physique des jeunes filles ou avis aux mères sur l'art de diriger leur santé et leur développement.* Paris: Hachette. http://gallica.bnf.fr/ark:/12148/bpt6k104230x.r=manuel+instruction+fille.langFR. Accessed 17 Feb 2015.

[14] Dufrénoy, Adélaïde. 1816. *La petite ménagère ou l'éducation maternelle (4 tomes).* Paris: A. Eymery. http://gallica.bnf.fr/ark:/12148/bpt6k54455967.r=.langFR. Accessed 17 Feb 2015.

specific rhetoric consisting of several expressions, like the injunction to 'Be within the family the ring that binds, the voice that consoles, the arm which supports, and through your actions and virtues make them love the name of God'.[15] This example places the girl's role within the mode of obligation and allows behavioural expectations to be made explicit alongside etched drawings depicting the girl amidst scenes of daily life, like other visual models of activities and behaviour.

To convince women to apply these strict rules and to make the models acceptable, the manuals' authors used different justifications that were first and foremost essentialist. Activities assigned to women were defined based on a belief in a feminine nature as specific and different from the masculine nature. The domestic economy was described as 'women's science *par excellence*',[16] and the art of 'performing housework and managing homes and families' was 'the woman's domain'.[17] Women's activities were valued and the authors emphasised the specialised expertise they required and the dedication they represented: 'The household duties, while menial in appearance, are sublime in reality, because they are summed up in these words: thinking of others'.[18]

Apart from Rousseau's *Emile* (1762), men had no written material for 'learning their gender', whereas women, via instruction manuals and magazines, received a good number of lessons to ensure their social role. This transmission occurred through a specific, prescriptive rhetoric, partly related to the practical nature of the knowledge they needed to learn to implement.

Readers accepted the imperative tone because the columnist was seen as an expert possessing and transmitting a superior set of knowledge. They were often well known to readers, and some, like Marcelle Auclair and later Ménie Grégoire, became central personalities of the magazine. They presented their advice as 'tips', 'tricks' and 'secrets' that they were sharing with their readership. The transmission of this valuable knowledge established trust and allowed for the use of a directive tone. The tone was mitigated by the columnist, who was presented as a friend:

> Readers of *Marie-Claire*, we are, above all, your friend, please ask our advice for all aspects of life, and we will work hard to be your happiness consultant.[19]

This climate of trust and friendship was built by a specific epistolary style that mimicked friendly correspondence. Beginning with the first issues, in a column entitled 'Parlons en amies' ('Girl talk'), a columnist addressed readers directly, signing the text with the initials M.-C. or the magazine's name, *Marie-Claire*, as you would the bottom of a letter. This signature, a convention of private correspondence, invoked proximity between the columnist and the readers. These codes were revisited in the 'Le courrier de Marie-Claire' ('Letters to Marie-Claire') section, in

---

[15] Juranville, Clarisse. 1879. *Le savoir-faire et le savoir vivre: guide pratique de la vie usuelle à l'usage des jeunes filles*. Paris: Librairie Larousse. http://gallica.bnf.fr/ark:/12148/bpt6k6149610s.r=manuel+instruction+fille.langFR. Accessed 17 Feb 2015.

[16] Juranville 1879: preface.

[17] Juranville 1879: 8.

[18] Juranville 1879: 20.

[19] Marie-Claire. 1938a. *Mettez votre visage en valeur*, 8–9.

which readers were identified by their first name. The response was written in the style of a discussion where one person asks the advice of someone more experienced and knowledgeable. The responses were signed by the first name of the columnist. This personal touch introduced feelings of connection. *Marie-Claire* was able to simultaneously embody the character of the columnist addressing readers and the readers themselves.

Many columnists made their mark on the magazine through the relationship they developed with their readers. Marcelle Auclair was on staff from its establishment in 1937 until publication halted in 1944 and returned in 1955 after its 1954 reappearance. Specialising at first in beauty, and later on in the post-war years in matters of morality and spiritual life, she responded to readers' letters and wrote prolifically. She dispensed advice and recommendations in the style of a friend, or at times a mother:

> I ask you to please be natural. [...] In terms of eyeshadow, I agree with your mother and urge you to use it only in extreme moderation; you have everything to gain.[20]

Marcelle Auclair had the kindness of a friend that readers could reencounter each week (or each month after the magazine's reappearance) and the knowledge of an older sister. This trust relationship was cultivated even beyond the magazine pages on 25 April 1938, when the Cercle des Amies de Marie-Claire (Marie-Claire Friends Circle) opened its doors, a house where readers could go for advice, classes or lectures, including some by Marcelle Auclair. Enhancing this climate of trust created a safe space for discussion, which in turn reinforced community cohesion.

Ménie Grégoire[21] had a similar role in the early 1970s. *Marie-Claire* was becoming 'the couple's magazine' with the emergence of the theme of sexuality, which Ménie Grégoire helped develop. To do this, she changed the format of addressing readers, privileging direct exchange in the *Questions Sur l'Amour* (Questions About Love) column, where columnists published readers' questions and their own answers. While readers' letters had been featured since the magazine's beginnings, never had they been more central or taken up as much space. This form of direct exchange, which she used in parallel to her radio show on RTL, in which listeners phoned in with questions that she answered on air, fostered closeness between the columnist and her readership. Ménie Grégoire's work went beyond this format to include her prolific writing on sexuality for *Marie-Claire*. Her articles' defining characteristic was that she would gather a wide range of women's testimonials. This shared intimacy gave significance to the exchange and strengthened readers' sense of community.

This process of transmission, led by a woman expert, was also found in the magazine's advertising content since the advertising material mimed the articles: a transmitter of feminine traits, usually a celebrity, was shown on the page speaking about the product and her experience with it. This transmitter could also be an omni-

---

[20] Marie-Claire. 1938b. *Jeunes filles, la beauté c'est la santé*, 17.

[21] Cardon, Dominique. 2003. Droit au plaisir et devoir d'orgasme dans l'émission de Ménie Grégoire. *Le Temps des médias* 1: 77–94. www.cairn.info/revue-le-temps-des-medias-2003-1-page-77.htm. Accessed 17 Feb 2015.

scient narrator with a hidden identity but whose knowledge was understood to be superior to that of the recipient.

The context of friendship and trust helped create a strong bond between the magazine and its readers, which likely explains its reader loyalty. However, the bond was limited since readers could only have a limited, rhetorical exchange. In a mode of vertical transmission, the columnist remained the expert imparting knowledge to her students.[22]

4.2.2   Transmitting by Sharing

Women bloggers, for their part, showcase topics that affect them and that either don't exist or rarely appear in women's magazines, through a high specialisation of subjects. For example, in the case of medically assisted procreation (MAP), bloggers discuss their experience as a couple and their often long and painful quest to procreate. These women share many intimate details with their readers, who consist predominantly of other so-called MAPettes and who in turn confide their challenges and successes. The vocabulary deployed is highly technical and the many abbreviations – DPO (day post-ovulation), gygy (for gynaecologist) and PDS (for blood test) – affirm the existence of a community dialogue that is indecipherable to unfamiliar or unaffected readers, recalling medical forums.

This sense of community based on experience sharing also appears in the comment sections, where encouragement, good luck wishes or advice for the blogger can be found. When she announced her pregnancy on her blog in an article on 15 May 2014, entitled 'Le dire tout bas, pour ne pas réveiller le mauvais œil…' ('A Whisper, So As Not to Wake the Evil Eye…'), Lucette received 66 positive reader comments.[23] Miss Infertility, the first to comment, wrote:

> Whispers from me: (Yeeeeeeeeeeeees!!!!!! Lucette, we both did it!!!!! This is amazing!!!!!!!). Got my fingers crossed for you! i took my second dose this morning, this is stressful!! Lots of love.

Bloggers forge relationships and know the history and experiences of one another. They regularly wish each other well in writing their posts. On Lucette's post of 13 October 2014, entitled 'Trouillothon',[24] she reminded her reader friends that even during her pregnancy she wouldn't forget the anxiety they might be going through at the moment of embryo implantation:

> Because today it is your turn, but together we are always stronger.

---

[22] Pasquier, Dominique. 2014. Les jugements profanes en ligne sous le regard des sciences sociales. *Réseaux* 183: 9–25. http://www.cairn.info/revue-reseaux-2014-1-page-9.htm. Accessed 17 Feb 2015.

[23] Chez Lucette. 2014a. *Le dire tout bas, pour ne pas réveiller le mauvais œil… .* https://chezlucette.wordpress.com/2014/05/15/le-dire-tout-bas-pour-ne-pas-reveiller-le-mauvais-oeil/.

[24] Chez   Lucette.   2014b.   *Trouillothon.*   https://chezlucette.wordpress.com/2014/10/13/trouillonthon/.

Motherhood is a theme in *Marie-Claire*, notably in topics related to childcare (1937–1944) and childhood education (1954–1970), but pregnancy itself as a subject is generally unexplored. However, it is widely addressed by bloggers who share the stories of their pregnancies month by month in the form of 'pregnancy updates', repurposing an older practice of 'pregnancy journals'.[25] These posts are illustrated with a photograph of the author's belly, which can be seen growing over the months.[26] This type of account, accompanied by self-produced images,[27] reinforces the uniqueness of each experience.

Bloggers also tell the story of their labour hour by hour, as seen in a number of blogs and posts.[28] Generally, they explain their desire to write not only to remember but also to share with other 'nullis' – a term they use to refer to nulliparous women. The stages and feelings attached to the experience are divulged down to the smallest details.

In these examples, knowledge related to motherhood is transmitted through individual stories rather than advice directives. Readers learn by way of many individual experiences, reinforced by the use of self-produced images.

Among beauty blogs, many posts narrate beauty routines. In 'Routine du soir bonsoir' ('Good evening, evening routine') on the blog *Woodybeauté*, dated 10 November 2014, a blogger narrates her nightly routine:

> In the evening, especially in winter, I hate putting water on my face, it's too chilly. So I need some practical and easy-to-use leave-on products. I'm a big fan of micellar water (see my many tests here, here and here) but with the return of the cold I wanted a more soothing product.

She then states her opinion on each product and describes the sensations experienced during use. The article is accompanied by a photograph of the products used arranged next to each other,[29] a recurrent visual device in the blogosphere. The distribution of this visual form from one blog to another[30] shows that bloggers both appreciate and appropriate this personalised experience sharing.

---

[25] Fine, Agnès. 2000. Écritures féminines et rites de passage. *Communications* 70: 121–142. http://www.persee.fr/web/revues/home/prescript/article/comm_0588-8018_2000_num_70_1_2066. Accessed 17 Feb 2015.

[26] Desperatecouchpotatoea. 2014a. *Journal de Grossesse – Saison 2, Episode 6 – Le paradoxe de la dernière ligne droite….* https://desperatecouchpotatoe.wordpress.com/2014/09/18/journal-de-grossesse-saison-2-episode-6-le-paradoxe-de-la-derniere-ligne-droite/.

[27] Gunthert, André. 2014. L'image conversationnelle. *Études photographiques* 31: 54–71. http://etudesphotographiques.revues.org/3387. Accessed 17 Feb 2015.

[28] Desperatecouchpotatoe. 2014b. *#Journal de grossesse, saison 2, épisode 8 et fin, dans la douleur tu enfanteras.* https://desperatecouchpotatoe.wordpress.com/2014/10/16/journal-de-grossesse-saison-2-episode-8-et-fin-dans-la-douleur-tu-enfanteras/; Maman au naturelle. 2014a. *Mon accouchement Naturel Partie 1: Le travail.* http://mamanaunaturelle.blogspot.fr/2014/11/mon-accouchement-naturel-partie-1-le.html; Maman au naturelle. 2014b. *Mon accouchement Naturel Partie 2: la naissance.* http://mamanaunaturelle.blogspot.fr/2014/11/mon-accouchement-naturelle-partie-2-la.html; Mon joli Cœur. 2014. *Mon accouchement (part 1), Une matinée pas comme les autres….* http://mon-jolicoeur.blogspot.fr/2014/11/mon-accouchement-part-1.html.

[29] Woodybeauté. 2014. *Routine du soir bonsoir !.* http://www.woodybeauty.com/2014/11/routine-du-soir-bonsoir.html.

[30] Olly Nolera. 2014. *Produits terminés #2 : mars/avril 2014.* http://ollynolera.blogspot.com/2014/05/produits-termines-mars-avril-2014.html.

Similarly to women's magazine columnists, the authors of posts like these share about their uses of beauty products. However, their experience is lent authenticity by the photographic evidence of the used product bottles. We know that columnists work for brands by creating positive editorial content, while here the photography serves as proof that the bloggers have truly purchased and used the products and have no hidden advertising agenda. Indeed, bloggers' demand for independence is a regularly recurring topic. In recent years, brands have taken note that bloggers, particularly 'influential' ones,[31] might become mediators of production and have sought to forge relationships and contracts with them to promote their goods.[32] In this context, bloggers have committed to specifying when their writing is connected to a partnership and when they are writing about a product that a company has provided them for free,[33] so as not to threaten the trust they have built up with their readers.

In a number of other cases, bloggers do not invent visual formulas but reclaim and repurpose media forms. Using tutorials, photographs or videos, they precisely describe step-by-step methods. On the blog *Lorylyn*, Laurianne explains on a self-produced video how to apply concealer.[34] Videos like this one can be quite intricately edited and even include music. Beauty bloggers also frequently use the before-and-after format to show a procedure's steps.[35] With these 'user manual' images, and by further individualising the exchange, bloggers reclaim the social function of gender-related practical knowledge transmission that women's magazine had taken charge of since the late 1930s.

In fashion blogs, bloggers often photograph themselves to show what they are wearing in their post. Mimicking magazines, they deploy a visual formula that comes from the fashion world. In women's magazines in the 1990s, editors published photographs of women out in the streets to show the authentic 'look'. *Street style* was characterised by full-length photographs of women posing in the street. This style was taken up by fashion photographers presenting their collections. Fashion bloggers have now seized upon these media visual codes while composing their own conduct and style of dressing.[36]

[31] Pasquier 2014.

[32] Rocamora, Agnès, and Djurdja Bartlett. 2009. Blogs de mode: les nouveaux espaces du discours de mode. *Sociétés* 104: 105–114. http://www.cairn.info/revue-societes-2009-2-page-105.htm. Accessed 17 Feb 2015.

[33] Pensée By Caro. 2014. *Les marques, la pub, le blog et moi.* http://www.penseesbycaro.fr/2014/10/les-marques-la-pub-le-blog-et-moi-et-moi-et-moi/.

[34] Lory lyn79. 2013. *Moi mon anti-cernes je l'applique suivant la méthode du Triangle !* http://www.lorylynmakeup.com/2013/06/moi-mon-anti-cernes-je-lapplique.html.

[35] NuellaSource. 2014. *Le Flawless concealer de Black Opal.* http://nuellasource.blogspot.fr/2014/04/le-flawless-concealer-de-black-opal.html.

[36] A moody girl's closet. 2014. *Fluo.* http://www.amoodygirlscloset.com/fluo.

As with fashion, culinary bloggers[37] share images of dishes they have prepared. For most, producing these images requires care[38] and is part of the photographic tradition of women's magazines that Barthes called 'ornamental cuisine'.[39] The search for polished images leads to posts providing technical guidance on how to achieve this type of photography.[40] However, unlike the bourgeois cooking that Barthes referred to, bloggers share easy recipes. Although in these examples, bloggers' visual production is imbued with a media-based model, the fact that they themselves have created the images and are the models also shows an inclination to appropriate that model.

4.3   Conclusion

When women speak in a way they qualify as feminine, they do so on themes that are quite similar to those of women's magazines, showing a consistency in these offerings. However, they break away from a global concept of femininity that suggests each of them has the same expectations or interests. By taking up blogging, they are appropriating functions that until now and for nearly a century have been controlled by the cultural industries, including the transmission of gender-specific knowledge. The magazines' authoritative style is disappearing to make room for individualised stories and experience sharing in which readers can find the information they need without receiving advice. The trust that magazines cultivated through rhetoric is now manifest in blogs, where communities are built and links are forged.

The appropriation of discourse occurs through the production and distribution of self-produced images that individualise exchanges while affirming a willingness to recognise oneself in the published visual models. Like instruction manuals and women's magazines, blogs fulfil a social function of gender transmission. While the male gender seems to be acquired less by 'learning' than by habit formation, in these blogs the feminine gender still seems to find expression through knowledge acquisition.

---

[37] Naulin, Sidonie. 2014. La blogosphère culinaire. *Réseaux* 183: 31–62. www.cairn.info/revue-reseaux-2014-1-page-31.htm. Accessed 17 Feb 2015.

[38] Chef Nini. 2014. *Mendiants de Noël*. http://www.chefnini.com/mendiants-noel/ Accessed 17 Feb 2015.

[39] Barthes, Roland. 1957. Cuisine ornementale. In *Les mythologies*, ed. Roland Barthes, 120–121. Paris: Editions du Seuil.

[40] Madame Gâteau. 2014. *Quelques conseils pour débutants en photographie culinaire*. http://www.barbaragateau.com/2014/05/quelques-conseils-pour-debutants-en.html.

References

Barthes, Roland. 1957. Cuisine ornementale. In *Les mythologies*, ed. Roland Barthes, 120–121. Paris: Editions du Seuil.

Cardon, Dominique. 2003. Droit au plaisir et devoir d'orgasme dans l'émission de Ménie Grégoire. *Le Temps des médias* 1: 77–94. www.cairn.info/revue-le-temps-des-medias-2003-1-page-77. htm. Accessed 17 Feb 2015.

Chermette, Myriam. 2009. *"Donner à voir"*, *La photographie dans Le Journal: discours, pratiques, usages (1892–1944)*. Ph.D. Université de Saint Quentin en Yvelines.

Chollet, Mona. 2012. *Beauté fatale, les nouveaux visages de l'aliénation féminine*. Paris: Zones.

Dardigna, Anne-Marie. 1978. *La presse féminine, fonction idéologique*. Paris: Maspero.

Fine, Agnès. 2000. Écritures féminines et rites de passage. *Communications* 70: 121–142. http://www.persee.fr/web/revues/home/prescript/article/comm_0588-8018_2000_num_70_1_2066. Accessed 17 Feb 2015.

Gunthert, André. 2014. L'image conversationnelle. *Études photographiques* 31: 54–71. http://etudesphotographiques.revues.org/3387. Accessed 17 Feb 2015.

Mayeur, Françoise. 2008. *L'éducation des filles en France au XIXe siècle*. Paris: Perrin (1st edn: Hachette 1979).

Menneveux, Richard. 2010. Be.com le nouveau féminin en ligne de Lagardère, *FrenchWeb.fr*. http://frenchweb.fr/be-com-le-nouveau-feminin-de-lagardere. Accessed 17 Feb 2015.

Naulin, Sidonie. 2014. La blogosphère culinaire. *Réseaux* 183: 31–62. www.cairn.info/revue-reseaux-2014-1-page-31.htm. Accessed 17 Feb 2015.

Pasquier, Dominique. 2014. Les jugements profanes en ligne sous le regard des sciences sociales. *Réseaux* 183: 9–25. http://www.cairn.info/revue-reseaux-2014-1-page-9.htm. Accessed 17 Feb 2015.

Rocamora, Agnès, and Djurdja Bartlett. 2009. Blogs de mode: les nouveaux espaces du discours de mode. *Sociétés* 104: 105–114. http://www.cairn.info/revue-societes-2009-2-page-105.htm. Accessed 17 Feb 2015.

Sullerot, Evelyne. 1963. *La presse féminine*. Paris: Armand Colin.

Sources

A moody girl's closet. 2014. *Fluo*. http://www.amoodygirlscloset.com/fluo

Chef Nini. 2014. *Mendiants de Noël*. http://www.chefnini.com/mendiants-noel/ Accessed 17 Feb 2015.

Chez Lucette. 2014a. *Le dire tout bas, pour ne pas réveiller le mauvais œil…*. https://chezlucette. wordpress.com/2014/05/15/le-dire-tout-bas-pour-ne-pas-reveiller-le-mauvais-oeil/

Chez Lucette. 2014b. *Trouillothon*. https://chezlucette.wordpress.com/2014/10/13/trouillonthon/

Desperatecouchpotatoea. 2014a. *Journal de Grossesse – Saison 2, Episode 6 – Le paradoxe de la dernière ligne droite…*. https://desperatecouchpotatoe.wordpress.com/2014/09/18/journal-de-grossesse-saison-2-episode-6-le-paradoxe-de-la-derniere-ligne-droite/

Desperatecouchpotatoe. 2014b. *#Journal de grossesse, saison 2, épisode 8 et fin, dans la douleur tu enfanteras*. https://desperatecouchpotatoe.wordpress.com/2014/10/16/journal-de-grossesse-saison-2-episode-8-et-fin-dans-la-douleur-tu-enfanteras/

Dufrénoy, Adélaïde. 1816. *La petite ménagère ou l'éducation maternelle (4 tomes)*. Paris: A. Eymery. http://gallica.bnf.fr/ark:/12148/bpt6k54455967.r=.langFR. Accessed 17 Feb 2015.

Fonssagrives, Jean-Baptiste. 1869. *L'éducation physique des jeunes filles ou avis aux mères sur l'art de diriger leur santé et leur développement*. Paris: Hachette. http://gallica.bnf.fr/ark:/12148/bpt6k104230x.r=manuel+instruction+fille.langFR. Accessed 17 Feb 2015.

Juranville, Clarisse. 1879. *Le savoir-faire et le savoir vivre: guide pratique de la vie usuelle à l'usage des jeunes filles.* Paris: Librairie Larousse. http://gallica.bnf.fr/ark:/12148/ bpt6k6149610s.r=manuel+instruction+fille.langFR. Accessed 17 Feb 2015.

L'am0ureuse. 2014. #*La Reine des Neiges version 2.* http://am0ureuse.wordpress.com/2014/05/13/ la-reine-des-neiges-version-2/

Lory lyn79. 2013. *Moi mon anti-cernes je l'applique suivant la méthode du Triangle !* http://www. lorylynmakeup.com/2013/06/moi-mon-anti-cernes-je-lapplique.html

Madame Gâteau. 2014. *Quelques conseils pour débutants en photographie culinaire.* http://www. barbaragateau.com/2014/05/quelques-conseils-pour-debutants-en.html

Maman au naturelle. 2014a. *Mon accouchement Naturel Partie 1: Le travail.* http://mamanauna-turelle.blogspot.fr/2014/11/mon-accouchement-naturel-partie-1-le.html

Maman au naturelle. 2014b. *Mon accouchement Naturel Partie 2: la naissance.* http://mamanau-naturelle.blogspot.fr/2014/11/mon-accouchement-naturelle-partie-2-la.html

Marie-Claire. 1937a. *Editorial.*

Marie-Claire. 1937b. *La mode sculpturale.*

Marie-Claire. 1937c. *Sommaire.*

Marie-Claire. 1938a. *Mettez votre visage en valeur*, 8–9.

Marie-Claire. 1938b. *Jeunes filles, la beauté c'est la santé*, 17.

Mon joli Cœur. 2014. *Mon accouchement (part 1), Une matinée pas comme les autres….* http:// mon-jolicoeur.blogspot.fr/2014/11/mon-accouchement-part-1.html

NuellaSource. 2014. *Le Flawless concealer de Black Opal.* http://nuellasource.blogspot. fr/2014/04/le-flawless-concealer-de-black-opal.html

Olly Nolera. 2014. *Produits terminés #2 : mars/avril 2014.* http://ollynolera.blogspot.com/2014/05/ produits-termines-mars-avril-2014.html

Pensée By Caro. 2014. *Les marques, la pub, le blog et moi.* http://www.penseesbycaro.fr/2014/10/ les-marques-la-pub-le-blog-et-moi-et-moi-et-moi/

Woodybeauté. 2014. *Routine du soir bonsoir !.* http://www.woodybeauty.com/2014/11/routine-du-soir-bonsoir.html

Part II
Gendered Representations. Introductory Remarks

Delphine Diaz and Régis Schlagdenhauffen

The topic of the second part of the book is gender as a critique of representations of supposedly masculine and feminine skills. Echoing the article on the telegraph in the previous section, the first contribution elucidates the representations of the *demoiselles du téléphone* through a controversy that took place in 1904 and that confronted a famous actress with the employees responsible for establishing telephone communications. This incident, which snowballed into an 'Affair' discussed by all the press of that time, shed light on really diverse representations of the feminity, confronting an 'emancipated' woman (with her own phone service) with the phone operators. Dominique Pinsolle contextualises Miss Sylviac's epic in the intricacies of the telegraph and telephone administration. His contribution tackles the different conceptions of femininity during the *Belle Époque* and analyses how the media of that time regarded women's relationships with information and communication technologies. The second contribution of this part applies a comparative perspective to the use of information and communications technology in France and Germany. Through a diachronic study, Marion Dalibert and Simona De Iulio highlight how in children's magazines, gender representations, age categories and uses of information and communications technology interact and are mutually formed.

D. Diaz (✉)
Laboratoire CERHiC EA 2616, Université de Reims Champagne-Ardenne,
57 rue Pierre Taittinger, 51096 Reims, France
e-mail: delphinediaz@gmail.com

R. Schlagdenhauffen
Université de Lorraine, Nancy, France
e-mail: regis.schlag@gmail.com

Chapter 5
The Sylviac Affair (1904–1910) or Joan of Arc Versus the *Demoiselles du Téléphone*

Dominique Pinsolle

Abstract In April 1904, the well-known French actress Ms. Sylviac had her phone service suspended by the telephone administration after being accused of insulting the *demoiselles du telephone* – France's then exclusively female staff of phone operators, who failed to connect her to the number she requested. The major newspapers (*Le Matin*, *Le Temps*, etc.) quickly transformed Ms. Sylviac into a symbol of helpless subscribers forced to turn the other cheek before an all-powerful, monopoly-abusing administration. The real question became whether telephone operators should be considered officials receiving special protections in cases of job-related insults. Beyond the actress's personal situation, the case highlighted the new balance of power being established between subscribers, the telephone administration and its employees.

On 6 April 1904, French actress Marie-Thérèse Chauvin (1863–1948), known as Ms. Sylviac, had her telephone subscription suspended by the government after she was accused of offending the *demoiselles du téléphone* – France's then exclusively female staff of phone operators, who failed to connect her to the number she requested. The next day, the newspaper *Le Matin* reported the story of Ms. Sylviac's 'telephonic excommunication'. The 'charming dramatic artist' stated that the 'epic scene' unfolded in her dressing room where the telephone was installed. At around 14:00, one of her friends, actress Rosa Bruck, made an urgent communication request. For 45 min, both women continued attempting to call out but failed to reach an employee. Ms. Sylviac then requested 728-00, the number for central management, where she could leave a complaint. The supervisor of Central Gutenberg (located near the Louvre) immediately intervened, blaming the subscriber for not having sought him out earlier, coming to the defense of his employees. The tone mounted, with Ms. Sylviac insisting on her point and calling in one of her servants

D. Pinsolle (✉)
Centre d'études des mondes moderne et contemporain (CEMMC), Université Bordeaux Montaigne, Pessac, France

UFR Humanités-Département d'Histoire, Université Bordeaux Montaigne,
33607 Pessac, France
e-mail: dominique.pinsolle@u-bordeaux-montaigne.fr

V. Schafer, B.G. Thierry (eds.), *Connecting Women*, History of Computing,
DOI 10.1007/978-3-319-20837-4_5

to corroborate her criticism of the telephone operators' coarse manners towards subscribers. Faced with the supervisor's dismissiveness, the actress lost composure and responded that 'his perfect little employees talk a little too much like milkmaids' (*Le Matin*, 7 April 1904). The phone line was cut. That evening at around 19:00, the phone rang and 'a stringy and ridiculous gentleman' announced to Ms. Sylviac that her subscription was suspended until further notice, pursuant to Article 52 of the Decree of 8 May 1901 determining telephone service regulation. In addition, the actress faced a possible fine. The incident was widely publicised. The press seized upon the case, an association of telephone subscribers was created, and the Sylviac Affair was discussed all the way up to the General Assembly. Yet her telephone privation was in no way an isolated case, nor was she the first to face administrative censure. In fact, in Paris in 1903 there were 10 suspensions for insults; in 1904 there were 11 (*Journal Officiel*, 6 February 1905: 176). Across the entire network, the newly created Association of Telephone Subscribers (*l'Association des Abonnés du Téléphone*) logged an annual figure of approximately 200 suspensions due to insults (*Bulletin de l'Association des Abonnés du Téléphone* (3), 1904: 1), while the Deputy Secretary's chief of staff at the Ministry of Posts and Telegraphs (*Ministère de Postes et des Télégraphes*) said this type of suspension occurred 'every 2 or 3 days' (*Le Temps*, 14 April 1904). But the incident with Ms. Sylviac was the first to cause controversy on a national scale. What explains this sudden political and media outrage? Why was Ms. Sylviac 'the straw that broke the camel's back', to borrow a phrase used by her supporters (*Bulletin de l'Association des Abonnés du Téléphone* (3), 1904: 1)? How was the case illustrative of the relationship between the telephone administration, the telephone network and the early twentieth-century telephone subscribers? We will see that although the actress's case became an object of political and media dramatisation, this was counterbalanced by the victim's identity as a woman whose social status opposed that of the *demoiselles du téléphone*. Finally, the case's magnitude shed light on the new relationship between the telephone administration and the subscribers that was in the process of establishing.

5.1   A Political and Media Dramatisation Transforms Ms. Sylviac into a 'Joan of Arc' Against the Telephone Administration

The Sylviac Affair erupted in a context of strong criticism against the telephone administration's management of the network. The Act of 16 July 1889 had ended the private monopoly held by the Société Générale des Téléphones, and since then the State had been regularly challenged, especially with the first 'phone crisis' that accompanied the 1900 report by Alexandre Millerand, then Minister of Posts and Telegraphs.[1] Very quickly, media commentary about Sylviac's case continued in this

---

[1] Bouneau, Christophe, and Alexandre Fernandez. 2004. *L'entreprise publique en France et en Espagne de la fin du XVIIIe siècle au milieu du XXe siècle: environnement, formes et stratégies.* Pessac: Maison des Sciences de l'Homme d'Aquitaine.

vein. Take, for example, Henri Rochefort's appropriation of Proudhon to declare that *L'État, c'est le vol* ('The State is theft'), and continuing with a simplified explanation of the dysfunction, he felt the case revealed:

> Ms Sylviac's adventure has demonstrated clearly what we experience every day, that the State is the king of thieves. The telephone administration was a single company that worked without a hitch. A gang of minister cops went into their offices one day and took it over *by force of arms*. At this moment, the telephone crisis erupted. (*L'Intransigeant*, 11 April 1904)

From the start, then, the Affair went beyond the case of a bullied actress. Behind what might have remained a passing headline was the issue of the State's relationship with the economy in an era when the notion of 'public services' was just developing.[2] This explains why the right exploited the scandal against the left-wing coalition that was then in power. *Le Figaro*, in particular, asserted that the unfortunate actress had

> allowed all those capable of reflection to see what the fate will be for the thirty-eight million citizens of our Republic on the day when the Bloc's socialist program is applied, and the State is the sole operator of the railways, transportation of all types, lighting, water, banking, mining, and all industries and trade. (*Le Figaro*, 21 April 1904)

Sylviac's telephone service was restored on 15 April. However, she was summoned to Judge Cail, who charged her with offending a public servant (*Le Matin*, 16 April 1904). In response to this prosecution by the postal administration (then led by Under-Secretary for Posts and Telegraphs, Alexandre Bérard), the Association of Telephone Subscribers was created by the Marquis Maurice de Montebello. The nephew of a former French ambassador to St. Petersburg, he was serving as the General Counsel of Canton de Montendre in Charente inférieure. A former official of the Colonial and Commerce Ministry (*Ministère des Colonies et du Commerce*), he had previously founded the French Commercial Alliance (*Alliance Commerciale Française*) to promote the development of French trade in the Far East. The organisation he founded to champion Ms. Sylviac drew 500 members in 4 days; a month later, it had grown tenfold (*L'Humanité*, 17 May 1904) at a time when Paris had 30–35,000 telephone subscribers among its 2.5 million residents – having grown from 8 to 10,000 15 years earlier (National Archives 637/AP/42 Marcel Sembat fund, 1904).

The Sylviac Affair immediately foregrounded the debate over phone malfunctions. Articles proliferated and her misadventure even inspired a musical entitled *Votre abonnement sera suspendu du... au...* ('Your subscription will be suspended from... to...'), by Gabriel Timmory, which opened in Paris on 11 May (*Le Matin*, 12 May 1904). The actress, herself a member of the Association of Telephone Subscribers, was anointed a 'new Joan of Arc' by Montebello at the first general meeting held on 16 May. Besides Montebello, the *New York Times'* Paris correspondent was enthused by Sylviac's 'Joan of Arc attitude' (*The New York Times*, 8 May 1904). But the comparison was not unanimous; it exasperated *L'Humanité* ('Encore Jeanne d'Arc!' 'Once again Joan of Arc!' 13 December 1904) and amused MP

---

[2] Lemercier, Claire. 2007. La construction d'un modèle français de service public avant 1914. *Regards croisés sur l'économie* 2: 47–54.

Marcel Sembat who, in his report on the 1905 budget for Posts and Telegraphs, noted with irony that 'a fan [of Ms. Sylviac] may venture so far as to proclaim that she is Joan of Arc' (Chambre des députés, n°1956, 8e législature, 1904 session). The Affair's drama culminated with this historical reference. Nevertheless, it was merely the result of a campaign by the era's major newspapers that had begun the day after the inciting event, first among them *Le Figaro*, which praised the 'gracious and valiant champion of the molested public' (*Le Figaro,* 13 April 1904) and proclaimed that '[i]f the French people was not the most ungrateful in the world, it would raise a statue of gold and ivory, with eyes of precious stones, to Ms. Sylviac' (*Le Figaro*, 21 April 1904).

The fact that the victim was a woman lent a special tone to the commentary. On 7 May 1904, for example, lawyers of the Paris Bar met to discuss State monopolies' power to interrupt contractual obligations. One of the speakers, praising the actress and decrying the inertia of ordinary taxpayers, exclaimed, 'It took a woman to shake us out of our torpor!' (*Le Matin*, 8 May 1904). Similarly, on 6 February 1905, while speaking to the Chamber of Deputies about 'administrative abuse' with regard to the telephone, Fernand Engérand, the Deputy of Calvados, said, 'It was enough for this abuse to reach a pretty woman and, worse still, a dramatic artist, to immediately trouble public opinion' (*Journal Officiel*, meeting of 6 February 1905). As MP Engérand's remark illustrates, the victim's gender only had an impact because she was also an actress whose charms prevented male commentators from remaining apathetic and who herself 'benefitted from the windfall to talk about herself'.[3] The combination between gender and social affiliation is what made Ms. Sylviac the ideal incarnation of unhappy subscribers in the eyes of the press and all their supporters. But while the victim's gender may serve the cause of telephone subscribers, it may also be a disservice, since it concerns 'just a woman'.

5.2   Sylviac's Fate, from the Perspective of her Gender and the Working Conditions of the *Demoiselles du Téléphone*

The fact that the telephone suspension in this story occurred during an attempt by women to converse can reduce its polemic to an amusing anecdote. There is humour when Louis Brunet, the radical socialist deputy of the Reunion Island at the Chamber of Deputies, interrupts Engérand as the latter evokes Sylviac's broad support, with a verse by Boileau: 'All Paris for Chimene has Rodrigue's eyes' (*Journal Officiel*, meeting of 6 February 1905). Indeed, the Affair's alleged seriousness was tempered by the victim's gender and by the widespread stereotype that women only used the phone for frivolous reasons, as shown in this explanation by *Le Temps* of why the telephone fascinates the French:

---

[3] Bertho, Catherine. 1981. *Télégraphes et téléphones de Valmy au microprocesseur*. Paris: Librairie générale française.

[The male] merchant appreciates this invention that facilitates orders and simplifies negotiations; the Parisian [woman] cherishes its easy, elegant conversational style that extends the buzz of the city into the living room and the bedroom. (14 April 1904)

In this quote, men are seen as using the phone for serious and professional tasks, while women are seen as using it to gossip about private or mundane issues.[4] In *Masculine Domination*, where he analyses typical discourse, Bourdieu asserts that 'telephone calls' are part of the social activities assigned to women that are aimed at maintaining relationships between the family and the exterior world. But Bourdieu indicates that '[t]his domestic work goes essentially unnoticed, or frowned upon (as for example with the ritual denunciation of women's taste for chitchat, including over the phone ...)'.[5] In this light, Ms. Sylviac is a romantic symbol subjected to considerable media staging, as well as derision by men who trivialise her case as being about phone gossip. Moreover, the actress's fate was widely relativised by women who worked on the other end of the telephone line. Indeed, the *demoiselles du téléphone* and their working conditions were at centre stage and overshadowed the empathy for Ms. Sylviac.

In effect, Ms. Sylviac enjoyed popularity as a subscriber standing up to the administration, but much less as a telephone user insulting the employees. At the time, the latter worked in notoriously difficult conditions, which did not always allow them to consistently meet the demands of the thousands of subscribers. These *demoiselles* had a tiring and repetitive job and endured constant pressure by subscribers,[6] as well as from a meddlesome hierarchy with an iron discipline. Moreover, they were badly paid: entry-level workers received slightly over 100 francs per month,[7] and they did not receive the same pay increase as clerks had 11 years earlier. The General Association of Postal, Telegraph and Telephone Workers (*Association Générale des Agents des Postes, Télégraphes et Téléphones*) unsuccessfully requested that the pay of 'women employees' be increased to what it had been prior to 1893, which was two-thirds of that of clerks. In doing so, they highlighted a 'fact duly established by the Administration, that work done in 1 year by three women is equivalent to that achieved by two men' (*Bulletin officiel de l'Association générale des Agents des Postes, Télégraphes et Téléphones* (47), November 1904: 332–333). From the Affair's beginnings, *L'Humanité* took up these women's defence, underscoring that their gender deepened their status as scapegoats:

Even though the *demoiselles du téléphone* have been exonerated, writing is still chiefly published about them, in short because the State is merely an entity despite the responsible person of Mr Bérard, and because it is more convenient to have someone in front of you to easily curse, such as women. (*L'Humanité*, 30 April 1904)

---

[4] Bertho 1981: 239.

[5] Bourdieu, Pierre. 2002. *La domination masculine*. 1st ed. 1998. Paris: Seuil.

[6] Bachrach, Susan. 1984. *Dames employées: the feminisation of postal work in nineteenth-century France*. New York: Haworth Press.

[7] Bertho 1981: 250.

Even within the Association of Telephone Subscribers, Montebello believed that 'the *demoiselles du téléphone* [...] are overworked and we truly must forgive them' (*Le Matin*, 2 May 1904). The association identified the goal of improving their conditions, because the quality of the phone network and therefore subscriber satisfaction depended on it. The bulletin published an issue on employee grievances and gave detailed information about their working conditions. It informed readers that out of 1,800 employees in the Paris network, only 1,400 were actually assigned to the telephone, a disparity explained by numerous absences,[8] while other tasks were entrusted to some employees. The *demoiselles du téléphone* worked 7 h per day, and according to the administration they received an average of 70 and up to 150 calls per hour. In addition to the insufficient number of employees, the Association of Telephone Subscribers cited defective equipment, an alarming assertion that appears not to be exaggerated when compared with the documents sent to Marcel Sembat to prepare his 1905 Posts and Telegraphs budget report. One of these documents states that 'telephony is threatened with collapse if we do not backtrack, if we do not create specialists in large offices to regulate equipment, to test telegraph lines and telephone circuits for all electric operations in order to facilitate the location of defects and the suppression of lines and devices' (National Archives, 637/AP/42 Marcel Sembat Fund, author unidentified, 1904).

It should also be underscored that the Sylviac case emerged as Georges Trouillot (Minister of Commerce, Industry, Posts and Telegraphs) had just tried unsuccessfully to convince then Minister of Finances Maurice Rouvier of the need for strong job creation to 'strengthen existing staff, whose duties are already so burdensome that service, on certain points, absolutely collapses' (National Archives, 637/AP/42 Correspondence with the Ministry of Finance, 1904).

Beyond the difficulties associated with physical working conditions, relations between subscribers and employees were often problematic. The *demoiselles du téléphone*, mostly young single girls,[9] generally came from the peasantry (hence, perhaps, the inspiration for Sylviac's 'milkmaids' insult) and the *petite bourgeoisie*.[10] Customers, meanwhile, were generally wealthy dignitaries and bourgeois who did not exactly appreciate the idea that employees might have access to their telephone conversations.[11] Even if these girls were absolutely obligated to respect the secrecy of communications, the curiosity associated with women inspired mistrust.[12] There were often strained relations, particularly because 'for wealthier subscribers, the *demoiselles du téléphone* are not citizens, they are servants'

---

[8] Le Quentrec, Yann. 2006. Les employées de bureau: un groupe professionnel féminin mais invisible et dévalorisé. In *Le bas de l'échelle. La construction sociale des situations subalterns*, ed. Pierre Cours-Salies and Stéphane Le Lay, 81–96. Paris: ERES.

[9] Bertho 1981: 250.

[10] Lhomme, Pierre. 2009. Les téléphonistes et leurs luttes jusqu'en 1945. In *Des demoiselles du téléphone aux opérateurs des centres d'appel*, ed. Colette Schwartz, Yveline Jacquet, and Pierre Lhomme, 27–44. Pantin: Le Temps des Cerises.

[11] Lhomme 2009: 28.

[12] Julliard, Virginie. 2004. Une "femme machine" au travail: la "demoiselle du telephone". *Quaderni* 56: 23–32.

(*L'Humanité*, 30 April 1904). Gender and class relations thus intertwined; a *demoiselle du téléphone* often found herself in a position of double subjugation by the user.

This explains the ambivalent commentary surrounding the Sylviac Affair: she complained as a wronged subscriber, was alternately extolled or mocked as a woman, was defended by the press as a respected artist and was criticised by the left as a wealthy socialite. Meanwhile she unwittingly placed the plight of the *demoiselles du téléphone*, whose working conditions were publicly denounced, at the centre of discussion. Moreover, their still unclear status was the subject of important decisions over the course of the scandal, which illustrated the new relations being established between users and the administration at the time.

5.3   Behind the Affair: The Establishment of New Relations Between Users and the Administration

From the outset, the criticism levied against Ms. Sylviac arose from the status of the *demoiselles du téléphone*: with the network subjected to a State monopoly, should they be considered civil servants and receive special protections if insulted in the exercise of their job duties? The question was significant because if an employee of a private company was insulted, the punishment was a mere fine of one to five francs, whereas insults against government employees were punishable by 16–200 francs under Article 224 of the Penal Code regarding offences directed at a functionary.[13] The matter was left to a judge to decide. On 18 May 1904, the actress was sent to the 11th Criminal Chamber, following the direction of the Under-Secretary of State of Posts and Telegraphs.

On 23 April, meanwhile, another victim of the administration, the Director of a paint and glaze shop, Mr Belloche, was also accused of disrespecting the *demoiselles*. His subscription was not suspended but a complaint was filed against him, and like Ms. Sylviac he was sent to a misdemeanour trial for 'insulting a functionary during the exercise of her job duties' (*Le Matin*, 14 May 1904). The cases were tried simultaneously; on 2 June, the judge found that a *demoiselle du téléphone* was indeed a citizen performing a public service, which automatically resulted in a conviction for Mr Belloche and a fine of 100 francs for an infraction of Article 224 of the Penal Code. Ms. Sylviac was acquitted because she had not voiced her insult directly but through the intermediary of a supervisor who was not himself subjected to any verbal aggression.

Mr Belloche immediately appealed the conviction. On 25 October, the Court of Criminal Appeals sided with him; the *demoiselles'* status was reduced to that of 'clerks' not overseen by a public service ministry, which annulled his sentence. The Attorney General at the Paris Court filed an appeal, but it was dismissed on 18 February 1905 by the Court of Cassation, whose decision established that the work

---

[13] Milhaud, Edgard. 1918. Les régies et leur evolution. *Annales de la régie directe* 103: 5–62.

of the *demoiselles du téléphone* 'implies neither allocation nor delegation of any part of the public authority'.[14] As agents of operation and not of authority, the *demoiselles* could not be protected by Article 224 of the Penal Code concerning functionaries.

This decision satisfied the Association of Telephone Subscribers, which believed the telephone would now be recognised as an ordinary commercial service to the benefit of its users (*Bulletin de l'association des abonnés au téléphone*, (9), 1905: 2). While Ms. Sylviac did not receive damages after her acquittal in 1907, Montebello's organisation enjoyed a strong position following the outcome of the Sylviac and Belloche case. After their first victory in the Court of Cassation, a second followed in 1910 when the administration amended the notorious Article 52 regulating telephone operation, which had allowed it to automatically suspend subscriber communications if the latter insulted an employee. Going forward, automatic suspension would no longer be enforced without prior warning and an allowance for the subscriber to explain their side; in cases of proven offenses, the penalty could now not exceed 2 days. Although Article 52 was stopped being applied in effect since the two cases under discussion (*Bulletin de l'Association des abonnés au téléphone*, (66), December 1909: 4), this change reflected the growing influence of organised subscribers.

Indeed, this decision was made in a context of emerging consumer mobilisations, which oscillated between an 'ethical' element that prioritised social goals and a 'consumerist' element that prioritised price controls.[15] In the Sylviac Affair, it wasn't price but service quality that subscribers felt was at issue. However, Montebello's association's demands clearly tended towards the 'consumerist' end of things, in the sense that one of their main objectives was for telephone users to be recognised and treated as consumers. This demand went beyond the scope of the Association of Telephone Subscribers. Marcel Sembat, for example, the former chairman of the Commission of Posts and Telegraphs, wrote a long article in 1909 in the Annals of Direct Governance (*Annales de la régie directe*) to welcome the outcome of the Sylviac Affair and emphasise that the decision represented a break in the status of the *demoiselles du téléphone*.[16] The Association of Telephone Subscribers' role as designated 'telephone communication consumers' revealed, in his eyes, that there was essentially no difference between a State-provided service and ordinary commerce:

> We made clear to the administration that an individual who buys two meters of tape is not exposed to exorbitant penalties over a quarrel with the vendor, and that common law sufficing to protect the milliner should also suffice to protect her sister who is entered into the telephone system instead of entering into a clothing shop. The administration was also forced to see that given the price of subscription, it has no more right to cut a subscriber's phone line than a grocer has the right to deliver a pound of sugar to a customer when a kilo is paid for under the pretext that the customer has misbehaved in his shop.[17]

---

[14] Milhaud 1918: 38.

[15] Chessel, Marie-Emmanuelle. 2012. *Histoire de la consommation*. Paris: La Découverte.

[16] Sembat, Marcel. 1909. L'organisation du contrôle du public. *Annales de la régie directe* 2: 33–37.

[17] Sembat 1909: 34.

Beyond the specific case of the telephone, Sembat concluded that socialists themselves must now incorporate the consumer into their economic and social model. Such ideas were in vogue at the time. In 1910, Armand Fenétrier founded the League of Consumers (*Ligue des consommateurs*), heralding the advent of a new and autonomous consumers' force alongside the working class and employers.[18] The following year, economist Charles Gide followed suit, expressing enthusiasm about the new phenomenon of 'consumer strikes'.[19] The Association of Telephone Subscribers' successes can be placed in this context where the consumer became a full participant both in the private sector and State-provided services.

In an era when 'public services' were still conceived of primarily within a 'framework of local and private management',[20] the challenge to the telephone administration's management catalysed a new set of questions concerning the State's relationship with service consumers. In this respect, the Sylviac Affair was a moment for reflection and significant decisions. As Edgard Milhaud underscored in 1918 in the Annals of Direct Governance: 'It is the very question of the industrial State's juridical nature, and the character of the relationship between the public and the industrial State, that this debate has engaged'.[21]

5.4 Conclusion

Ms. Sylviac's story was 'the straw that broke the camel's back' for several reasons. First, the fact that the victim was a popular actress was the determining factor in the media's dramatisation of her case. Her gender and class combined to give the scandal a particular twist that resulted in the equally revelatory and ridiculous comparison with Joan of Arc. But the fact that Ms. Sylviac was a woman is ultimately merely anecdotal, as it is primarily her social affiliation that attracted media attention and drew her most virulent critics. It is not for nothing that the actress's own efforts to be talked are part of the story. But it's only because the press rushed into what quickly became a mini-scandal that the 'Sylviac Affair' had such an impact, despite the male taunts and the criticism of *L'Humanité* among others. The attention that the actress enjoyed is explained by the fact that her case generated two debates. On one hand, the controversy, which represents one moment among years of criticism of the administration's management of the telephone network, raises questions of State monopoly and its relevance to the issue. On the other hand, decisions made about the status of the *demoiselles du téléphone* and the administration's ruling on

---

[18] Fénétrier, Armand. 1910a. Les grèves de consommateurs. *La Revue de solidarité sociale* 68: 19–21; Fénétrier, Armand. 1910b. Les consommateurs s'organisent. *La Revue de solidarité sociale* 70: 52–53.

[19] Pinsolle, Dominique. 2013. Les grèves des abonnés du gaz en France (1892–1914): des grèves de consommateurs parmi d'autres? *TST* 25: 130–148.

[20] Lemercier 2007: 54.

[21] Milhaud 1918: 38.

the Sylviac and Belloche cases show the new balance of power between users and the administration that was being established and, more generally, the new role of consumers in society. Behind an apparently frivolous anecdote of an artist outraged by the shut-off of her phone, we find the larger questions of the economic role the State can and should play in telephony and beyond.

References

Bachrach, Susan. 1984. *Dames employées: the feminisation of postal work in nineteenth-century France*. New York: Haworth Press.

Bertho, Catherine. 1981. *Télégraphes et téléphones de Valmy au microprocesseur*. Paris: Librairie générale française.

Bouneau, Christophe, and Alexandre Fernandez. 2004. *L'entreprise publique en France et en Espagne de la fin du XVIIIe siècle au milieu du XXe siècle: environnement, formes et strategies*. Pessac: Maison des Sciences de l'Homme d'Aquitaine.

Bourdieu, Pierre. 2002. *La domination masculine*. 1st ed. 1998. Paris: Seuil.

Chessel, Marie-Emmanuelle. 2012. *Histoire de la consommation*. Paris: La Découverte.

Fénétrier, Armand. 1910a. Les grèves de consommateurs. *La Revue de solidarité sociale* 68: 19–21.

Fénétrier, Armand. 1910b. Les consommateurs s'organisent. *La Revue de solidarité sociale* 70: 52–53.

Julliard, Virginie. 2004. Une "femme machine" au travail: la "demoiselle du telephone". *Quaderni* 56: 23–32.

Le Quentrec, Yann. 2006. Les employées de bureau: un groupe professionnel féminin mais invisible et dévalorisé. In *Le bas de l'échelle. La construction sociale des situations subalterns*, ed. Pierre Cours-Salies and Stéphane Le Lay, 81–96. Paris: ERES.

Lemercier, Claire. 2007. La construction d'un modèle français de service public avant 1914. *Regards croisés sur l'économie* 2: 47–54.

Lhomme, Pierre. 2009. Les téléphonistes et leurs luttes jusqu'en 1945. In *Des demoiselles du téléphone aux opérateurs des centres d'appel*, ed. Colette Schwartz, Yveline Jacquet, and Pierre Lhomme, 27–44. Pantin: Le Temps des Cerises.

Milhaud, Edgard. 1918. Les régies et leur evolution. *Annales de la régie directe* 103: 5–62.

Pinsolle, Dominique. 2013. Les grèves des abonnés du gaz en France (1892–1914): des grèves de consommateurs parmi d'autres? *TST* 25: 130–148.

Sembat, Marcel. 1909. L'organisation du contrôle du public. *Annales de la régie directe* 2: 33–37.

Archives and Printed Sources

1904. Bulletin officiel de l'Association générale des Agents des Postes, Télégraphes et Téléphones 47.

Archives Nationales. 1904a. 637/AP/42. *Bulletin officiel de l'Association générale des Agents des Postes, Télégraphes et Téléphones* 47: 332–333.

Archives Nationales. 1904b. 637/AP/42, Le ministre du Commerce, de l'Industrie, des Postes et des Télégraphes au ministre des Finances (26 Feb 1904), in file 'Correspondance avec le Ministère des Finances' (5 Feb–31 Mar).

Archives Nationales. 1905. 637/AP/42, fonds Marcel Sembat, Budget des Postes, Exercice 1905, Documents préparatoires, 'Simples remarques sur le fonctionnement des services électriques à Paris et dans les Départements, au point de vue technique et au point de vue de l'exploitation' (6 Nov 1904). Bulletin de l'Association des abonnés du téléphone 1: 2.

Bulletin de l'Association des Abonnés au Téléphone (1904–1914).

Chambre des députés. 1904. 8th legislature, 1904 session, addendum to the minutes of the session of 13 July 1904. *Rapport fait au nom de la commission du budget chargé d'examiner le projet de loi portant fixation du budget général de l'exercice 1905*, by deputy Marcel Sembat (1956): 49 (held at the French National Library).

Chapter 6
The Representational Intertwinement of Gender, Age and Uses of Information and Communication Technology: A Comparison Between German and French Preteen Magazines

Marion Dalibert and Simona De Iulio

Abstract Gender, preadolescence and the use of information and communication technology are not stable and static entities in the field of media. Rather, they are constantly shaped by images and texts. This chapter aims to examine their representational intertwinement and to cross-analyse gender and age imaging with ICT use. The primary issue treated in this paper concerns the way preteen magazine imagery 'marks' ICT use according to gender and age (and vice versa). Are certain technologies and their usage patterns associated with a particular gender? How does media imagery participate in the mutual shaping of gender, technology and age group? In different national contexts, to what extent does imagery of computers and video game use contribute to modelling preadolescence, an age category that did not exist even a few decades ago? This text seeks to respond to these questions by drawing on the results of an exploratory research on ICT imagery found in German and French preteen magazines over the last 30 years.

The media creates a space upon which 'social identities'[1] and their assigned categorical attributes (gender, age, social class, etc.) are put on display for the public.[2]

---

[1] Goffman, Erving. 1975. *Stigmate: les usages sociaux des handicaps*. Paris: Éditions de Minuit.

[2] Quéré, Louis. 1992. L'espace public: de la théorie politique à la métathéorie sociologique. *Quaderni* 18: 75–92; Charaudeau, Patrick. 1997. *Le discours d'information médiatique: La construction du miroir social*. Paris: Nathan; Voirol, Olivier. 2005. Les luttes pour la visibilité. Esquisse d'une problématique. *Réseaux* 129–130: 89–121; Ollivier, Bruno. 2009. Présentation générale: Les identités collectives : comment comprendre une question politique brûlante ? In *Les identités collectives à l'heure de la mondialisation*, ed. Ollivier Bruno, 7–28. Paris: CNRS Editions.

M. Dalibert (✉) • S. De Iulio
Laboratoire GERiiCO, Université Lille 3, Domaine univ du "Pont de Bois",
59653 Villeneuve-d'Ascq, France
e-mail: marion.dalibert@univ-lille3.fr; simona.deiulio@univ-lille3.fr

© Springer International Publishing Switzerland 2015   89
V. Schafer, B.G. Thierry (eds.), *Connecting Women*, History of Computing,
DOI 10.1007/978-3-319-20837-4_6

Moreover, insofar as it acts as a 'signifying agent'[3] within 'imagined communities',[4] the media participates in the production and circulation of meanings about these identities that thereby become stereotypes. The notion of stereotype refers to the problematics of the specification and differentiation of social groups.[5] Our use of it here is close to that of Henri Boyer's conceptualisation of 'representation' (2008).[6] For us, a stereotype results from a process of identification and categorisation that is carried out upon a group sharing certain categorical attributes. This sociodiscursive process aims to characterise the group as having certain behaviours and practices, and the result is not necessarily static nor must it always be framed as caricature. Indeed, we refer to extremely exaggerated and simplified stereotypes as 'hyperbolic stereotypes'.

In this sense, the media develops and establishes normative representations of femininity and masculinity and may be defined as 'technologies of gender'.[7] It thus contributes to the construction of 'hegemonic' representations and stereotypes[8] that are not entirely stable, being subject to processes of resignification, evolution, rupture, opposition and counter-representation.

As such, the subjects of gender, preadolescence and ICT use are all objects of discourse that are constructed by written and/or visual media – sometimes in contradictory fashion – but that are not fixed yet in the field of media and communications. Here, we seek to examine their representational intertwinement and to cross-analyse imagery of gender, age and ICT use. We examine whether the imagery in preteenmagazines 'marks'[9] the use and operation of ICT by gender and age (and vice versa). Specifically, we are focused on the representation of the uses of new technologies in German and French preteen magazines over the last 30 years. We attempt to identify common representational trends and discontinuities in both countries during this period. Were certain technologies and modes of use associated with particular genders? How did media representations participate in the mutual shaping of gender, technology and age group? In each country, to what extent did imagery of uses of the computer or video games contribute to creating a model of a specific age group that had not existed just a few decades earlier, namely, that of the 'preadolescents' or 'preteens'?

In the following pages, we attempt to answer these questions by drawing on the results of an exploratory research on ICT imagery in French and

[3] Hall, Stuart. 2007. *Identités et cultures. Politiques des Cultural Studies*. Paris: Editions Amsterdam: 91.

[4] Anderson, Benedict. 1996. *L'imaginaire national. Réflexions sur l'origine et l'essor du nationalisme*. Paris: La Découverte.

[5] Amossy, Ruth, and Anne Herschberg-Pierrot. 1997. *Stéréotypes et clichés. Langue, discours, société*. Paris: Nathan université.

[6] Boyer, Henri. 2008. Stéréotype, emblème, mythe. Sémiotisation médiatique et figement représentationnel. *Mots* 88: 99–113.

[7] de Lauretis, Teresa. 2007. *Théorie queer et cultures populaires. De Foucault à Cronenberg*. Paris: La Dispute.

[8] Hall 2007.

[9] Brekhus, Wayne. 2005. Une sociologie de l'"invisibilité": réorienter notre regard. *Réseaux* 129–130: 243–272.

Germanpreteenmagazines. Our comparative study focuses on a corpus of images published since 1983 in three German magazines, *Micky Maus*, *Geolino* and *Zeit Leo*, and two French magazines, *Le Journal de Mickey* and *Okapi*. These magazines rely heavily on illustrations, and we identified and collected all the images featuring ICT, including the Internet and multimedia (computer, tablet), telecommunications (telephone, fax, Minitel), audio (microphone, radio, transistor, Walkman) and still or moving image capture (still camera, video camera, film, video games, television). We thus gathered a heterogeneous body of images: photos, drawings, cartoons and computer graphics.

Whether they were used as advertisements or as illustrations supplementing editorial content (the various sections and articles), the photographs presented in these magazines and in our corpus showcase scenes of ICT being used in scripted manners with children posed as the users of it. They were not taken in a natural context showing real actions and therefore do not capture spontaneous uses of technology in action. To use Ervin Goffmann's terminology,[10] these photographs represent 'hyperritualised' scenes depicting social types rather than specific individuals. The hyperritualised aspect appears still more accentuated in the drawings gathered, including some inspired by comic strips, which show a gendered use of ICT by preteens, often with undertones of caricature.

In total, this quantitative and qualitative analysis includes a set of 680 images, 413 from French magazines and 267 from German journals. The corpus is uniform in terms of the age of its intended audience (9–13). However, it is not chronologically homogeneous, leaving gaps because academic and public libraries do not automatically archive media that is produced for young people. As a result, we were only able to obtain partial collections from individuals. In France, we gathered images from issues of *Le Journal de Mickey* dating from 2000 to 2014 and issues of *Okapi* dating from 1983 to 2014. In Germany, the images collected are from issues of *Micky Maus* dating 1990 to 2011, issues of *Geolino* dating 2011 to 2014 and issues of *Zeit Leo* dating 2011 to 2014.

6.1 Preadolescence, a Nebulous but Gendered and Technologised Age

The emergence of preadolescence as a transition age between the end of childhood and the beginning of puberty is a relatively recent phenomenon. While the term 'prepubescent' circulated in Europe's medical community from the beginning of the twentieth century, it was not until the 1940s in the USA that the commercial sectors of fashion and cosmetics began to identify a new social group – girls at the threshold of adolescence – and to shape it into a market segment to which it could offer 'intermediate' lines of merchandise.[11] Beginning in the late 1980s, US marketers became

---

[10] Goffmann, Ervin. 1979. *Gender advertisements*. London: Mc Millan.
[11] Cook, Daniel T., and Susan B. Kaiser. 2004. Betwixt and be Tween. Age, ambiguity and the sexualization of the female consuming. *Journal of Consumer Culture* 4(2): 203–227.

increasingly focused on children on the cusp of adolescence, recognising their growing purchasing power and specific consumer behaviours. In the 1990s, in the USA and later in Europe, preadolescence became a 'target' to 'capture'[12] for a panoply of brands and products: clothing, accessories, body care, cultural activities,[13] media content[14] and new digital technologies.

By the late 1990s, this result of social categories created by marketers drew the attention of sociologists and anthropologists studying childhood, culture and consumption. Dick Hebdige[15] found that, in the social imaginary and commercial world alike, the figure of the teenager was fading into a youth of an ever-lowering age. But this new transitional period was surrounded by semantic murk, as the normativity of market segmentation paradoxically produced an unclear, nebulous result. Nicoletta Diasio and Virginie Vinel view preadolescence as an 'age of diversity': 'calendar age, biological age, social age, and school class do not correspond'.[16] As suggested by the neologism 'tween', the name North American marketers have attributed to this group, these preadolescents are situated *in between*, at an uncertain intermediate point. To define preadolescence according to biological age is therefore less than straightforward, as the boundaries fluctuate from one advertiser to another, being delimited variously at ages 8–12, 8–14 or 11–12.

Preadolescence thus seems to be characterised by instability, and market and media discourse find themselves modelling and normalising a nebulous and elusive age.[17] Figuratively speaking, this work of representation follows an iconographic tradition constructed over the last two centuries that represents puberty's biological metamorphosis as the body's inscription into a gender. In line with ancient physiognomic tradition, growing up is optically accompanied by the acquisition of gendered traits and an increasingly significant cleavage between the masculine and the feminine.

In recent years, academic and professional literature in the field of marketing and communication has frequently visualised the current generation of children on the border of adolescence as one of the early adopters who are experienced and passionate about digital technologies (computers, mobile phones and smartphones, tablets, e-books, MP3 players, etc.) to which they are supposedly accustomed from birth, as suggested by the labels attributed to them like 'digital natives' or 'Net Generation'. Unlike their 'digital immigrant' adult counterparts, who were born into a world

[12] Cochoy, Frank (ed.). 2004. *La captation des publics. C'est pour mieux te séduire, mon client....* Toulouse: Presses universitaires du Mirail.

[13] Octobre, Sylvie. 2004. *Les loisirs culturels des enfants de 6 à 14 ans.* Paris: La Documentation française.

[14] Pasquier, Dominique. 1999. *La culture des sentiments. L'expérience télévisuelle des adolescents.* Paris: MSH; Monnot, Catherine. 2009. *Petites filles d'aujourd'hui. L'apprentissage de la féminité.* Paris: Autrement.

[15] Hebidge, Dick. 1988. *Hiding in the light: on images and things.* London: Routledge.

[16] Diasio, Nicoletta, and Virginie Vinel. 2014. La préadolescence: un nouvel age de la vie? *Revue des sciences sociales* 51: 8–13.

[17] De Iulio, Simona. 2014. Entre catégorisation et indétermination : l'imagerie des frontières de l'enfance dans la presse féminine et dans la presse « jeune ». *Revue des sciences sociales* 51: 26–33.

where digital technology did not yet exist, today's preteens should belong to a generation of so-called digital natives, who allegedly don't need to familiarise themselves with new technologies that come to them 'naturally' from the cradle onward.[18] Marketing thus apprehends age as the determining factor in the ICT use, and some authors even distinguish a 'Computer Generation' that is born between 1975 and 1987 and that is composed of 'native speakers' of the computer language, from an 'Internet Generation', that is born from 1988 onward[19] and that is perfectly integrated and at ease in digital network environments.

Sociologists studying ICT use, for their part, have no shortage of questions regarding the limits and even the dangers of these classifications and their normativity, as well as the 'effect of erasure on other social divisions that create fissures in these generational constructions'.[20] Media studies also advise caution and urge us not to forget about the fragmentation of social and cultural identities present among ICT users: '[t]alk of digital natives may make it harder for us to pay attention to the digital divide in terms of who has access to different technical platforms and the participation gap in terms of who has access to certain skills and competencies or for that matter, certain cultural experiences and social identities'.[21] Meticulous observation of the everyday practices of young people helps to abandon the caricature of the preteen digital native. It can also highlight the specific ways in which ICT participates in the experience and construction of gender and identity, something that appears to increasingly escape adult control and to be more and more organised by the marketing and media world.[22]

As we will show later in the remaining of this chapter, preteenmagazines offer particularly rich material for studying advertising and media representations of the mix between age, gender and ICT uses and appropriation, as well as for examining the identity profile of preadolescence generated in Germany and in France over the last three decades.

6.2   Stronger Diversity in France, Counter-Representations in Germany

In Germanpreteenmagazines, images of analogue and digital technological devices primarily appear in advertising. Until the end of the 1990s, in the pages of *Micky Maus,* video game consoles, computers, cameras, toy phones and other

[18]Prensky, Marc. 2001. Digital natives, digital immigrants. *On the Horizon* 9(5): 1–6. MCB University Press; Palfrey, John, and Urs Gasser. 2008. *Born digital. Understanding the first generation of digital natives.* New York: Basic Books.

[19]Block, Martin P., and Don E. Schutz. 2008. *Media generations – media allocation in a consumer-controlled marketplace.* Washington: Prosper Publishing.

[20]Lobet-Maris, Claire. 2011. Âge et usages informatiques. *Communications* 1: 19–28.

[21]Jenkins, H. 2007. Reconsidering digital immigrants ... the official weblog of Henry Jenkins. http://henryjenkins.org/2007/12/reconsidering_digital_immigran.html. Accessed 25 July 2015.

[22]Pasquier, Dominique. 2005. *Cultures lycéennes: la tyrannie de la majorité.* Paris: Autrement.

technological objects were placed at the centre stage in ads boasting their performance with fact-based arguments citing ease of use, portability and variety of functions. It was not until the 2000s that the magazine's advertising images began to
feature the users of these devices. The new images were almost exclusively of boys
showing and/or using a technical device and making claims about it to the young
readers. Girls were absent in most advertisements. When they were included, they
often appeared younger and smaller than the boys and were never placed at the
centre but rather were relegated to the sides or background, from where they atten-
tively or admiringly observed the centrally featured male characters using the
device. Beginning around 2010, German advertising imagery started moving
towards a representation linking technological devices and uses with imaginary
worlds: for example, one Nintendo Gameboy advertisement depicts boys on a bus
playing with their consoles, out of which Pokemon figures magically emerge. The
media of photography and comic strips merge, and the technological device becomes
a tool activating the imagination and allowing young users to connect with one
another, as well as to the fantastical universe produced by the cultural industry of
childhood.

Unlike the German corpus, in which ICTs appear mainly in advertisements,
French magazines also feature it in their editorial content, which is frequently laid
out and illustrated in the format of newspaper cartoons or comic strips. The images'
discourse is not necessarily centred on technology, but on the environment into
which technology is placed, such as urban public spaces (streets, parks); a family
home, including the living, kitchen or bedroom; school (classrooms, playgrounds);
work (businesses); cultural venues (libraries, concert and theatre halls); and social
centres (cafes). These environments serve, first, to construct a 'model' of the family
structure centred on the heterosexual 'white' couple[23] and their two children (often
a boy and a girl), and second, to link gender with social roles – and consequently to
ICT use. As an example, *Le Journal de Mickey* regularly depicts a father figure in
the living room watching television, while the mother works in the kitchen.

In addition to the characters' division of labour by gender and age reflecting
power relations, representations of social identities are often relatively static.
Indeed, the French corpus shows very little diversity in its construction of preadolescence (and even in its treatment of adults) that might 'trouble' the norms of femininity and masculinity[24] as they are reiterated over the course of the images.
Characters are systematically gendered and endowed with an age so that their depictions enable readers to differentiate between boys and girls, men and women and
fathers and mothers. The visual markers of gender and age are embodied in hair-
style, clothing (its shape, colour and pattern) and accessories (including ICTs).
Feminine characters have long hair (varying according to the age being portrayed)
and wear skirts and jewellery, barrettes or scrunchies, and their clothes/accessories

[23] Dyer, Richard. 1997. *White*. London: Routledge.

[24] Butler, Judith. 1990. *Gender trouble: feminism and the subversion of identity*. London: Routledge.

have patterns (flowers, hearts) and/or colours (pink, purple) associated with femininity. Masculine characters have short hair (with long hair sometimes used to mark adolescence) and wear pants, T-shirts or button-down shirts. This grammar of representation, which is linked to the importance of drawing in the French corpus, catalyses a typification of the characters by gender.

These trends are more nuanced in the German corpus. In the photos of advertisements in *Micky Maus*, the ICT user type is a muscular, smiling boy who is confident, dominant, competitive and a winner. But the masculinities featured in German media's staged imagery cannot be reduced to a reproduction of heterosexist norms of hegemonic masculinity.[25] Indeed, other images are shown: boys displaying a wider range of emotions; transgressing the ideal of the strong, athletic body; or aestheticising and caring for their bodies differently. In the rare advertisements where they are associated with ICT, girls appear calm, thoughtful and open. Their smallness and fragility contrasts sharply with the strength of the autonomous, adventurous, agile and aggressive heroines that populate the video games[26] advertised in the magazine.

Even if the German corpus accounts for more qualitatively varied femininities and masculinities, girls are quantitatively fewer than in the French corpus. Indeed, in *Okapi*, *Le Journal de Mickey* and *Micky Maus* alike, boys are over-represented even as the magazines cater to a mixed audience. A count of the number of male and female characters, and the number of times they are shown as ICT users, indicates a strong gender differential. In total, 71 % of the characters in images found in the German *Micky Maus* are marked by the male gender, while images in France's *Le Journal de Mickey* are 68 % male; in *Okapi* they are 61 % male. The difference is rendered even more striking when considering the number of women represented in the images who use technology: a mere 15 % in *Micky Maus* and 24 % in *Le Journal de Mickey*. *Okapi* shows more balance, with 43 % of its depictions of technology users marked by the female gender. However, this (quasi) parity in ICT use is relatively recent, as girls were almost non-existent in the 1980s – making up only 11 % of characters and 7 % of users – while from 2010 to 2014, 42 % of characters and 48 % of users were marked by the female gender. This relative balance beginning in the 2010s correlates more to the magazine's editorial policy than to the national context, since if you compare it to *Le Journal de Mickey*, only 35 % of the latter's were female characters from 2010 to 2014, and these characters represented only 23 % of technology users. It should be added that various public debates contributed to this development, like the discussion on gender equality *[parité]* in the late 1990s and on diversity in 2005. Differences also exist between magazines in how they stage ICTs, even if these may somewhat reflect national specificities.

---

[25] Connell, Raewyn. 2014. *Masculinités. Enjeux sociaux de l'hégémonie*. Paris: Editions Amsterdam.

[26] Lignon, Fanny. 2013. « Des jeux vidéo et des adolescents » A quoi jouent les jeunes filles et garçons des collèges et lycées ? *Le Temps des médias* 21: 143–160.

6.3 Gendered Representations of ICT Use

The German and French corpuses have commonalities and differences in their rep-resentations of technology use. Whether in the French or German preteenmaga-zines, ICT was primarily associated with masculinity in the 1980s. Its use was feminised beginning in the 1990s with the image of the computer. However, the technology was mostly represented in a masculine context during the 1980s and 1990s, being shown accompanied by young boys who were often alone, using it to play video games or to explore its technical aspects. This imagery participated in the construction of the male figure of the computer 'geek'.

Beginning in the 2000s, the computer took hold visually in different worlds (school, home, work) and was shown in association with both genders. In 2010, it became the most widely represented technology in the French corpus, overtaking television. In the images, girls and boys used the family computer without distinc-tion, but their uses differed. The former were shown using their keyboard to develop and maintain social skills and relationships with others, whether romantic or friendly, which was not the case for boys. Adolescent girls were regularly shown drafting an email or communicating over social networks like Facebook or Twitter.

The association between femininity and relationships with others was also pres-ent in telephone use (landline and mobile), in both the German and French corpus. Adolescent girls were shown calling their friends (other girls) to socialise or chat since they are supposedly 'talkative'. In *Okapi* and *Le Journal de Mickey*, illustra-tions and photographs from the 1980s and 1990s show adolescent girls with a tele-phone to their ear, smiling and/or with their mouth open, sometimes lying on a bed; in the 2000s, they were portrayed exchanging romantic or friendly texts in their bedrooms or the schoolyard. This type of staging is also found in the German corpus where, for adolescent girls, the phone is associated with having contact with others as well as with feelings or romantic relationships. But a few counterexamples exist, like one advertising image featuring a girl in boy's clothes, rollerblading with two other boys during a school holiday, with the mobile phone portrayed as the guaran-tor of her independence and security. In contrast to girls, preteen boys in the French corpus use the phone to perform an action (calling for a service, subscribing to a magazine, calling the police), and the words they exchange are often specified in bubbles (which is never the case for girls). In advertisements, masculinity may also be linked with the laptop's technological aspect and its (complex) manufacturing process. In the German *Micky Maus*, meanwhile, the mobile phone often appears in advertising discourse because it helps construct the figure of the cool boy who is admired by girls.

One of the peculiarities of the French corpus is that in addition to linking girls' use of certain technologies to relationships with others, girls are depicted as having cultural practices that often mirror those of television, which on the scale of 'cul-tural legitimacy'[27] are more depreciated than those of boys. For example, in the

---

[27]Bourdieu, Pierre. 1979. *La distinction. Critique social du jugement*. Paris: Les Éditions de Minuit; Lahire, Bernard. 2004. *La Culture des individus. Dissonances culturelles et distinction de soi*. Paris: La Découverte.

2000s, microphones and amplifiers had an increased presence of images, reflecting the development of amateur musical practices. But while boys were shown practising rock or hip-hop, musical genres legitimised in the 1990s, adolescent girls were shown within the world of popular television music. In the 2010s, for example, they were regularly depicted singing songs from the musical television series *Violetta*. Occasionally, they appeared in images of teenage rock bands, but they were always in the minority, averaging three boys to one girl, and with some images of bands featuring no girls at all.

The demonstration of socially hierarchical gendered cultural practices is also apparent in images featuring the television. In both *Okapi* and *Le Journal de Mickey*, masculine uses are linked to major sporting events on one hand – like the Olympics and the World Cup – which boys and/or their fathers watch from the living room sofa and to societally valued practices like watching the news on the other hand. Adolescent girls and their mothers, for their part, are almost systematically shown having a devalued use of television: whatever the age, they are represented watching television shows 'for girls'[28] that are populist and/or sentimental, like *Hélène et les Garçons [Hélène and boys]*, *Plus Belle la Vie [More beautiful life]* or *Lizzie McGuire*. In *Le Journal de Mickey*, the use of television is strongly associated with masculinity and signifies a (very) asymmetrical construction of gender relations: the mother is nearly always associated with domestic and double day work (ironing, cooking, etc.) – and therefore not TV watching – while the father sits on the couch watching television to relax, sometimes accompanied by his children. This pitfall is not visible in *Okapi* or in the Germanmagazines.

Apart from gender-differentiated use of ICT, other technologies are also presented as masculine only, like video games and digital media players, even though teenage girls increasingly use them since the 2010s. Whether in France or Germany, images depicting video games usually show male preteens, joystick in hand, playing together. When girls are visible, they are often outnumbered. And when they are shown alone in the French corpus, it is because they are playing games related to 'care work' – a domain traditionally associated with femininity,[29] like games about the protection of the planet. The German corpus includes ads in which girls are presented as the marketing target for video games with a significant affective dimension (like pet care) or which connect to practices that are conventionally regarded as feminine (such as dance). But in the German corpus, girls can also be seen playing 'serious' video games whose main purpose is learning.

Even if it has been feminised in recent years, the portable music player (cassette, CD or MP3) is a technology associated with masculinity. It is characteristically used as a visual marker of preadolescence: the headphone, shown over the ears or around the neck of boys, tends to be an accessory in the grammar of preteen representation.

This description of the logics of the ICT representation (the most visible among the corpus) indicates a process of stereotypification. The demonstration of their uses

---

[28] Biscarrat, Laetitia. 2015. Le genre de la réception. Stéréotypes de genre et fictions sérielles. *Communication* 33/2: forthcoming.

[29] Molinier, Pascale. 2010. Au-delà de la féminité et du maternel, le travail du care. *L'Esprit du temps* 58: 161–174.

contributes to characterising and differentiating preteen boys from preteen girls. Certainly this process is not static; it evolves over time and reflects differences between magazines and countries. Nevertheless, we may observe that France is more normative than Germany, where femininities and masculinities can be troubled.

6.4 Conclusion

The imagery of preteenmagazines for readers ages 9–13 has contributed in recent decades to shaping, developing and recirculating visual stereotypes of preteens and ICTs. These stereotypes appear highly polarised in terms of gender, and analysing the corpus reveals a markedly different treatment of boys versus girls vis-à-vis ICT use. The emergence of different models in the German corpus, however, seems to confirm the hypothesis that 'far from escaping the traditional conception of differences of the sexes, which tends to reduce gender to a binary opposition between the masculine and the feminine, [the media] is also a site of counter-discourses and counter-models, which displace, rework, and reconfigure the dominant conception'.[30] On one hand, certain stereotypical traits and behaviours are associated with a staged imagery intersecting age, masculinities and femininities and the use of ICTs; on the other hand, these hegemonic representations are part and parcel of dissident versions and counterexamples with which the readership of German preteen magazines, or part of it, is also supposed to identify.

Media and advertising imagery of the insertion of ICT into everyday life does not, then, erase gender differences. Nevertheless, the materiality and functionality of the technical devices populating the pages of German and French preteenmagazines also interweave with social norms, values, symbols and cultural traits that appear highly gendered. Even the diverse uses of technology that have become ordinary, like the telephone, television, mobile phone and computer, are accompanied by differences in what are supposed to be the interests and practices of girls versus those of boys. The comparison also shows that although they are strongly anchored to the dominant models of masculinity and femininity, gendered representations of ICT are culturally and historically situated and subject to change.

The results of this work therefore confirm the pursuit of advertisers to turn digital devices into identity objects for preteen culture,[31] so that in these stereotyped images, headphones, MP3 players and video game consoles become visual markers of childhood at the border of adolescence. The analysis of our corpus, however, invites us to question the thesis of a spontaneous or 'natural' adherence by the

---

[30] Julliard, Virginie, and Nelly Quemener. 2014. Le genre dans la communication et les médias : enjeux et perspectives. *Revue française des sciences de l'information et de la communication* 4. http://rfsic.revues.org/693. Accessed 8 Apr 2014.

[31] Octobre, Sylvie (ed.). 2010. *Enfance et culture. Transmission, appropriation et representation.* Paris: La Documentation Française.

younger generation to new technical devices that they intuitively and effortlessly know how to use. Over the past few decades, French and German preteen magazines have sought to bring digital technology into the world of preteen objects, everyday practices, knowledge and values. Editorial content and advertising discourse within the analysed magazines have aimed at teaching its youngest readers how to operate CD-ROMs or leading them to discover the mobile phone, computer and Internet. Meanwhile, preteen magazines have contributed to creating a very complex network of relationships between the form and content of the various media forms involved in the emergence of a transmedia culture. In this way, the images in these magazines reveal their ambition to act as mediators between young readers and a technological world that is still opaque and unfamiliar.

References

Amossy, Ruth, and Anne Herschberg-Pierrot. 1997. *Stéréotypes et clichés. Langue, discours, société*. Paris: Nathan université.

Anderson, Benedict. 1996. *L'imaginaire national. Réflexions sur l'origine et l'essor du nationalisme*. Paris: La Découverte.

Biscarrat, Laetitia. 2015. Le genre de la réception. Stéréotypes de genre et fictions sérielles. *Communication* 33/2: forthcoming.

Block, Martin P., and Don E. Schutz. 2008. *Media generations – media allocation in a consumer-controlled marketplace*. Washington: Prosper Publishing.

Bourdieu, Pierre. 1979. *La distinction. Critique social du jugement*. Paris: Les Éditions de Minuit.

Boyer, Henri. 2008. Stéréotype, emblème, mythe. Sémiotisation médiatique et figement représentationnel. *Mots* 88: 99–113.

Brekhus, Wayne. 2005. Une sociologie de l'"invisibilité": réorienter notre regard. *Réseaux* 129–130: 243–272.

Butler, Judith. 1990. *Gender trouble: feminism and the subversion of identity*. London: Routledge.

Charaudeau, Patrick. 1997. *Le discours d'information médiatique: La construction du miroir social*. Paris: Nathan.

Cochoy, Frank (ed.). 2004. *La captation des publics. C'est pour mieux te séduire, mon client....* Toulouse: Presses universitaires du Mirail.

Connell, Raewyn. 2014. *Masculinités. Enjeux sociaux de l'hégémonie*. Paris: Editions Amsterdam.

Cook, Daniel T., and Susan B. Kaiser. 2004. Betwixt and be Tween. Age, ambiguity and the sexualization of the female consuming. *Journal of Consumer Culture* 4(2): 203–227.

De Iulio, Simona. 2014. Entre catégorisation et indétermination : l'imagerie des frontières de l'enfance dans la presse féminine et dans la presse « jeune ». *Revue des sciences sociales* 51: 26–33.

de Lauretis, Teresa. 2007. *Théorie queer et cultures populaires. De Foucault à Cronenberg*. Paris: La Dispute.

Diasio, Nicoletta, and Virginie Vinel. 2014. La préadolescence: un nouvel age de la vie? *Revue des sciences sociales* 51: 8–13.

Dyer, Richard. 1997. *White*. London: Routledge.

Goffman, Erving. 1975. *Stigmate: les usages sociaux des handicaps*. Paris: Éditions de Minuit.

Goffmann, Ervin. 1979. *Gender advertisements*. London: Mc Millan.

Hall, Stuart. 2007. *Identités et cultures. Politiques des Cultural Studies*. Paris: Editions Amsterdam.

Hebidge, Dick. 1988. *Hiding in the light: on images and things*. London: Routledge.

Jenkins, H. 2007. Reconsidering digital immigrants … the official weblog of Henry Jenkins. http://henryjenkins.org/2007/12/reconsidering_digital_immigran.html. Accessed 25 July 2015.

Julliard, Virginie, and Nelly Quemener. 2014. Le genre dans la communication et les médias : enjeux et perspectives. *Revue française des sciences de l'information et de la communication* 4. http://rfsic.revues.org/693. Accessed 8 Apr 2014.

Lahire, Bernard. 2004. *La Culture des individus. Dissonances culturelles et distinction de soi.* Paris: La Découverte.

Lignon, Fanny. 2013. « Des jeux vidéo et des adolescents » A quoi jouent les jeunes filles et garçons des collèges et lycées ? *Le Temps des médias* 21: 143–160.

Lobet-Maris, Claire. 2011. Âge et usages informatiques. *Communications* 1: 19–28.

Molinier, Pascale. 2010. Au-delà de la féminité et du maternel, le travail du care. *L'Esprit du temps* 58: 161–174.

Monnot, Catherine. 2009. *Petites filles d'aujourd'hui. L'apprentissage de la féminité.* Paris: Autrement.

Octobre, Sylvie. 2004. *Les loisirs culturels des enfants de 6 à 14 ans.* Paris: La Documentation française.

Octobre, Sylvie (ed.). 2010. *Enfance et culture. Transmission, appropriation et representation.* Paris: La Documentation Française.

Ollivier, Bruno. 2009. Présentation générale: Les identités collectives : comment comprendre une question politique brûlante ? In *Les identités collectives à l'heure de la mondialisation*, ed. Ollivier Bruno, 7–28. Paris: CNRS Editions.

Palfrey, John, and Urs Gasser. 2008. *Born digital. Understanding the first generation of digital natives.* New York: Basic Books.

Pasquier, Dominique. 1999. *La culture des sentiments. L'expérience télévisuelle des adolescents.* Paris: MSH.

Pasquier, Dominique. 2005. *Cultures lycéennes: la tyrannie de la majorité.* Paris: Autrement.

Prensky, Marc. 2001. Digital natives, digital immigrants. *On the Horizon* 9(5): 1–6. MCB University Press.

Quéré, Louis. 1992. L'espace public: de la théorie politique à la métathéorie sociologique. *Quaderni* 18: 75–92.

Voirol, Olivier. 2005. Les luttes pour la visibilité. Esquisse d'une problématique. *Réseaux* 129–130: 89–121.

Part III
ICT and Professionalization. Introductory Remarks

Delphine Diaz and Régis Schlagdenhauffen

The professionalization of women in the field of information and communication technology is a natural extension of some aspects outlined in previous sections. The first contribution, Giuditta Parolini's UK case study of Rothamsted Statistics Department, illuminates one element that has long been in the shadows: the participation of many women in the early days of computing. Subverting the traditional image of computing as a masculine field, she explains the sociogenesis of women's early role, showing that as of 1920 women were already active participants in that process. Based on the testimony of former employees, she highlights the singular part they played, showing the contradiction between their professional status as 'technicians' and the fact that they were not fully regarded as such by their male colleagues. Chantal Morley and Martina McDonnell's contribution extends the discussion begun by G. Parolini by offering a comparative study of women in computing in France, Finland and the United Kingdom between 1960 and 1990. Despite different national contexts, the authors observe many similarities in gender divisions within the information and communication technology professions. These points in common partly explain the over-representation of men in these professions, but do not allow to step up a new deal. In order to do so, Karen Lee Ashcraft and Catherine Ashcraft reflect on diversity interventions and demonstrate the part that history could (and should) play. Showing that women taking second place in certain occupational sectors is not specific to Europe or to ICT, they start a dialogue between European and American histories, and between civil aviation and ICT

D. Diaz (✉)
Laboratoire CERHiC EA 2616, Université de Reims Champagne-Ardenne,
57 rue Pierre Taittinger, 51096 Reims, France
e-mail: delphinediaz@gmail.com

R. Schlagdenhauffen
Université de Lorraine, Nancy, France
e-mail: regis.schlag@gmail.com

history, showing how Civil Aviation gradually confined women to care functions. Their emergence in other professional bodies reconfigured the essentialized forms of masculine and feminine attributes without allowing an equal professional recognition of men and women, which proves the existence of the 'glass ceiling' that women face in such professions and in many others.

Chapter 7
From Computing Girls to Data Processors: Women Assistants in the Rothamsted Statistics Department

Giuditta Parolini

Abstract Over 200 women worked as computing assistants in the Rothamsted statistics department during the twentieth century. They were employed in the analysis of field and laboratory experiments and in the examination of the returns of agricultural surveys. Before World War II they did calculations with pen, paper, slide rules and electromechanical calculating machines, but during the 1950s, when the department underwent an early process of computerisation, their tasks shifted to data processing. Only sparse records exist on the work of these women, and their contribution to the activity of the Rothamsted statistics department has never been assessed, consigning them to invisibility. Combining the literature currently available on laboratory technicians with the one on human computers and data processors, the paper will provide a *longue durée* perspective (1920s–1990) on the work of the female assistants in the Rothamsted statistics department, addressing two distinct aspects. On the one hand it will examine how the tasks of these women evolved with the computing technologies available in the department. On the other hand the paper will reflect on the invisibility of these assistants, who are never explicitly accounted as contributors to the scientific activity of the Rothamsted statistics department, despite being a conspicuous component of its staff.

Since the 1980s women's presence in ICT has drawn the attention of historians, sociologists and professionals engaged in the field. Historical case studies, collections of oral histories, quantitative and qualitative sociological investigations and meetings of professionals associations have addressed the issue.[1]

---

[1]Lovegrove, Gillian, and Barbara Segal. 1991. *Women into computing: selected papers 1988–1990*. Berlin: Springer. [in collaboration with the British Computer Society]; Light, Jennifer S. 1999. When computers were women. *Technology and Culture* 40(3): 455–483; Grier, David A. 2001. Human computers: the first pioneers of the information age. *Endeavour* 25(1): 28–32, Grier, David A. 2007. *When computers were human*. Princeton: Princeton University Press; Abbate, Janet (ed). 2003. Special Issue on women and gender in the history of computing. *IEEE Annals of*

G. Parolini (✉)
Technische Universität Berlin and Berliner Zentrum für Wissensgeschichte,
10623 Berlin, Germany
e-mail: giudittaparolini@gmail.com

© Springer International Publishing Switzerland 2015
V. Schafer, B.G. Thierry (eds.), *Connecting Women*, History of Computing,
DOI 10.1007/978-3-319-20837-4_7

This growing literature has mostly examined educated women, who received training in mathematics, engineering or computer science before entering the field. Yet, this is not fully representative of the female participation in computing during the twentieth century. Routine tasks, such as doing basic arithmetic or punching cards and paper tape, were often entrusted to women without higher education, whose contribution to computing is even more concealed than the one given by their university-trained colleagues.[2]

In the context of scientific research, these blue-collar women,[3] who worked as human computers or data processors, are certainly akin to technical figures. They share the routine nature of their job, the lack of recognition and the scarcity of sources for examining their role in science with the seventeenth-century assistants of Robert Boyle described by Steven Shapin (1989)[4] in his seminal contribution on the "invisible technician".

Combining the current literature on laboratory technicians with the one on human computers and data processors, the paper will address a case study on women, gender and ICT taken from the history of statistics. It will investigate the female assistants who were engaged as human computers and data processors in the statistics department of Rothamsted Experimental Station, a British institution for agricultural research. The Rothamsted statistics department was both a statistical and a computing centre,[5] similarly to the Mathematical and Statistical Service run by George W. Snedecor at Iowa State College and examined by D. A. Grier (2007: 159–169).[6] In both cases statistical methods and computing power were mostly devoted to the solution of problems in agricultural research.

From the 1920s, when the department was founded, until the 1990s, when data processing was outdated by the availability of improved computer technologies, over 200 women worked alongside the scientific staff of the Rothamsted statistics

---

the History of Computing 25(4): 4–8, Abbate, Janet. 2012. Recoding gender: women's changing participation in computing. Cambridge, MA: MIT Press; Margolis, Jane, and Allan Fisher. 2003. Unlocking the clubhouse. Cambridge, MA: MIT Press; Cohoon, Joanne, and William Aspray. 2006. Women and information technology: research on underrepresentation. Cambridge, MA: MIT Press; Misa, Thomas J. (ed.). 2010. Gender codes: why women are leaving computing? Hoboken: Wiley/IEEE Computer Society.

[2] Haigh, Thomas. 2010. Masculinity and the machine man: gender in the history of data processing. In Gender codes: why women are leaving computing? ed. Thomas J. Misa, 51–71. Hoboken: Wiley/IEEE Computer Society; Hicks, Mary. 2010a. Meritocracy and feminization in conflict: computerization in the British Government. In Gender codes: why women are leaving computing? ed. Thomas J. Misa, 95–114. Hoboken: Wiley/IEEE Computer Society, Hicks, Mary. 2010b. Only the clothes changed: women operators in British computing and advertising, 1950–1970. IEEE Annals of the History of Computing 32(4): 5–17.

[3] Misa 2010: 8.

[4] Shapin, Steven. 1989. The invisible technician. American Scientist 77(6): 554–563.

[5] Parolini, Giuditta. 2013. "Making sense of figures": statistics, computing and information technologies in agriculture and biology in Britain, 1920s–1960s. Doctoral dissertation. University of Bologna, Parolini, Giuditta. 2014. The emergence of modern statistics in agricultural science: analysis of variance, experimental design and the reshaping of research at Rothamsted Experimental Station, 1919–1933. Journal of the History of Biology. doi:10.1007/s10739-014-9394-z.

[6] Grier 2007: 159–169.

department contributing to the analysis of agricultural experiments and surveys. At first they did calculations with pen, paper, slide rules and electromechanical calculating machines, but after the World War II, when the department underwent an early process of computerisation, their tasks shifted to data processing jobs, such as punching paper tape and cards, and later in time the use of word processors.

Only sparse records exist on the work of these women and their contribution to the activity of the Rothamsted statistics department has never been assessed, consigning them to invisibility. Writing these women back into the history to which they belong "in action if not in memory"[7] is essential not only to further our knowledge of the female participation in computing but also to gain a deeper understanding of the statistical research performed at Rothamsted.

The paper will provide a *longue durée* perspective on the work of these women assistants covering most part of the twentieth century (1920s–1990). It will address two distinct aspects. On the one hand it will examine how the tasks of these female technicians changed over time and evolved with the computing technologies available in the department. On the other hand the paper will reflect on the invisibility of these women, who are never explicitly accounted as contributors to the scientific activity of the Rothamsted statistics department, despite being a conspicuous component of its staff.

7.1 Technicians in Science

As argued by Steven Shapin, an enriched understanding of laboratory practices in science requires unravelling the role of the technicians who worked alongside scientists. Yet, as Shapin remarks, the persistence of "individualistic and revelatory models of scientific activity" has provided "a cultural basis for the invisibility of technicians and other support personnel, and for our tendency to see science predominantly as thought rather than as work".[8] According to Shapin, thus, historical research has "to document and to clarify the significance of technicians' work", but must also "explain why it was that they were largely transparent to the gaze of those who employed them".[9]

A literature devoted to the role of technicians in science has stemmed from Shapin's contribution.[10] In addressing the social dimension of the scientific enterprise from the technicians' perspective, this literature has emphasised the difficulty to produce even a portrait of the technician. On the one hand, in fact, information on technicians' work and careers is scarce at best and often completely absent, and on the other hand, "there are many sorts of technician, with varying degrees of competence, qualifications and experience".[11] Due to this intrinsic ambiguity, the label of

---

[7] Light 1999: 483.

[8] Shapin 1989: 561.

[9] Shapin 1989: 556.

[10] E.g. Iliffe, Rob. 2008. Guest editorial: technicians. *Notes and Records of the Royal Society of London* 62(1): 3–16.

[11] Iliffe 2008: 5.

technicians can be applied both to the college-educated women who programmed the ENIAC[12] and to the women without higher education appointed as computers and data processors in the Rothamsted statistics department.

Despite the many differences, a few common elements recur time and again. First of all, technicians perform tasks that are considered mere routine. In so doing they have scarce or absent career perspectives, being often the fate of the senior staff to supervise and train junior technicians. What is most striking of technicians is their social distance from the scientific staff. Even though they work in the same environment as scientists, technicians live in a world apart.

All these features apply to the female assistants in the Rothamsted statistics department, but they are not peculiar of these women. Other twentieth-century groups of female technicians employed in scientific laboratories display a similar pattern of low-status recognition. An example widely cited[13] is the one of the "scanning girls" engaged since the late 1930s in the examination of nuclear emulsions in high-energy physics.[14] Despite lacking a background in physics, these women were trained to scrutinise the emulsions using high-power microscopes in order to find significant particle events. Interestingly, while their contribution to the process of discovery was acknowledged at the beginning, in time the names of these female technicians disappeared, leaving them almost invisible by the early 1950s. During the same decade the Cambridge crystallographers engaged in the study of the molecular structure of myoglobin and haemoglobin and hired young women on short-term contracts to do densitometer readings of precession films and perform the related calculations.[15] These women were named *computors* within the laboratory, although doing computations was only one of their tasks. Even though they "were seen as belonging to the 'inner sanctum' of the work and ranked higher than other assistant personnel in the laboratory",[16] these women make only a cursory appearance in the history of the Medical Research Council Laboratory of Molecular Biology in Cambridge.

The examples now mentioned draw attention on the subordinate role that female technicians had during the twentieth century. They raise questions on gender, practical knowledge, professional recognition and participation in the scientific enterprise, the same issues that will be at the core of my analysis of the assistants in the Rothamsted statistics department. The female assistants at Rothamsted had only a basic mathematical and computing knowledge, but without them the statistics department would not have been able to fulfil its scientific mission, as the contribution of the assistant staff was essential in the analysis of the agricultural and biological experiments and surveys that accumulated in the department from year to year. The women assistants, in fact, were engaged in the routine number crunching and data processing that was part and parcel of this statistical analysis.

---

[12] Light 1999: 474.

[13] Iliffe 2008: 10.

[14] Galison, Peter. 1997. *Image and logic: a material culture of microphysics.* Chicago: The University of Chicago Press: 33, 198–200.

[15] de Chadarevian, Soraya. 2002. *Designs for life: molecular biology after World War II.* Cambridge: Cambridge University Press.

[16] de Chadarevian 2002: 124 footnote.

Before the computerisation of the department, the assistants were in charge of the arithmetic (e.g. computations of squares and square roots and conversion of measuring units) required by the application of the statistical method known as analysis of variance to the laboratory and field results. They also took part in the analysis of agricultural surveys calculating, averages and errors for the data collected. In both cases the guidelines for the work of these women were set by the local statisticians. When digital computers became available in the department, the involvement of the assistants in number crunching was superseded by activities such as tape/card punching and subsequent verification of the data. Again the assistants worked under the management of the scientific staff that organised the clerical work and distributed the tasks.

7.2   Female Labour in Computing

Computing has been for long time a labour-intensive enterprise.[17] "[M]en and women, young and old, well educated and common" took part in it as human computers.[18] Some computers worked alone and without any financial return, as Emma Gifford who devoted several years of her life to the calculation and publication of an extensive table of natural sines,[19] some instead were members of larger organisations and supported themselves and their families with the income of their labour, like Mary Edwards who worked for the British *Nautical Almanac* in the second half of the eighteenth century.[20]

If in the seventeenth and eighteenth centuries human computers could usually rely only on slide rules, a few collections of mathematical tables, and their personal enterprise, in the nineteenth-century mechanical calculating machines and punched-card equipment entered into accounting and scientific computation easing the burden of number crunching. After World War II, with the availability of electronic computers, the labour of calculation progressively shifted from human beings to machines as suggested by the change in the meaning of the word *computer*.

Yet, computerisation did not coincide with the prompt dismissal of human computers. When electronic computers began to spread in scientific research, military projects and in business, new job opportunities in programming, data processing and key-punching emerged for the former human computers. For instance, the ENIACprogrammers were selected among the women who were previously engaged in the computation of gunnery tables using desk calculators and a differential analyser at the US Army's Ballistic Research Laboratory.[21]

---

[17] Grier 2007: 6.

[18] Grier 2001: 28.

[19] Campbell-Kelly, Martin, Mary Croarken, Raymond Flood, and Eleanor Robson. 2003. *The history of mathematical tables: from Sumer to spreadsheets*. Oxford: Oxford University Press: 9.

[20] Croarken, Mary. 2003. Mary Edwards: computing for a living in 18th century England. *IEEE Annals of the History of Computing* 25(4): 9–15.

[21] Light 1999: 469.

Gender is a crucial category in understanding the contribution of technicians to computing labour. Since the nineteenth-century gender played a part in the selection of human computers because, for a long time, women were a cheaper workforce than men.[22] In punched-card installations female labour was largely employed for data entry, but management and supervision of the machines usually were a male prerogative.[23] In the computer age women engaged as data processors remained low-status clerical workers in the office economy.[24]

In the 1940s a gendered understanding of computing work promoted the association of women with software – at that stage programming was perceived as a technical and routine chore – in contrast to the male-dominated manufacture of hardware. However, only a decade later programming was already a male enterprise,[25] and nowadays computing professionals and educators are left wondering how to remedy the scarce presence of women in computer science.[26]

A process of occupational sex typing[27] maintained the assistants work in the Rothamsted statistics department as a female occupation over the twentieth century. Yet, gender alone cannot explain why the female assistants constantly remained in the periphery of the scientific enterprise. To address this issue it is necessary to take into account the labour organisation in the statistics department and how the tools and practices adopted shaped the role of the female technicians. The information available to pursue this research is scarce, but combining institutional records, archive materials and oral histories, we can follow the female assistants in the Rothamsted statistics department for a large part of the twentieth century.

7.3   Women Assistants in the Rothamsted Statistics Department

From the 1920s to 1990s, over 200 women worked as assistants in the Rothamsted statistics department. A few were secretaries and typists, but the overwhelming majority was employed in the analysis of field and laboratory experiments and in the examination of the returns of agricultural surveys (Table 7.1). These women had no university education and were usually selected among the local population. Up to the 1950s they were full-fledged human computers, but with the computerisation of the department, they began to undertake the more clerical tasks related to data processing. They always worked under the supervision of a statistician, usually a male statistician, and they were (almost) never named in the reports of the scientific

---

[22] Grier 2007: 83.

[23] Haigh 2010.

[24] Hicks 2010b.

[25] Ensmenger, Nathan. 2010. *The computer boys take over: computers, programmers and the politics of technical expertise*. Cambridge, MA: MIT Press.

[26] Cohoon and Aspray 2006; Misa 2010.

[27] Haigh 2010: 52–55.

Table 7.1 Female assistants engaged in computing/data processing (1920s–1990)

Year	No. of female assistants engaged in computing/data processing	Year	No. of female assistants engaged in computing/data processing	Year	No. of female assistants engaged in computing/data processing
1923/1924	*1* W. D. Christmas A. D. Dunkley	1952	*18*	1972	*19*
1925/1926	*1* W. D. Christmas A. D. Dunkley	1953	*20*	1973	*17*
1927/1928	*2* W. D. Christmas A. D. Dunkley	1954	*20*	1974	*17*
1929	*3*	1955	*19*	1975	*14*
1930	*3*	1956	*20*	1976	*16*
1931	*2*	1957	*19*	1977	*16*
1932	*2*	1958	*21*	1978	*12*
1933	*3* J. W. West	1959	*20* A. G. Davies	1979	*11*
1934	*3* J. W. West	1960	*21*	1980	*10*
1935	*4* J. M. Wilson	1961	*25*	1981	*8*
1936	*4* J. M. Wilson	1962	*26* B. M. Cooper	1982	*10*
1937	*5*	1963	*23*	1983	*10*
1938	*4*	1964	*28*	1984	*6*
1939-1945	*11*	1965	*28*	1985	*7*
1946	*12*	1966	*27*	1986	*6*
1947	*12*	1967	*27* D. E. T. Thomas	1987	*5*
1948	*15*	1968	*21*	1988	*5*
1949	*15*	1969	*19*	1989	*5*
1950	*17* W. J. Walters	1970	*20*	1990	*4*[a]
1951	*18*	1971	*20*		

[a]This number has been obtained considering the compensation between retirements during the year and new appointments. Counting the women assistants from the staff lists gives a reliable estimation of the magnitude of their number, but the total is subject to shifts of some units because: (a) clerical roles (secretary, typists, etc.) were not always explicitly indicated; (b) women who did not leave the job upon marriage were listed at first under their maiden's name and afterwards with their married name, and it is not always possible to trace them; and (c) the women who worked only for a few months were not mentioned in the staff lists. The names of the few men who worked in the statistics department as assistants are explicitly reported. The table has been compiled using the Rothamsted Experimental Station reports (1923/1924–1987) and AFRC Institute of Arable Crops Research reports (1988–1990)

activity of the department, except the staff lists. Until 1990 in the staff lists women were mentioned with their full name, while men were only listed with initials of their first name, offering therefore a straightforward criterion for discrimination between male and female staff. Although providing only essential information, the lists allow to reconstruct how the number of the female assistants changed during the period examined, for how long these women remained in the department on average and how the role of the female assistants was identified.

The first female assistant in the Rothamsted statistics department, Kathleen Abbott, is listed in the station report for the years 1923/1924. She is classified as an assistant computer, and during the 1920s and 1930s a few more women were hired in the department with the same qualification. Before World War II, however, only 11 female assistants in total are mentioned in the station reports. This is not surprising as the exponential growth of the Rothamsted statistics department began only during the 1940s and strengthened in the decades after World War II.[28] By 1948 there were already 15 women assistants; in 1953, 20; and in 1964, 28. After the war these women were just accounted as assistant or clerical staff, without further specifications.

During the 1950s and 1960s, the number of the female assistants constantly increased despite the computerisation of the department. But the female assistants at Rothamsted were never involved in programming the first mainframe available for the local statisticians, a prototype computer named Elliott 401.[29] Programming was always performed by the scientific staff – during the 1950s and 1960s the programming staff was all male – but even when the computations were entrusted to the computer, several tasks, such as punching the paper tape with the input data or converting the units of the experimental results, were still done by hand by the female assistants. This clerical labour decreased over time with the availability of more sophisticated mainframes, but in the 1950s, 1960s, 1970s and even 1980s, the women assistants had a role to play in the statistics department. Only in 1968 the assistant staff suddenly diminished because an autonomous computer department was created at Rothamsted, and some of the female assistants previously working in the statistics department were transferred there.

In 1978 the staff list of the statistics department began to offer a more articulate description of the female assistants. The women engaged as secretaries, typists or in other administrative roles were listed aside from the women engaged in the computing work, for the first time classified as data processors. There were 12 data processors in that year and there was a hierarchy among them, with senior and junior staff listed apart. The number of data processors in the department oscillated around ten until 1984, when it began to diminish again, and in 1987 the women assistants were deprived of their status as data processors and merely listed as administrative officers or administrative assistants. In the late 1980s and early 1990s, there were still

---

[28] Parolini 2013: Chap. 4.

[29] Parolini 2013: 226–244.

four to five women assistants in the statistics department and their role was merely labelled as "data preparation".

The different denominations reflect the change in the tasks assigned to the female assistants who shifted from being human computers, solely engaged in calculations, to data processors who devoted their time to key-punching, data entry and filing. Sometimes the assistants also contributed to run the computer, when the statistics department was in charge of its own mainframe. Vera Wiltsher, a former data processor, used to do "overtime" on the Elliott 401. "You put the program tape in and then you run the tape and you got an output tape, which you had to print out", recalls Wiltsher,[30] who began to work at Rothamsted in 1961, when she was 17. Wiltsher remained in the statistics department until February 1967, when she left for a few years to raise her children. She came back to the department in 1979 to work on the analysis of surveys. For this work she had to use punched cards instead of the already-familiar paper tape and she recalls: "It was so different from anything I had ever touched before!".[31]

In the early 1980s the female assistants had to deal with the new systems for data entry and word processing that progressively replaced punched cards with key-to-disc systems. According to the station reports, the operators liked the new equipment, which improved their working conditions[32] and reduced the time for preparing the yield book of the field experiments,[33] but on the other hand the assistants had to learn new keyboard operations.

The women who remained in the Rothamsted statistics department for several years therefore experienced a constant transformation of their tasks in relation to the new technologies available. Moving from one technology to the other forced the female assistants to learn from scratch new skills and follow different work practices. This is a reminder that the know-how of the laboratory technician is first and foremost a know-how related to machines. For instance, both Vera Wiltsher, already mentioned, and Brenda Watler, another data processor who worked in the statistics department in the period 1972–1989, suggested that a decisive change for them was related to the type of computer input adopted, that is paper tape or punched cards. Unlike Vera Wiltsher who began to work at Rothamsted when she was in her teens, Brenda Watler arrived in the statistics department while she was in her early 40s and had already acquired an experience with punched cards working for the insurance company Friends Provident. At Rothamsted Watler had to learn all about paper tape and oral histories collected with Wiltsher, and Watler suggests that for both women the change of medium, from tape to cards for Wiltsher and vice versa for Watler, was a challenge.

---

[30] Parolini 2013: 257.

[31] Parolini 2013: 256.

[32] Rothamsted Experimental Station. 1981. *Report for 1980 Part 1*. Harpenden: Rothamsted Experimental Station: 269.

[33] Rothamsted Experimental Station. 1982. *Report for 1981 Part 1*. Harpenden: Rothamsted Experimental Station: 276.

7.4   A Job for Women

During the 70-year period examined, less than ten men – an extremely small percentage when compared with the over 200 female assistants – are listed among the computing/data processing staff of the Rothamsted statistics department (Table 7.1). Evidently men considered the role of assistant in the statistics department an unsuitable occupation.

The economic conditions were certainly not appealing. The pay of the assistant staff in the statistics department was not high. Before World War II, when the finances of the department were rather scarce, mostly young and inexperienced women were appointed as human computers. The weekly entry pay for these young assistants, just mentioned as "girls" in some correspondence of the 1930s, was 7s 6d, less than the weekly income for the Rothamsted female cleaners in the same period.[34]

The young women who entered in the department before World War II were expected to quit the job in a few years for marrying. But even after the war, when female employment became more socially acceptable and married women worked for several years as assistants in the statistics department, the situation remained unchanged. The female assistants never had a career progression. Such is the case of a married woman called Verona Roberts who entered in the department in the 1940s and remained there until the 1970s. During this time Roberts was engaged in the computing work related to the survey of fertiliser practice, an annual investigation into the use of fertilisers in farming that the Rothamsted statistics department began during World War II and carried on for decades. At her retirement in 1975, the station report could just commend Roberts' "devoted work" for the survey, as a summary of her 32-year service in the department.[35]

Only in the late 1970s, the staff lists adopted an explicit distinction between junior and senior roles in data processing, giving to the female assistants a semblance of a progression. But it was only a meagre improvement, as the tasks of the senior members were not different from the ones of the junior staff. Brenda Watler, who is listed among the senior data processors since 1978, remembers in fact that she used to share the work of all the other assistants.

The low salary and the absence of perspectives here described were certainly the main elements that made the job of assistant in the statistics department unappealing for a male workforce. On the other hand the assistant role was considered suitable for women because, for a large part of the twentieth century, they were not expected to have proper careers. This situation is not peculiar of the research institution here examined, but representative of a general trend in Britain, as argued by Mary Hicks in her examination of gender patterns in the computerisation of the

---

[34] For the definition of the human computers in the department as girls, see below the correspondence of the computers Pennells and Rolt with the local statisticians. For the weekly wages of the assistant staff, see the archive of Rothamsted Research (RRes), LAT 45.2.

[35] Rothamsted Experimental Station. 1976. *Report for 1975 Part 1*. Harpenden: Rothamsted Experimental Station: 332.

British civil service.[36] There is certainly a third cultural component that acted after World War II and that Hicks points out. In British advertising, the image of the computer operator was stereotypically female and perceived as a "low-cost, high-turnover, relatively unskilled worker".[37] This enduring stereotype certainly contributed to identifying the role of assistant in the Rothamsted statistics department as a female job.

7.5   From Human Computers to Data Processors

As observed by David Grier, the stories of human computers "are often difficult to tell, as the vast majority of computers left no record of their lives beyond a single footnote to a scholarly article or an acknowledgment in the bottom margin of a mathematical table".[38] The Rothamsted computers did not even have these brief mentions. The only insight into the working life of the Rothamsted human computers is offered by the unsuccessful request of wage increase filed in December 1931 by two women, Florence Pennells and Kitty Rolt.[39]

Pennells and Rolt appealed to the then head of the department, Ronald Aylmer Fisher, for a better salary. They were earning, respectively, 22s 6d and 12s per week, while a (male) assistant statistician earned in the same period about £7 per week. Asking for more money, they complained that their work as assistant computers was a much harder chore than the one of the other girls employed as assistants in the station.[40]

Yet, the role of assistant computers was not perceived as a real professional qualification at Rothamsted. For instance, a colleague of Florence Pennells and Kitty Rolt moved from the assistant staff in the department of statistics right to the task of laboratory attendant in the department of chemistry, when the grant that supported her computing work expired. Her departure prompted the request of pay rise by Pennells and Rolt.

Fisher's answer suggests a sympathetic attitude towards his computing girls. "I shall certainly feel responsible for seeing that you are not driven to work harder than is good for your health, or indeed beyond what is necessary to attain full competence in computing practice", he wrote them and committed himself to support their request if they could prove a "real increase" in their computing capacity.[41] He invited

---

[36] Hicks 2010a.

[37] Hicks 2010b: 3.

[38] Grier 2007: 8.

[39] The correspondence between the women computers, the statisticians in the department and the station director is held in the Fisher Papers at the Barr Smith Library, the University of Adelaide (hereafter BSL), and in the archive of Rothamsted Research [ref. STATS 7.11] (hereafter RRes).

[40] Letters from F. Pennells and K. Rolt to R. A. Fisher, 3rd and 12th December 1931, BSL.

[41] Letter from R. A. Fisher to F. Pennells and K. Rolt, 5th December 1931, RRes. For the qualification of the computers as 'girls' see Letter from R. A. Fisher to F. Yates, 5th December 1931, RRes.

them to show to Frank Yates, the assistant statistician in charge of the computing staff, which calculating machines they could use "skilfully and quickly for the different routine processes required" and, "what is very valuable when there is a shortage of machines", he invited the human computers to show the tasks for which they were "able to use the slide rule or logarithm tables".[42]

The Rothamsted computers of the 1930s were taught not only how to manage desk calculators, slide rules and mathematical tables but also basic notions of statistics, because, from time to time, they were called to handle a bit of statistics on their own. For instance, in the absence of Fisher's assistant statisticians, Pennells and Rolt had to examine a set of data related to a sheep experiment. The Rothamsted farm manager wanted the human computers "to work out some correlations" for him, and Pennells and Rolt resorted to Frank Yates for advice, still unsure about their statistical competences.[43]

The work undertaken by the woman computers in the 1930s was not very different from the tasks of their female colleagues in the 1940s and 1950s. Tabulators were introduced at Rothamsted in the 1940s, but until the second half of the 1950s, experiments and surveys were mainly analysed by hand and using desk calculators. Only in the late 1950s and during the 1960s, when the Rothamsted statistics department developed effective computer programmes for the analysis of agricultural and biological experiments and surveys, the tasks of the women assistants shifted from computing to data processing.

Vera Wiltsher remembers: "We were employed as data processors, which means we assisted in running the computer. [...] You had to punch the tape, and then you put it through the verification program. Another person would find out any mistakes you had made. Also you had to do a lot of hand-work because the output we were getting was not very sophisticated, so you had to do a lot of calculations, standard errors etc. To do all these computations we used calculating machines. [...] You had to work with a colleague because everything was double checked".[44]

Frank Yates, who promoted the computerisation of the Rothamsted statistics department, claimed that computerisation made it unnecessary to train "computers in the complexities of routine computation, such as the analysis of variance".[45] Although the human computers interacted with more advanced technologies, in fact, they progressively lost control on the calculations performed in the department and they became just scientific clerks, with a deskilling of the computing tasks for which the female assistants had been employed at Rothamsted since the 1920s.

However, if number crunching began to be computerised in the 1950s, all the operations concerned with the preparation of the data for the analysis of experiments and surveys and the distribution of the computer output to the experimental

---

[42] Letter from R. A. Fisher to F. Pennells and K. Rolt, 5th December 1931, RRes.

[43] Letter from F. Pennells and K. Rolt to F. Yates, 29th December 1931, RRes.

[44] Parolini 2013: 256.

[45] Yates, Frank. 1960. The use of electronic computers in the analysis of replicated experiments, and groups of experiments of the same design. *Bulletin de l'Institut Agronomique et des Stations de Recherches de Gembloux* 1: 201–210: 210.

scientists were automated only very slowly. Therefore, the women assistants did not vanish from the statistics department, but remained there and progressively acquired the role of data processors, a function that was still crucial in the analysis of experiments and surveys.

The transformation of the computers into data processors was a long and continuous process that lasted more than two decades and co-evolved with the computing technologies available in the department. For instance, the memories of Vera Wiltsher refer to the work with the Elliott 401, the first mainframe available at Rothamsted. When a second more advanced computer, a Ferranti Orion, arrived in the statistics department in the 1960s, she remembers that "you had not to do hand calculations because the computer did all by itself and also the output was much more sophisticated".[46] But the improved technologies emphasised the clerical features of the assistants over their technical skills, contributing to isolate them in a world apart within the statistics department.

7.6   Conclusion: On the Invisibility of the Women Assistants at Rothamsted

Gender was not the main element that contributed to the invisibility of the female assistants in the Rothamsted statistics department. It was the lack of authority[47] to preside over scientific work that relegated these women to invisibility. They "did not have anything to do with the scientific side", they "just did the punching of the tape and verified it, and the tape was sent off to be run".[48]

The female technicians were not perceived by the statisticians as equals and their practical labour was not acknowledged as akin to research, although it was essential for the department. The analysis of agricultural and biological experiments and surveys, in fact, did not require only sound statistical knowledge, but more prosaically hands able to interact with the computing technologies available and to transform experimental results and survey returns in figures that the statisticians could then evaluate and convey through publications in journals and books and in the yearly reports of the institution that were for decades one of the principal commitments for the statistics department.

It is likely that the computers themselves felt unimportant in the scientific enterprise, as a clear division in terms of competences, financial rewards and career perspectives between scientific and assistant staff was traditionally enforced at Rothamsted, and the female assistants in the statistics department were local people who had realistic expectations over an employment in the agricultural institution.

---

[46] Parolini 2013: 258.
[47] Shapin 1989: 560.
[48] Vera Wiltsher in Parolini 2013: 257.

On the other hand, as "[t]echnicians' work is fixed to a particular location in a way that scientific work is not",[49] the stories of these women give an immediate outlook on how computerisation and data management changed statistical work at Rothamsted. The fluctuations of the number of the female assistants from year to year and the shift of their role from human computers to data processors allow us to evaluate the impact that technologies had on the organisation of the department.

These women offer also a perspective on scientific research that is complementary to the scientists' own claims. For instance, Frank Yates, the statistician who promoted the computerisation of the department, argued that already with the Rothamsted first mainframe, the Elliott 401, the clerical work involved in the preparation of the computer input and output was reduced to a minimum, but the memories of Vera Wiltsher tell a different story.[50]

To the historian's gaze the female assistants in the Rothamsted statistics department cannot and should not remain invisible, unless we accept to perpetuate partial histories of the scientific enterprise that neglect the development of scientific practices in favour of theoretical achievements.

Acknowledgement I am grateful to Mrs Brenda Watler (interviewed in August 2014) and Mrs L. Vera Wiltsher (interviewed in September 2011) for sharing with me their memories of the years spent in the Rothamsted statistics department. I thank the Lawes Agricultural Trust for the permission to quote from the materials held in the archives of Rothamsted Research.

References

Abbate, Janet (ed). 2003. Special Issue on women and gender in the history of computing. *IEEE Annals of the History of Computing* 25(4): 4–8.

Abbate, Janet. 2012. *Recoding gender: women's changing participation in computing.* Cambridge, MA: MIT Press.

Campbell-Kelly, Martin, Mary Croarken, Raymond Flood, and Eleanor Robson. 2003. *The history of mathematical tables: from Sumer to spreadsheets.* Oxford: Oxford University Press.

Cohoon, Joanne, and William Aspray. 2006. *Women and information technology: research on underrepresentation.* Cambridge, MA: MIT Press.

Croarken, Mary. 2003. Mary Edwards: computing for a living in 18th century England. *IEEE Annals of the History of Computing* 25(4): 9–15.

de Chadarevian, Soraya. 2002. *Designs for life: molecular biology after World War II.* Cambridge: Cambridge University Press.

Ensmenger, Nathan. 2010. *The computer boys take over: computers, programmers and the politics of technical expertise.* Cambridge, MA: MIT Press.

Galison, Peter. 1997. *Image and logic: a material culture of microphysics.* Chicago: The University of Chicago Press.

Grier, David A. 2001. Human computers: the first pioneers of the information age. *Endeavour* 25(1): 28–32.

Grier, David A. 2007. *When computers were human.* Princeton: Princeton University Press.

---

[49] Iliffe 2008: 6.

[50] Parolini 2013: 240.

Haigh, Thomas. 2010. Masculinity and the machine man: gender in the history of data processing. In *Gender codes: why women are leaving computing?* ed. Thomas J. Misa, 51–71. Hoboken: Wiley/IEEE Computer Society.

Hicks, Mary. 2010a. Meritocracy and feminization in conflict: computerization in the British Government. In *Gender codes: why women are leaving computing?* ed. Thomas J. Misa, 95–114. Hoboken: Wiley/IEEE Computer Society.

Hicks, Mary. 2010b. Only the clothes changed: women operators in British computing and advertising, 1950–1970. *IEEE Annals of the History of Computing* 32(4): 5–17.

Iliffe, Rob. 2008. Guest editorial: technicians. *Notes and Records of the Royal Society of London* 62(1): 3–16.

Light, Jennifer S. 1999. When computers were women. *Technology and Culture* 40(3): 455–483.

Lovegrove, Gillian, and Barbara Segal. 1991. *Women into computing: selected papers 1988–1990.* Berlin: Springer. [in collaboration with the British Computer Society].

Margolis, Jane, and Allan Fisher. 2003. *Unlocking the clubhouse.* Cambridge, MA: MIT Press.

Misa, Thomas J. (ed.). 2010. *Gender codes: why women are leaving computing?* Hoboken: Wiley/ IEEE Computer Society.

Parolini, Giuditta. 2013. *"Making sense of figures": statistics, computing and information technologies in agriculture and biology in Britain, 1920s–1960s.* Doctoral dissertation. University of Bologna.

Parolini, Giuditta. 2014. The emergence of modern statistics in agricultural science: analysis of variance, experimental design and the reshaping of research at Rothamsted Experimental Station, 1919–1933. *Journal of the History of Biology.* doi:10.1007/s10739-014-9394-z.

Rothamsted Experimental Station. 1976. *Report for 1975 Part 1.* Harpenden: Rothamsted Experimental Station.

Rothamsted Experimental Station. 1981. *Report for 1980 Part 1.* Harpenden: Rothamsted Experimental Station.

Rothamsted Experimental Station. 1982. *Report for 1981 Part 1.* Harpenden: Rothamsted Experimental Station.

Shapin, Steven. 1989. The invisible technician. *American Scientist* 77(6): 554–563.

Yates, Frank. 1960. The use of electronic computers in the analysis of replicated experiments, and groups of experiments of the same design. *Bulletin de l'Institut Agronomique et des Stations de Recherches de Gembloux* 1: 201–210.

Chapter 8
The Gendering of the Computing Field in Finland, France and the United Kingdom Between 1960 and 1990

Chantal Morley and Martina McDonnell

Abstract This chapter documents the role that women played in the computing field in three different European countries from the late 1960s into the early 1990s: Finland, a latecomer to the computer industry which was then deemed of national importance, France which boasted several computer manufacturing companies and where IT service companies played an important role in the early history of computing, and the United Kingdom, also involved in computer manufacturing, but where the public sector played a major role. We will see that despite national differences, similarities exist concerning the role women played in the computer industry and that the masculinisation of the profession can be attributed to similar causes. Initially, jobs were considered unskilled and marked out as women's work. When women acquired the necessary skills to play a more important role, various forms of discrimination slowly discouraged them from staying in computer science. The study of these three countries at the moment when computing was introduced into the public and private sectors and became a major tool for management and strategic decisions shows how software activities were socially constructed as masculine.

The history of computerscience in the United States clearly shows that women played active roles in its beginnings. They were largely responsible for operating the first American electronic calculators, and several of these women took part in major developments in computer software and computer languages.[1] Starting in the 1960s and during the two following decades, an ever-increasing number of women entered the new field of computer programming.[2] In Europe as well, computer program-

---

[1] Gürer, Denise. 1995. Pioneering women in computer science. *Communications of the ACM* 58(1): 45–54; Goyal, Amita. 1996. Women in computing: historical roles, the perpetual glass ceiling, and current opportunities. *IEEE Annals of the History of Computing* 18(3): 36–42.

[2] Ensmenger, Nathan L. 2012. *The computer boys take over: computers, programmers, and the politics of technical expertise.* Cambridge, MA: MIT Press; Abbate, Janet. 2012. *Recoding gender – women's changing participation in computing.* Cambridge, MA: MIT Press.

C. Morley (✉) • M. McDonnell
Institut Mines-Télécom, Télécom École de Management, Evry, France
e-mail: chantal.morley@telecom-em.eu; martina.mcdonnell@telecom-em.eu

© Springer International Publishing Switzerland 2015
V. Schafer, B.G. Thierry (eds.), *Connecting Women*, History of Computing,
DOI 10.1007/978-3-319-20837-4_8

ming jobs from the late 1960s into the early 1990s were largely held by women. In this chapter, we will document this trend by contrasting the situation in three different countries: Finland, a latecomer to the computer industry which was then deemed of national importance, France which boasted several computer manufacturing companies and where IT service companies played an important role in the early history of computing, and lastly the United Kingdom, also involved in computer manufacturing, but where the public sector played a major role. We will see that despite national differences, similarities exist concerning the role women played in the computer industry and that the masculinisation of the profession can be attributed to similar causes.

8.1   The Role of Women in the Institutionalisation of Computing in Finland

This section draws heavily on the work of Vehvilaïnen (1997, 1999),[3] who explored the culture and practices of computing in Finland by examining the archives of the Finnish Information Technology Society and the autobiographies of Finnish pioneers in computerscience. Women in Finland withdrew from the information technology field in the early 1990s as they did in most Western countries. However, for 20 years, from the 1960s to the 1980s, Finland presented a paradox: On the one hand, many women were involved in key activities of IT such as programming and analysis, but on the other hand, they were almost completely absent from the decision-making process which contributed to the institutionalisation of IT in Finland. In this section, we will first show how women were kept out of the spheres of decision-making despite Finland's reputation as a pioneer in female/male equality (in 1906, it was the first country in the world to introduce women's right to vote and equal access to public office). We will then track women's involvement in the field of information technology in Finland.

8.1.1   The Participants in the Development of IT in Finland

Compared with other Western countries, Finland is considered to be a latecomer to computing. The first Finnish computer, the ESKO, based on the German computer G1, was not built until the late 1950s. After World War II, the aim was

---

[3] Vehviläinen, Marja. 1997. Gender and expertise in retrospect: pioneers in computing in Finland. In *Women, work and computerisation: spinning a web from past to future*, ed. Anna Frances Grundy et al., 435–448. Proceedings of the 6th international IFIP conference. Berlin: Springer; Vehviläinen, Marja. 1999. Gender and computing in retrospect: the case of Finland. *IEEE Annals of the History of Computing* 21(2): 44–51.

twofold – reduce Finland's dependence on German technology and at the same time strengthen national culture. Nonetheless, the first computer in operation in Finland was an IBM650 bought by the Finnish Postal Bank in 1958, and the ESKO, already obsolete, was donated to the University of Helsinki. Despite this late start, there was a rapid increase in the number of computers, and 10 years later, more than 160 computers were in operation in Finland. Although initially dependent on foreign technical knowledge and expertise, Finland soon gained its technological independence. Three different institutions played a major role in this national and patriotic project.[4] Women however were almost totally absent in this early stage.

The first institution involved was the *Punched Card Association* (renamed the *Computer Association* in 1960). It published a journal aimed at disseminating knowledge of electronic machines. Membership was selective and members had to be considered experts (either those with considerable experience or those who had worked in top management positions). Only 3 % of the members were women, none held a leadership or editorial position, and working groups were all male. At the beginning of the 1970s, the Association modified its rules and encouraged computer professionals, which included many women, to become members. The participation of these women in discussions on professional practices has been widely documented in the Association's journal. Nevertheless, no articles were written by women in this journal until as late as the 1980s.

The Association of Data Processing (ADP), which also played a key role, was founded in 1961 by Otto Karttunen, a former World War II army officer. Its aim was to organise training in computerscience across Finland. It was run rather like a 'secret society'[5] – membership was limited to those who held leadership or management positions in computing. Until the end of the 1960s, no women had joined the 'club'. ADP members believed they had a mission to promote national progress, and its most influential members wrote to each other as 'my good brother'.[6] The *ADP* and the *Computer Association* were actively involved in setting up computer departments and services in both the public and private sector. Both groups also worked on defining the *ADP* training programmes and on developing the methods that organised work and practices in computing.

The third institution that influenced the development of computing in Finland was IBM. This company dominated the computer market in Finland in the 1950s and was also the unique source of computer training in Finland for several years (from the end of 1950s to the beginning of 1960s). IBM, like many other companies, was male dominated, and women long remained a minority despite government measures in favour of gender equality.

---

[4] Paju, Petri. 2008. National projects and international users: Finland and early European computerization. *IEEE Annals of the History of Computing* 1(4): 77–91.

[5] Vehviläinen 1999: 46.

[6] Vehviläinen 1999: 46.

8.1.2   The Place of Women in IT Professions in Finland

In Finland, the male-dominated founding bodies and the absence of critical debate among decision-makers resulted in the information technology (IT) world becoming a closed culture implicitly linked to men. Nevertheless, decision-makers increased the number of training programmes that were open to all, regardless of sex or social class, in order that Finland reached a level enabling it to be a player on the international scene. Women benefited greatly from this opportunity. Between 1960 and 1980, the percentage of female programmers rose from 7 % to over 30 % and the number of female analysts from 9 % to 30 %. However, the entry of women into computer professions must also be seen as part of a wider societal evolution. As early as the 1960s, female/male equality gave rise to much debate and led to measures being taken, notably in the field of education and childcare. Women entered the job market on a broad scale, and rapidly the number of women with high school diplomas had exceeded the number of men. By 1980, 30 % of all computer professionals were women.

Computer programmers were recruited on the basis of tests. Many women applied and were hired. Nevertheless in the 1960s, women's expertise was undervalued. They had little chance of promotion, and the experts continued to be men.[7] The situation evolved during the 1970s, when universities began to offer courses in computerscience. Soon 30 % of students in these courses were women, and these women went on to hold senior positions in companies and institutions. In many universities between 1980 and 1990, almost 50 % of those studying information technology were female. This figure began to decline from 1990 onwards. Moreover, technical universities continued to harbour a predominantly male culture, and few female students applied. In the 1980s, only 8–10 % of students in these schools were women and this figure decreased during the 1990s.

8.1.3   The Case of Finland: Concluding Remarks

To sum up, computerscience in Finland, introduced and developed in the 1950s, was considered to be of strategic and national interest. Only men and often old comrades-in-arms were involved in its promotion and development. Women were absent not only in the national decision-making spheres but also from associations and publications. On the other hand, as soon as they were given the opportunity, they chose to study information technology and to work in computer-related jobs. The case of Finland illustrates that the determining factor in branding the field of computing as masculine was not so much men and women's relationships to technology but rather the fact that a small group of socially dominant men occupied the terrain in terms of both decision-making and visibility. Furthermore, the increasing number of women

---

[7]Vehviläinen 1997: 441.

in university IT courses, in contrast to the almost total absence of women in similar courses in technical institutions, makes it clear that it is not the discipline that is at issue here (IT courses being similar in both types of institutions) but rather a difference of culture. Technical universities retained practices that discouraged women from entering the field. To illustrate the role of gender in limiting access to certain areas, Vehvilaïnen reported in reference to Otto Karttunen: 'In Karttunen's world, there were three kinds of women: (1) those related to machines within the routines of scientific management, (2) the attractive secretaries and (3) one token woman who was able to make men laugh during the lunch break'.[8]

8.2 The Role of Women in the Development of Computing in France

France lagged behind Finland and other European countries in granting political equality to women; women's right to vote and to hold public office was not won until after World War II. However, women were admitted to study sciences at university as early as the second half of the nineteenth century. Nevertheless, the more renowned and highly respected French engineering schools continued to maintain a male-only policy well into the twentieth century.[9] In 1917, the loss of a great number of young men during World War I convinced leaders of the need to allow women to access engineering jobs. Thus, four engineering schools opened their doors to women. In 1925, a female engineer, Marie-Louise Paris, frustrated that only few women were being admitted into these schools, set up an engineering school exclusively for women, the *Ecole PolytechniqueFéminine* (EPF). However, women would have to wait until 1972 for all engineering schools to be co-educational, notably the highly prestigious *Ecole Polytechnique*. A second institutional mechanism contributed to prevent women from accessing positions of power in computing: the 'engineering corps'.[10] Since the eighteenth century, the French State has recruited engineers on a very selective basis. These engineers become government employees and are organised into 'engineering corps' according to their area of expertise – mining, civil engineering, telecommunications engineering, etc. The majority of these engineers are former students of the *Ecole Polytechnique*. They then follow additional courses at the other engineering schools (Mines, Ponts et Chaussées, Télécom, etc.). During the period 1960–1990, this 'engineering corps', notably the graduates from the *Ecole Polytechnique*, played an important role in industrial development in France,[11] acting as key decision-makers in government

---

[8] Vehvilӓinen 1999: 48.

[9] Marry, Catherine. 2004. *Les femmes ingénieurs: une révolution respectueuse*. Paris: Belin.

[10] Canepa, Daniel, Jean-Martin Folz, and Florian Blazy. 2009. Mission d'étude sur l'avenir des corps d'ingénieurs de l'Etat. http://www.ladocumentationfrancaise.fr/rapports-publics/094000145/. Accessed 3 Mar 2015.

[11] Canepa et al. 2009.

bodies and state-owned companies (in the fields of electricity, nuclear energy, telecommunications, armaments, aeronautics, transport, etc.). In addition, the *Ecole
Polytechnique* alumni represented an influential network in French politics and economics.[12] This was notably true in the development of computing in France.

8.2.1   The Major Players in the Development of Computing in France

The French State played a major role in the early development of computerscience
and computer industry in France. In 1954, SEA (Société d'Electronique et
d'Automatisme) secured a military contract, thus allowing France to join the 'club'
of manufacturers of large computers. The French State continued to intervene
throughout the turbulent history of computing, both politically and economically, in
particular in the creation and mergers of computer manufacturing firms – CII
(Compagnie Internationale pour l'Informatique), Bull, Unidata, CII-Honeywell-
Bull, R2E, SEMS, etc.[13] A government programme, the 'Plan Calcul', was launched
in 1966 with the aim of developing a national computer manufacturing industry. In
addition to the construction of large computers, the world's first microcomputer
(Micral) was developed in France in 1972 thanks to a government contract. The
State continued to support the development and commercial distribution of minicomputers. As a result, the total number of computers in use increased considerably.
While in 1962 there were only 600 computers installed in France, by 1970 there
were 1300. Other major players in the computerisation of both companies and public sector bodies were the IT service companies. Their mission was to provide qualified personnel and turnkey solutions. They flourished between 1958 and 1973 and
were more numerous in France than elsewhere.[14] Several were set up as subsidiaries
of banks or major industrial firms (Crédit Lyonnais, Société Générale, Crédit du
Nord, France Telecom, Schlumberger, Péchiney and Alcatel). Thousands of companies specialised in programming were formed between 1965 and 1969, but more
than half had folded 10 years later.[15] However, the majority of the firms which were
to play a decisive role in IT services at an international level (Sema, SESA, SOPRA,
CGI, STERIA, Sligos) were started by engineering graduates of *Ecole
Polytechnique*.[16]

---

[12] Kosciusko-Morizet, Jacques-Antoine. 1973. *La 'Mafia' polytechnicienne*. Paris: Seuil.

[13] Griset, Pascal (ed.). 1999. *Aux origines de l'informatique française: entre Plan Calcul et
UNIDATA, 1963–1975*. Paris: Editions Rive Droite, Institut d'Histoire de l'Industrie.

[14] Lacombe, Frank, and Philippe Rosé. 2011. *Entreprises de services et économie numérique: une
radiographie des SSII*. Paris: CIGREF éditeur.

[15] Lacombe and Rosé 2011: 31.

[16] Bret, Christian. 2005. L'histoire des 40 premières années des SSII en France à travers leurs hommes et leurs activités. *Entreprises et Histoire* 3: 9–14.

8.2.2 The Women Involved in the Growth of IT in France

Between 1960 and 1975, women were almost entirely absent from decision-making and entrepreneurial spheres with regard to the development of computing. Firstly, they were late in gaining access to the various 'engineering corps', notably those which dominated the history of IT as shown with the case of the *Ecole Polytechnique*, and it was not until the 1980s that a few female engineers were admitted to the influential 'corps des mines' or 'corps des télécommunications'. Despite this, women were interested and active in computerscience. We can see this by examining three different areas: computer design, computer science studies and IT professions.

In computer design, in the second half of the 1950s, two female engineers, Alice Recoque (ESPCI, Ecole Supérieure de Physique et de Chimie Industrielles, graduate engineer) and Françoise Becquet (EPF, Ecole Polytechnique Féminine, graduate engineer), designed a small conversational machine, the CAB 500, a forerunner of the personal computer and SEA's biggest commercial success. Following the merger of SEA with the newly formed company CII in 1966, Alice Recoque was put in charge of the design of CII's Mitra range of minicomputers, notably the Mitra 15 at the end of the 1960s. The latter was also very successful both technically and commercially.[17] These minicomputers were not within the scope of the 'Plan Calcul', which may explain why a woman was placed in charge of research in what was then termed 'small computers'. Despite her achievements,[18] Alice Recoque never reached a position of responsibility either in the public or private sector.

Concerning higher education, women in France as in Finland were attracted to computerscience studies. In 1972, women represented less than 5 % of students in engineering schools, but the highest percentage of women (9 %) were in engineering schools specialising in computer science.[19] Ten years later, in 1983, the percentage of female engineering students in schools specialising in computer science peaked at over 20 %. Then numbers began to fall, with a sharp decrease at the end of the 1980s, despite the fact that the overall number of women entering engineering schools continued to increase during this period. The case of the INSA engineering school in Rennes is noteworthy. For three consecutive years, male/female parity was more or less achieved (percentage of women in 1978, 47 %; 1980, 55 %; 1981, 50 %).[20] In a study carried out on ten engineering schools in France, Isabelle Collet showed that in the 1970s, the number of female computer science graduates was relatively high in comparison to the number of male graduates, given the higher percentage of male students in engineering schools overall. However, she pointed

---

[17] Mounier-Kuhn, Pierre-Emmanuel. 1990. Genèse de l'informatique en France 1945–1965. *Culture Technique* 21: 21–35.

[18] Recoque, A. 2007. Miria a validé l'ordinateur personnel avant qu'IBM ne le découvre. *Code source, hebdomadaire des 40 ans de l'INRIA* 1: 6.

[19] Marry 2004: 109.

[20] Collet, Isabelle. 2005. *La masculinisation des études d'informatique. Savoir, pouvoir et genre*. Thèse de doctorat en Sciences de l'Education, Université Paris X.

out that at the end of the 1980s, the figures for female graduates in computer science remained stable, whereas the number of male graduates soared. In 1979, male/female parity was reached, with approximately 100 students overall, whereas in 1989 there were about 120 female students and 400 male students.[21]

Lastly, many women clearly chose to work in the field of computerscience. A study conducted in 1969[22] showed that 30 % of EPF (Ecole Polytechnique Féminine) graduates worked in computing. For other engineering schools, the trend was less pronounced. However, the author noted that 17 % of all female engineering graduate students aged 30 and under chose to work in computing. At the beginning of the 1980s, a government report on the range and variety of jobs held by women noted that the computer science field was evidently not marked by gender stereotypes as were the fields traditionally dominated by men. The authors of the report were optimistic: 'We may therefore hope that the advent of new technologies and the ensuing changes in work organization will allow women, if they are able to seize the opportunity, to find their place in the new technical fields'.[23] In the 1980s, many IT service firms trained graduates, and recruitment was very open. In 1982, 35 % of computer scientists were women. However, by the end of the 1980s, the trend began to revert: In 2002, women represented 20 % of the computer science workforce,[24] and by 2011, the IT engineering profession figured among the 20 professions which contributed most to job segregation.[25] Concerning entrepreneurship, few women set up IT service firms. For example, in 1974, Marie-Therese Bertini developed a structured programming method that encountered some success. Nevertheless, MBT, the company she set up in 1985, never reached international scope although it is still operating. Despite her expertise, she was not invited to participate in the 'Merise' project, i.e. the development of a national information system development methodology.

8.2.3   The Case of France: Concluding Remarks

Women had little access to certain positions – decision-makers or key players – during the early period where there was a rapid development of IT. This was due to their late entry into the institutions that played a major role in this development. As regards to setting up a business, women encountered more obstacles than men for two major reasons. First, they did not belong to the alumni network of the 'grandes

---

[21] Collet 2005: 31.

[22] De Peslouan, Geneviève. 1974. *Qui sont les femmes ingénieurs en France?* Paris: PUF.

[23] Appert, Monique, Anne-Marie Grozelier, and Cécile Baron. 1983. Diversification de l'emploi féminin: insertion professionnelle des femmes formées dans des métiers traditionnellement masculins. *Dossier de recherche du CEE* 8, AFPA-CEE éditeur, quoted by Collet 2005: 55, our translation.

[24] DARES. 2004. Vingt ans de métiers: L'évolution des emplois de 1982 à 2002. *Premières Synthèses* 43: 2.

[25] DARES 2013. La répartition des hommes et des femmes par métiers. Une baisse de la ségrégation depuis 30 ans. *Dares Analyse* 79: 1–13.

ecoles', a major advantage in France in terms of securing partners and clients. Second, until 1965 according to French law, married women were not entirely independent legally. They required their husbands' permission to open a bank account, to manage family property and their own personal property and even to hold a job. Nevertheless, early on, female engineers were interested in the new and exciting area of computers and computing. To women at that time, the field appeared very open, as Françoise Becquet who started working for the manufacturer SEA in the late 1950s explained: 'It didn't matter if you were a man or a woman, a French national or a foreigner as long as you worked diligently and did the job well'.[26]

At the beginning of the 1980s, more and more women moved into the area of software. Nonetheless, a detailed study[27] clearly showed that women were the first, voluntarily or not, to leave the field as soon as the sector was hit by a crisis. IT once again became a male activity in the early 1990s. 'It is certain that IT jobs and careers are open to women. Neither their knowledge, interest or competence in the field can be questioned. Women are present in IT. However, it will be difficult for them to say they are computer engineers. Often they have the impression of being guests in the profession and of being welcome for their subsidiary 'feminine' qualities', concluded a study of female scientists, some of whom had spent their entire career in IT service companies (Collet and Ingarao 2002: 79, our translation).[28]

8.3 Women and IT in the Public Sector in the United Kingdom

In the United Kingdom, as early as the nineteenth century, the struggle for equal rights for women gave rise to diverse social movements. At the turn of the twentieth century, most British universities were open to women, although the most prestigious universities were the last male-only strongholds: Oxford (1920) and Cambridge (1948). In 1928, women obtained the right to vote. 1954 saw the introduction of a policy of equal salaries for men and women in the civil service. Between the years 1955 and 1985, the public sector occupied an ever-increasing position in the country's economy[29] with the welfare state and the wave of nationalisations (banks, industry, transport, etc.). Along with Germany and the United States, the United Kingdom was a pioneer in the computer industry (e.g. Colossus Mark 1 in

---

[26] Becquet, Françoise. 2010. *Exposition « Courbevoie, berceau de l'informatique française »*, *Souvenirs de Françoise Becquet*. http://sea.museeinformatique.fr/Souvenirs-de-Francoise-BECQUET_a2.html?com. Accessed 3 Mar 2015, our translation.

[27] Stevens, Hélène. 2007. The professional fate of woman engineers in the computer sciences: unexpected reversals. *Sociologie du travail* 49: 443–463.

[28] Collet, Isabelle, and Maud Ingarao. 2002. *La place des femmes dans les SSII*. Rapport au Ministère des affaires sociales, du travail et de la solidarité- Service des droits des femmes et de l'égalité professionnelle.

[29] Clark, Tom, and Andrew Dilnot. 2002. *Long-term trends in British taxation and spending*. The Institute for Fiscal Studies, Briefing Note 25. London.

1944, EDSAC and Manchester Mark in 1949, Elliott 152 in 1950, LEO 1 in 1951, Ferranti Mark 1 in 1951, DEUCE in 1955, Pegasus in 1956). Computers were widely used to support growth in the public sector. Contrary to what one might think, women did not receive equal treatment with men in this new area of activity. The 'meritocracy' ideal was to suffer as work in the field of computing required higher qualifications and was better paid. The obstacles notwithstanding, many women worked as operators and programmers. However, faced with discrimination, certain pioneering women decided to set up their own IT businesses.

8.3.1 Female Computer Scientists in the Civil Service and the Nationalised Industries

This section draws heavily on the work of Marie Hicks, which focused on gender in the history of computerisation in British government from 1950 (2010, 2011).[30] Before 1960, operating calculators required trained staff for command entry, fine-tuning of cables and replacing faulty tubes. These jobs were called 'machine positions' in the civil service job classification system and were almost exclusively held by women. In 1954, it was decided that these positions would not be covered by the equal salaries legislation. Furthermore, the few existing male operators were shifted to higher paid jobs with better prospects of promotion. Electronic computers began to be installed in civil service and government departments at the end of the 1950s. This required the staff to acquire new technical capabilities but also management skills as the number of computer-related projects increased.

Women, who had been hired to write code for the calculators, progressed to programming computers. By 1963, 70 % of programmers were women. Nevertheless, it was considered inappropriate for women to hold management positions, especially as the ever-increasing need for programmers meant attracting more men into the profession. Moreover, it was customary for young women to give up working when they married. Initially, programmers were recruited internally from middle management within the civil service which was heavily male dominated (90 % men). Senior women programmers, although required to train the new young male recruits, had no prospects of promotion. This wave of recruitments was relatively unsuccessful, partly because the aptitude tests were ill adapted and did not guarantee that recruits would be competent programmers. Yet despite the preference for recruiting men, women for a variety of reasons did not abandon the programming field. In the first place, women increasingly chose to continue working after marriage, and secondly, there was a growing need for programmers. Also following the 1965 economic crisis, wages in the civil service were frozen, notably those of the IT

[30] Hicks, Marie. 2010. Only the clothes changed: women operators in British computing and advertising, 1950–1970. *IEEE Annals of the History of Computing* 32(4): 5–17, Hicks, Marie. 2011. Meritocracy and feminization in conflict: computerization in the British government. In *Gender codes: why women are leaving computing*, ed. T.J. Misa, 157–192. Hoboken: Wiley.

staff which made the jobs less attractive. Young men did not rush to join a sector of activity which was predominantly female and thus with low prospects. In the end, the government decided to recruit externally, targeting those under 25. No qualifications were required and no reference was made to gender in the job advertisements. Many women applied and were hired to be operators and programmers, and the principle of equal pay was better respected. Nevertheless, female programmers and operators gradually left the profession due to discrimination encountered in their career path. For example, at the end of the 1960s, the high salaries women earned were considered an anomaly and they were refused promotion, while their male colleagues were promoted. Women became increasingly rare in computer departments.[31]

In her research on women in computing, Janet Abbate (2012: 117–119)[32] pointed out the difficulty, in both Great Britain and the United States, for a qualified female IT engineer to come back to a salaried job after maternity leave. She describes the case of two female British computer engineers who had been working for computer manufacturing companies – Bobby Hersom at Elliott Brothers and Mary Berners-Lee (the mother of Tim Berners-Lee) at Ferranti – and who regretted having to quit their jobs after the birth of their first child. They then had to be content with working freelance.

But discrimination also led two British women, both of whom held degrees in mathematics and were enthusiastic about the fledgling computer industry, to set up their own software companies.

8.3.2 Two Pioneering Women in the Software and IT Service Industry

Dina St Johnston, née Vaughan, began her career in 1947 working in a research institute while continuing to follow evening classes at Croydon Polytechnic.[33] She passed the entrance exams to two major universities (Bedford and Royal Holloway), but 90 % of the places were reserved for World War II veterans, and the remaining 10 % were allotted to men. She finally enrolled in London University and obtained a degree in mathematics. However, the company she was working for refused her a promotion (which was systematically granted to men under similar circumstances). She therefore changed jobs and went to work for Elliott Brothers, a computer manufacturing company. There, she learned computer programming and soon proved to be brilliant. She married a colleague at Elliott Brothers and in 1959 left the firm to

---

[31] Hicks 2011: 161.

[32] Abbate 2012.

[33] Lavington, Simon. 2009. An appreciation of Dina St Johnston 1930–2007 founder of the UK's first software house. *The Computer Journal* 52(3): 378–387; Porter, Collin. 2008. Dina St Johnston 1930–2007 Obituary. *The Institution of Railway Signal Engineers IRSE*. Proceedings 2007/2008: 17.

set up her own company. She founded the first private sector IT service company in the United Kingdom (Vaughan Systems and Programming). It specialised in software for industrial control and automation systems (warehouse automation, flight reservation systems, railway signalling systems). The company even built small dedicated computers such as the *Vaughan 4M* which introduced an automatic system for locating trains. Dina Vaughan continued programming until 1996 when she sold her company to retire.

Three years after Dina St Johnston, Stephanie Shirley also set up her own company. She had joined the research department of the London Postal Services in 1951.[34] She took evening classes and obtained an honours degree in mathematics in 1956. She discovered computerscience and became enthusiastic. She worked on several important computer-related projects for the post office. Although she was eligible for promotion, having received a degree in mathematics, she was not promoted. The members of the promotion panel refused to consider appointing a woman to that higher grade. She left the postal services in 1959 and went to work for a software development company that was a subsidiary of two computer manufacturing companies, GEC computers and ICT. She led a team carrying out tests on a new computer. She was very well paid; however, the 'glass ceiling' once again reappeared. When she made suggestions to the project steering committee, she was asked not to intervene in the project management meetings on non-technical subjects and to keep to her role as technician. She thus understood that she would never be able to move up the ladder in the company, and she decided to become her own boss.[35] She was also hoping to have children and wanted to continue on working afterwards. In 1962, at the age of 29, she set up a software development company (*Freelance Programmers*) using the name Steve Shirley.[36] She adopted this name so that potential clients would not know she was a woman until the first face-to-face meeting. She recruited women who wanted to work part-time in order to look after their children. All the analysts and programmers were women who worked freelance from home. The company soon became a British success story: In 1965, there were 65 employees, almost exclusively female until the 1975 Sex Discrimination Act required the company to hire more male employees. By 1986, 16 % of employees were men.

In an interview, Stephanie Shirley quotes one of her female employees who had difficulty persuading the Inland Revenue Service that she had earned her money honestly working at home and looking after two children[37]! By 2009, the company, then known as *F International*, boasted 1000 employees in three different countries (the United Kingdom, Denmark and the Netherlands), with sales of $10 million and an annual growth rate of 30 %. The name of the company was subsequently changed

---

[34] Abbate 2012: 125–143.

[35] Abbate 2012: 126.

[36] Abbate 2012: 138.

[37] Shirley, Steve, and Eliza G.C. Collins. 1986. A company without offices. *Harvard Business Review* 64: 127–136.

to *Xansa* and was bought by the French IT service company Steria in 2007. Stephanie Shirley was honoured with the title of 'Dame' in 2000 for her contribution to the British computersoftware industry.

8.3.3 *The Case of the United Kingdom: Concluding Remarks*

After World War II, the United Kingdom invested in computers to compensate for its decline as a world power. The public sector adopted IT early on. The civil service equality policies notwithstanding, computer coding was initially considered as women's work, badly paid and with no prospects for promotion. These jobs were then voluntarily redefined as male because it became imperative to reposition computing as a male field to meet the challenges of computerisation. On the other hand, stereotypes concerning women's technical incompetence were unknown. Later, in the years 1960–1980, other factors contributed to preventing women from establishing themselves in computer science. The first factor was low pay, as male/female work categories were maintained circumventing the 1954 law on equal pay. Finally, when higher salaries were offered because of the need to recruit more staff in computer departments, women employees were soon considered to be overpaid, and their career advancement was blocked, but this was not true for male employees. The second factor was the question of careers. Despite a 1969 government campaign to encourage young women to join the workforce, women were not really supposed to have a career, in particular if they had children. Employers were not encouraged to train or promote women and most believed women would leave employment early on. The last and perhaps most important factor was that, by not allowing female computer scientists, regardless of their abilities, to hold management positions, most of these women remained in subordinate positions. Nevertheless, women showed a real interest and enthusiasm for the computer industry. This is clearly illustrated by the successful pioneer female start-ups in IT services which expanded employing only women but also paid decent wages.

8.4 Differences and Common Traits

Historical studies on women in IT in Europe are as yet rare or incomplete, and it is virtually impossible to establish a strict comparison of the situations of Finland, France and the United Kingdom. It is interesting nonetheless to examine the three countries during the period between 1960 and 1990 despite the fact that the data for each country focused on different aspects of the situation. In the first place, in all three cases, there was a strategic commitment to invest in the manufacturing of computers and the State played a role in this. On the other hand, the countries differed in terms of female/male equality. Finland had a pioneering role, the United

Kingdom was well known for women's movements and equal rights, while in France, women only gained access to certain educational institutions and economic independence in 1960.

Despite these differences, common traits can be identified concerning women in computing professions. First, we see that women took advantage of any opportunity that arose to enter the field: In Finland, young women applied in great numbers to study the new field of computerscience; in France, computer engineering became the most popular job choice among young female engineering graduates; in the United Kingdom, great numbers of young, unqualified women took up programming jobs in the civil service. We then see that the stereotype of women's presumed technical incompetence, which later became so pervasive, rarely came into play until the late 1980s. At the outset, technical incompetence was not identified with women in this relatively new field. One possible explanation is that the countries considered as pioneers in the field of computing, notably the United States and the United Kingdom, employed women to operate and code the early computers. This implies that women in these countries were familiar with and worked in proximity with computers. Nevertheless, it must be noted that as early as the 1950s, advertisers used images of women to convey the simplicity of using computers and thus to promote sales. Such advertising campaigns may have given rise to the idea that women working in the field of computer science were less skilled.[38] Moreover, we observe that in the early days of computer technology, certain structural barriers kept women out of the decision-making spheres and out of the highly visible positions in the field – for example, the all-male composition of the founding bodies of Finnish computing, i.e. the army, IBM, etc., and the gendered practices such as the old boys' club mentality; in France, women being prevented from accessing both the 'engineering corps' and entrepreneurship; and in the United Kingdom, the barriers to women's career advancement both in the public sector and in the computer construction industry. The study of these three countries at a moment when computing was introduced into the public and private sectors and became a major tool for management and strategic decisions shows how software activities were socially constructed as masculine. Lastly, we note a turning point at the end of the 1980s. Although the number of women studying computer science or working in computing continued to increase, the trend was beginning to reverse: The percentage of women declined slowly as large numbers of men hastened to join a promising sector that provided well-paid employment. And when the computer manufacturing industry entered a crisis, women's withdrawal from the field continued, as they were nowhere firmly established in decision-making spheres or positions of power and responsibility. This appears to have particularly affected female computer scientists in France. Many of them chose to move into non-technical professions. And in the United Kingdom, the civil service recruitment and career advancement policies favoured men, thereby pushing women out of computing in the public sector.

---

[38] Hicks 2010.

The over-representation of men in computerscience in the 1990s has also been documented in the United States[39] and elsewhere in Europe, notably in Germany.[40] Starting in the mid-1980s and increasingly throughout the following decade, technological innovations and social practices around computers raised new and additional issues. The diffusion of home computers contributed to creating new gendered spheres and practices in households.[41] The hacker phenomenon, recognised as an emerging culture,[42] and the communities which emerged from the free software movement led by Richard Stallman in the United States in 1985 followed by Linus Torvalds in Finland in 1991 contributed to a widespread representation of computing as a male activity.[43] As computers and computing moved beyond the professional sphere, computer technology emerged as a masculine culture.[44] Nevertheless, our study shows that women had already begun to leave computing before the advent of microcomputers and network technology. Thus, women in IT should be studied within the broader context of the long-term evolution of computing technology, industry and communities.

References

Abbate, Janet. 2012. *Recoding gender – women's changing participation in computing*. Cambridge, MA: MIT Press.
Appert, Monique, Anne-Marie Grozelier, and Cécile Baron. 1983. Diversification de l'emploi féminin: insertion professionnelle des femmes formées dans des métiers traditionnellement masculins. *Dossier de recherche du CEE* 8, AFPA-CEE éditeur.
Becquet, Françoise. 2010. *Exposition « Courbevoie, berceau de l'informatique française », Souvenirs de Françoise Becquet*. http://sea.museeinformatique.fr/Souvenirs-de-Francoise-BECQUET_a2.html?com. Accessed 3 Mar 2015.
Bret, Christian. 2005. L'histoire des 40 premières années des SSII en France à travers leurs hommes et leurs activités. *Entreprises et Histoire* 3: 9–14.
Canepa, Daniel, Jean-Martin Folz, and Florian Blazy. 2009. Mission d'étude sur l'avenir des corps d'ingénieurs de l'Etat. http://www.ladocumentationfrancaise.fr/rapports-publics/094000145/. Accessed 3 Mar 2015.

---

[39] Klawe, Maria, and Nancy Leveson. 1995. Women in computing: where are we now? *Communications of the ACM* 38(1): 29–35.

[40] Oechtering, Veronika, and Roswitha Behnke. 1995. Situations and advancement measures in Germany. *Communications of the ACM* 38(1): 75–82.

[41] Miquel, C. 1991. *Mythologies modernes et micro-informatique. La puce et son dompteur*. Paris: L'Harmattan; Jouët, Josiane. 1987. Le vécu de la technique. La télématique et la micro-informatique à domicile. *Réseaux* 5(25): 119–141; Grundy, A.F., and J. Grundy. 1996. *Women and computers*. Bristol: Intellect Books.

[42] Turkle, Sherry. 1984. *The second self. Computers and the human spirit*. New York: Simon & Schuster.

[43] Collet, Isabelle. 2006. *L'informatique a-t-elle un sexe? Hackers, mythes et réalités*. Paris: L'Harmattan.

[44] Wajcman, J. 1991. *Feminism confronts technology*. Cambridge: Polity Press.

Clark, Tom, and Andrew Dilnot. 2002. *Long-term trends in British taxation and spending*. The Institute for Fiscal Studies, Briefing Note 25. London.

Collet, Isabelle. 2005. *La masculinisation des études d'informatique. Savoir, pouvoir et genre*. Thèse de doctorat en Sciences de l'Education, Université Paris X.

Collet, Isabelle. 2006. *L'informatique a-t-elle un sexe? Hackers, mythes et réalités*. Paris: L'Harmattan.

Collet, Isabelle, and Maud Ingarao. 2002. *La place des femmes dans les SSII*. Rapport au Ministère des affaires sociales, du travail et de la solidarité- Service des droits des femmes et de l'égalité professionnelle.

DARES. 2004. Vingt ans de métiers: L'évolution des emplois de 1982 à 2002. *Premières Synthèses* 43: 2.

DARES 2013. La répartition des hommes et des femmes par métiers. Une baisse de la ségrégation depuis 30 ans. *Dares Analyse* 79: 1–13.

De Peslouan, Geneviève. 1974. *Qui sont les femmes ingénieurs en France?* Paris: PUF.

Ensmenger, Nathan L. 2012. *The computer boys take over: computers, programmers, and the politics of technical expertise*. Cambridge, MA: MIT Press.

Goyal, Amita. 1996. Women in computing: historical roles, the perpetual glass ceiling, and current opportunities. *IEEE Annals of the History of Computing* 18(3): 36–42.

Griset, P. (ed.). 1999. *Aux origines de l'informatique française: entre Plan Calcul et UNIDATA, 1963–1975*. Paris: Editions Rive Droite, Institut d'Histoire de l'Industrie.

Grundy, A.F., and J. Grundy. 1996. *Women and computers*. Bristol: Intellect Books.

Gürer, Denise. 1995. Pioneering women in computer science. *Communications of the ACM* 58(1): 45–54.

Hicks, Marie. 2010. Only the clothes changed: women operators in British computing and advertising, 1950–1970. *IEEE Annals of the History of Computing* 32(4): 5–17.

Hicks, Marie. 2011. Meritocracy and feminization in conflict: computerization in the British government. In *Gender codes: why women are leaving computing*, ed. T.J. Misa, 157–192. Hoboken: Wiley.

Jouët, Josiane. 1987. Le vécu de la technique. La télématique et la micro-informatique à domicile. *Réseaux* 5(25): 119–141.

Klawe, Maria, and Nancy Leveson. 1995. Women in computing: where are we now? *Communications of the ACM* 38(1): 29–35.

Kosciusko-Morizet, Jacques-Antoine. 1973. *La 'Mafia' polytechnicienne*. Paris: Seuil.

Lacombe, Frank, and Philippe Rosé. 2011. *Entreprises de services et économie numérique: une radiographie des SSII*. Paris: CIGREF éditeur.

Lavington, Simon. 2009. An appreciation of Dina St Johnston 1930–2007 founder of the UK's first software house. *The Computer Journal* 52(3): 378–387.

Marry, Catherine. 2004. *Les femmes ingénieurs: une révolution respectueuse*. Paris: Belin.

Miquel, C. 1991. *Mythologies modernes et micro-informatique. La puce et son dompteur*. Paris: L'Harmattan.

Mounier-Kuhn, Pierre-Emmanuel. 1990. Genèse de l'informatique en France 1945–1965. *Culture Technique* 21: 21–35.

Oechtering, Veronika, and Roswitha Behnke. 1995. Situations and advancement measures in Germany. *Communications of the ACM* 38(1): 75–82.

Paju, Petri. 2008. National projects and international users: Finland and early European computerization. *IEEE Annals of the History of Computing* 1(4): 77–91.

Porter, Collin. 2008. Dina St Johnston 1930–2007 Obituary. *The Institution of Railway Signal Engineers IRSE*. Proceedings 2007/2008: 17.

Recoque, A. 2007. Miria a validé l'ordinateur personnel avant qu'IBM ne le découvre. *Code source, hebdomadaire des 40 ans de l'INRIA* 1: 6.

Shirley, Steve, and Eliza G.C. Collins. 1986. A company without offices. *Harvard Business Review* 64: 127–136.

Stevens, Hélène. 2007. The professional fate of woman engineers in the computer sciences: unexpected reversals. *Sociologie du travail* 49: 443–463.

Turkle, Sherry. 1984. *The second self. Computers and the human spirit.* New York: Simon & Schuster.

Vehviläinen, Marja. 1997. Gender and expertise in retrospect: pioneers in computing in Finland. In *Women, work and computerisation: spinning a web from past to future,* ed. Anna Frances Grundy et al., 435–448. Proceedings of the 6th international IFIP conference. Berlin: Springer.

Vehviläinen, Marja. 1999. Gender and computing in retrospect: the case of Finland. *IEEE Annals of the History of Computing* 21(2): 44–51.

Wajcman, J. 1991. *Feminism confronts technology.* Cambridge: Polity Press.

Chapter 9
Breaking the "Glass Slipper": What Diversity Interventions Can Learn from the Historical Evolution of Occupational Identity in ICT and Commercial Aviation

Karen Lee Ashcraft and Catherine Ashcraft

Abstract This chapter examines parallels in the evolution of two occupational identities – commercial airline flying and ICT work – and the implications for current diversification interventions. We begin by conceptualizing occupational identity and diversification through the "glass slipper" metaphor. We then demonstrate the empirical potential of this framework with a cross-case analysis of how these dynamics are at play in the historical evolution of the aforementioned professions. Finally, we consider how these cases, weighed together, implicate scholars and practitioners, especially research on technical-scientific work and so-called diversity interventions in ICT occupations.

This chapter explores the history of occupational identity – how tasks congeal into a recognizable line of work whose collective "brand" radiates from association with certain practitioners. We specifically examine parallels in the evolution of two occupational identities in the United States and Europe: commercial airline flying and ICT work. At first, these may seem too different to sustain comparison, but we maintain their mutual relevance as forms of labor involving communication technologies, whose elite technical status was originally in doubt yet eventually won. It is *how* such status was achieved, and the ways in which this process called upon gender and other vectors of difference, that concerns us here.

K.L. Ashcraft (✉)
Department of Communication, University of Colorado, Boulder, CO, 80309, USA
e-mail: Karen.ashcraft@colorado.edu

C. Ashcraft
National Center for Women & Information Technology, University of Colorado,
231 ATLAS Bldg, 1125 18th St, Boulder, CO, 80309, USA
e-mail: Catherine.ashcraft@colorado.edu

© Springer International Publishing Switzerland 2015
V. Schafer, B.G. Thierry (eds.), *Connecting Women*, History of Computing,
DOI 10.1007/978-3-319-20837-4_9

As argued in a recent theory of the "glass slipper",[1] histories of occupational identity are vital to trace because work often comes to be known and evaluated by the company it keeps – that is, by the practitioners aligned with it and, especially, by their embodied social identities. If societal estimations of work depend on who does it, then the nature and value of an occupation are *founded upon* gender and other such relations of inequality. Occupational status, in other words, is not independently secure. Nor does it "happen" to coincide with social identity hierarchies, as commonly assumed. Rather, cultural, economic, and institutional questions regarding occupational status (e.g., what kind of work is this, what is it worth, and how should it be configured and performed?) are resolved *by* and *through* the systems of privilege and disadvantage that constitute embodied difference. Consequently, the character of any occupation cannot be taken at face value, as if ordained by inherent properties that can be trusted to endure regardless of affiliated workers. Instead, we can expect that an occupation's status will be unsettled by, and alter with, significant shifts in its practitioner profile.

We argue, accordingly, that *reading the historical evolution of occupational identity is a crucial prerequisite to designing and implementing meaningful contemporary diversification efforts.* Initiatives to enhance the presence of "women and minorities" in such desirable occupations as ICT, for example, must proceed with caution, mindful of the gender and difference dynamics that rendered the work "desirable" in the first place, and which continue to afford its possibilities and risks. Without such historical consciousness, even the most well-intentioned diversity programs are likely to reproduce familiar forms of inequality.

The chapter begins by conceptualizing occupational identity and diversification through the "glass slipper" metaphor. Next, we demonstrate the empirical potential of this framework with a condensed account of the first author's diachronic research on occupational identity in the context of commercial aviation.[2] This provides a useful comparison against which we then read the gendered history of ICT.[3] Finally, we consider how these cases, weighed together, implicate scholars and practitioners, especially research on technical-scientific work and so-called diversity interventions in ICT occupations. We conclude that *tactically shifting reconstructions of an occupation's figurative practices must accompany, if not precede, efforts to diversify its actual, usual, or even figurative practitioners.*

---

[1] Ashcraft, Karen Lee. 2013. The glass slipper: "incorporating" occupational identity in management studies. *Academy of Management Review* 38(1): 6–31.

[2] E.g., Ashcraft, Karen Lee. 2005. Resistance through consent? Occupational identity, organizational form, and the maintenance of masculinity among commercial airline pilots. *Management Communication Quarterly* 19: 67–90, Ashcraft, Karen Lee. 2007. Appreciating the "work" of discourse: occupational identity and difference as organizing mechanisms in the case of commercial airline pilots. *Discourse & Communication* 1: 9–36; Ashcraft, Karen Lee, and Dennis K. Mumby. 2004. *Reworking gender: a feminist communicology of organization.* Thousand Oaks: Sage.

[3] E.g., Ensmenger, Nathan. 2010a. Making programming masculine. In *Gender codes: why women are leaving computing*, ed. Tom Misa, 115–142. Hoboken: Wiley, Ensmenger, Nathan. 2010b. *The computer boys take over: computers, programmers, and the politics of technical expertise.* Cambridge: MIT Press; Hicks, Marie. 2010. Meritocracy and feminization in conflict: computerization in the British government. In *Gender codes: why women are leaving computing*, ed. Tom Misa, 115–142. Hoboken: Wiley.

9.1 Occupational Identity and Diversification: An Introduction to the "Glass Slipper"

Our work in this chapter hinges on the claim that the nature and worth of work are malleable and contestable, not innate or otherwise self-evident. While tasks may dictate certain requirements (e.g., one thing must repeatedly lift another) and affordances (e.g., a preference for bodies, human or machine, that can lift), these by no means determine how we come to understand the act of lifting, what other tasks it logically accompanies, what constitutes effective performance, who or what best does it, for what value, and so forth. These are matters of interpretation and dispute. It therefore takes *identity work*, or ongoing social construction of the "essential" character of an occupation, to establish the identity *of* work.

"Technical-scientific" work, for instance, may appear to be a natural category for differentiating among occupations. But the connotation and pairing of these terms, as well as the swift reflex with which we apply the category to distinguish "complex" labor from "simpler" toil, are outcomes of social construction. That nursing is cast primarily as caring, when it arguably teems with technical tasks; that computing and engineering are designated technical, even as they demand intuitive and emotional knowing[4]; that birthing babies has transformed over time from a mystical and spiritual endeavor into a scientific and medical task[5]; that public relations swung from "hard" analytical work entailing "killer instincts" toward the "soft" work of "massaging" impressions; that flying morphed from a daredevil trick into an artistic pastime, then again into elite technical-scientific labor (as we will show) – these and countless illustrations affirm the enormous range of potentiality latent in work and hint at the extent of persuasion required to establish "technical-scientific" renditions over others. In sum, occupations, like organizations, assume collective selves, and the formation of these summative identities takes convincing, although contestation is more and less intense in particular historical moments.

On what grounds does such persuasion occur? Addressing the case of accounting, Kirkham and Loft[6] provide a pithy summary: "Whilst the nature and extent of any differences between the required skill, knowledge or expertise to undertake different accounting tasks remains contestable, such disputes are frequently resolved by reference to the class of person or persons who undertake them." Indeed, there is little question that work is known by the company it keeps. Abundant evidence from an area of inquiry known as occupational segregation studies confirms the claim that "occupations and activities, as well as people,

---

[4] Kelan, Elisabeth K. 2008. Emotions in a rational profession: the gendering of skills in ICT work. *Gender, Work and Organization* 15(1): 49–71.

[5] Hearn, Jeff. 1982. Notes on patriarchy: professionalization and the semi-professions. *Sociology* 16(2): 184–202.

[6] Kirkham, Linda M., and Anne Loft. 1993. Gender and the construction of the professional accountant. *Accounting, Organizations and Society* 18(6): 507–558: 508.

have gender identities",[7] or as Ashcraft[8] puts it, "acknowledging that occupations have collective identities means opening our eyes to their social identities as well."

The social identities of occupations can stem from their demographic alignment with certain groups of people, known as *physical* or *nominal* association, and/or from their ideational or emblematic alignment with particular embodied identities, known as *symbolic* or *ideological* association.[9] Physical association involves actual or usual practitioners, whereas symbolic association entails figurative practitioners.

Integrating research on both forms of association, Ashcraft proposes the metaphor of a "glass slipper" to capture "the alignment of occupational identity with embodied social identities as it yields systematic forms of advantage and disadvantage".[10] The glass slipper metaphor is specifically instructive because it helps to expose and foreground (a) occupational identity as an invention that becomes naturalized (like the glass slipper, made with a magic "poof" that later serves up material proof of merit); (b) the central role of contextually specific embodied social identities (not only women, but dainty foot size) in constructing the collective identities of occupations; (c) a tendency for occupational identity to over-emphasize features (like foot size) that favor certain practitioners yet bear thin relation to the actual work; (d) the strain of squeezing into an occupational identity mold made against you (as felt by Cinderella's "ugly stepsisters"); (e) the common pattern of dis/advantage spreading from figurative practitioner to entire occupation, engulfing actual and would-be practitioners (e.g., juxtapose the glass slipper of royalty alongside the duller shoe of a handmaiden, next to the dirty boot of domestic servants); and (f) the invisibility as well as fragility of dis/advantages created in the construction of occupational identity (i.e., a glass slipper is transparent and breakable).

As this suggests, the glass slipper advances growing recognition of the importance of symbolic association between bodies and work and, especially, the making of figurative practitioners. To date, however, the bulk of occupational segregation research has emphasized nominal association between bodies and work, or demographic alignments with the stable social (gender and race) categorizations of practitioners' physical bodies. Three broad explanations of how work and bodies become aligned have resulted from this work (for further detail and citations[11]). The first, which we abridge as **(1) bodies define work**, maintains that the major social classifications of actual practitioners influence how the work will come to be interpreted. Nursing, for example, owes its reputation as a caring profession largely to its longstanding association with white, well-educated women. The second, which we

---

[7] Kirkham and Loft 1993: 511.

[8] Ashcraft 2013: 8.

[9] Britton, Dana M. 2000. The epistemology of the gendered organization. *Gender and Society* 14: 418–434.

[10] Ashcraft 2013: 16.

[11] See Ashcraft 2013.

call **(2) work summons bodies**, reverses the direction of influence to claim that occupational content is processed through ready social norms, such that workers with corresponding social identities are hailed, through formal job ads or more subtle modes of identification. Hence, "nurturing occupations are more likely to become female dominated," though of course this is mediated by many factors.[12]

The third explanation places bodies and work in a recursive or bidirectional relation. This approach, which we condense as **(3) mutual influence**, holds that work becomes materially configured around the social identity of its customary practitioner in ways that perpetuate this "normal" match. In essence, we discriminate against (or privilege) certain people *by* discriminating against (or privileging) the occupations that bear their imprint, thereby preserving the highest-quality work for already privileged people. As nursing is built around women, for example, actual job quality erodes (e.g., mere *semi*-profession[13]), increasing the likelihood that only feminized workers will populate the work en masse.

Summarized simply, reigning explanations present three alternatives: chicken *or* egg or chicken *and* egg. These choices portend bleak prospects for diversity interventions. "Bodies define work" suggests that desirable work will not remain so if you significantly diversify the bodies aligned with it. Conversely, but no more optimistically, "work summons bodies" suggests that the re-coding of tasks (toward features linked to marginalized populations) is necessary in order to achieve diversification. Meanwhile, "mutual influence" agrees with both predictions of occupational decline, adding that the recursive relation between the character of work and the socially marked bodies that do it ignites a momentum difficult to extinguish. In short, raising the estimation of work aligned with marginalized people, or sustaining high estimations of an occupation once substantially diversified, appears to be a virtual impossibility.

This is precisely the mire into which most strategic diversification initiatives wade, yet few show adequate consciousness of or capacity to contend with the hazards entailed.[14] Given the preponderance of evidence, we must stress that it is in fact *reckless*, however well intentioned, to usher new bodies or task representations into an occupation as if its status as desirable work is independently anchored. To put the matter bluntly, programs focused primarily on bringing more "women and minorities" into (usually white) male-dominated professions direct marginalized populations toward occupational "promised lands" that will only remain so if the program is marginally successful (i.e., only a nonthreatening "handful" manage to cross

---

[12] Charles, Maria, and David B. Grusky. 2004. *Occupational ghettos: the worldwide segregation of women and men*. Stanford: Stanford University Press: 17.

[13] See Abbott, Andrew. 1998. Professionalism and the future of librarianship. *Library Trends* 46(3): 430–443.

[14] Among the rare programs that demonstrate such awareness is the campaign to increase the presence of men in nursing. But this is also an effort to change the public image and thereby raise the status of nursing – that is, to achieve a higher level of professionalization long denied on largely gendered grounds. Whatever gains such a strategy may bring to nursing, this is a form of diversification that ultimately perpetuates the very gender inequality it fights, surrendering to and exploiting the sexist principle that work aligned with men is regarded as more valuable.

over; for further discussion and support[15]). In short, the more successful the program, the more probable the eventual slide from promised land to wasteland. But if we concede that such diversity efforts are irresponsible and effectively doomed, with what are we left but surrender?

It is our contention that the **(4) glass slipper** articulates a fourth explanation that both better accommodates historical evidence and signals possible directions forward. With its sharper eye for symbolic association, the glass slipper points to the historical and ongoing social construction of occupational identity as a pivotal, constitutive activity that mediates the relation between the character of work and embodied social identities. Here, occupational identity is defined as "an evolving, co-constructed answer to two questions revolved in relation to one another: 'What is this line of work (e.g., account*ing*), and who does it (e.g., account*ants*)?'".[16]

This approach takes particular interest in the construction of *figurative* practitioners who serve as occupational "brands".[17] Such characters act as a proxy for the character of work; that is, they minimize the need for elaborate persuasion that the content, value, practice, and administration of work should be arranged in a particular way. Figurative practitioners promote reflex and closure rather than reflection and debate. In this sense, they distill occupational identity, performing continual acts of justification and naturalization in flashes of image, identification, and affect. These are the central characters that drive and validate the glass slipper effect, dis/advantaging the occupation as a whole and those who can/cannot embody the scripted performances they evoke. They arise from complex local articulations, which draw on such discursive resources as the physical bodies and social categorizations of actual or typical incumbents and other "foils" in the surround, task features, and the material organization of work. Crucially, figurative practitioners face challenges, shift shape, and fail; they may become settled for a time, but they are never determined.

Hence, the upshot of the glass slipper for diversity interventions is this: Meaningful forms of occupational equality necessitate careful, creative reconstructions of specific, situated occupational identities. In particular, they require attention to the birth and maturation of figurative practitioners now taken for granted. "Occupational rebranding" in this more critical mode depends upon, and begins with, sensitivity to the history of occupational identity. In other words, *reading the historical evolution of occupational identity is a crucial prerequisite to designing and implementing meaningful contemporary diversification efforts.*

In what follows, we enact such reading, turning to the origins of two occupations that may at first glance seem dissimilar: commercial airline flying and ICT. It is

---

[15] See Ashcraft, Karen Lee. 2006. Back to work: sights/sites of difference in gender and organizational communication studies. In *The SAGE handbook of gender and communication*, ed. Bonnie Dow and Julia T. Wood, 97–122. Thousand Oaks: Sage.

[16] Ashcraft 2013: 15, original emphasis.

[17] Ashcraft, Karen Lee, Sara Louise Muhr, Jens Rennstam, and Katie R. Sullivan. 2012b. Professionalization as a branding activity: occupational identity and the dialectic of inclusivity-exclusivity. *Gender, Work and Organization* 19(5): 467–488.

worth noting that, while rarely read in this way today, commercial aviation was initially promoted *as* a communication technology – a tool that would forever change our relation to other humans by enabling travel, interaction, and exposure to cultural difference around the globe. There is also a striking historical similarity between the infancy of both occupations that merits closer consideration. Namely, their designation as elite technical work was by no means guaranteed and required considerable persuasion, which hinged around gender. As we read both cases, we therefore ask how, amidst a host of possibilities, the identity of their work evolved as both "technical" and the "natural" province of particular bodies.

9.2   Privilege by Dis/Association? The Evolution of the Figurative Commercial Airline Pilot

The account offered here is a highly condensed version of fuller analyses provided elsewhere, based on the first author's extensive historical, empirical research on the evolution of professional identity in commercial aviation.[18] We intend this synopsis as a productive comparison alongside which to weigh our subsequent focal analysis, which integrates and interprets historical research on the occupational identity of ICT.

In the first two decades of the twentieth century, images of flight and fliers abounded. As Hopkins[19] helpfully traces, there was the "intrepid birdman" of traveling airshows – a figure who, in modern terms, was a cross between circus performer, magician, and rock star, staging death-defying feats for large, awed audiences. Similarly, though their performances were more impromptu and small scale, roving "barnstormers" flew into community fields, amazed locals with flying tricks, and offered lessons to the brave. The WWI ace introduced a sense of duty, honor, order, and patriotism to flight, whereas Hollywood celebrity pilots amplified the suave and glamor. Perhaps most famous by the 1920s was the rugged individualism of the airmail pilot, admired for his courage and valuable service, not to mention his reputation for rowdiness. Common among these circulating images was allegiance to a particular strain of masculinity: larger-than-life "lone wolves," driven by uncommon appetites for risk and adventure, physically capable and aggressive, sexually potent. As one commentator of the time gushed, "Something has kept these chaps young, and it isn't asceticism either. When they play poker they play all night. When they smoke they smoke too much. When they drink their glasses leak, and when they make love complaints are rare".[20] Make no mistake, implied the emerging pilot figure: Flying is a difficult, daring task reserved for the most robust of manly heroes.

---

[18] E.g., Ashcraft 2005, 2007; Ashcraft and Mumby 2004.

[19] Hopkins, George E. 1998. *The airline pilots: a study in elite unionization.* Cambridge, MA: Harvard University Press.

[20] Lay, Beirne Jr. 1941. Airman. *Fortune*: 23: 122–123.

Not surprisingly, these early "superman" images facilitated not only public fascination with flight but also pervasive fear of flying, the sort that is bad for business.[21] Refusing to settle for public reception as mere entertainment, the aviation industry responded with at least two notable image campaigns. Each one strategically mobilized embodied social identities to sell the safety of flight. And they eventually collided to create a cockpit monopoly for (a narrow version of) white masculinity, premised on the exclusion and control of women and other feminized figures, who suddenly found themselves locked out of the cockpit and stuck in the cabin.

The first campaign was supported by the *general* aviation industry, whose primary interest at the time was to popularize flying as a safe and pleasurable "everyman" pursuit in order to sell private planes and flight lessons. Interestingly, a campaign appealing to the common man exploited a contrasting public image of flight and fliers in the early twentieth century, one that had begun to captivate the public with an evident counter-narrative to the dominant superman myth – namely, the "ladyflier" or "ladybird" image. Personified by Amelia Earhart and a host of long-forgotten female pilots, the ladyflier was the subject of a media frenzy that crested for about a decade (for a detailed analysis of this period and the vital role played by ladyfliers[22]). Ladybirds were promoted as the epitome of modern womanhood, independent, adventurous, and – vitally – beautiful. In sponsored performances, ladyfliers were overtly instructed to act in a hyperfeminine manner (e.g., to primp in public). As Corn[23] masterfully shows, ladybirds were deliberately used by airplane manufacturers, salesmen, and flight schools[24] to shame men into flying with the explicit message: If *she* can do it, flying must be easy and safe; these ships are so durable, almost any pilot (even the flightiest!) will do.

Related dynamics were unfurling in European contexts as well; indeed, several of the early US ladyfliers (including the first African-American woman aviator, Bessie Coleman) received their training in France. As an international public increasingly romanticized ladyfliers, commentators of the day began to wonder out loud whether flying was so difficult after all, and whether it might not be better understood as women's work. One mused, for example, that ladyflier exploits reveal the true nature of pilots concealed by the mythical superman. "They are highly coordinated, sensitive types" marked by "delicacy, the long fingers and slender lines of physically sensitive people".[25] Around the same time, the *New York Times* observed, in a story on ladyfliers: "Flying an airplane need not, after all, be hard

---

[21] Hopkins 1998.

[22] See Corn, Joesph J. 1979. Making flying "unthinkable": women pilots and the selling of aviation, 1927–1940. *American Quarterly* 31: 556–571.

[23] Corn 1979.

[24] The authors' grandfather, who ran his own flying school and later became a career commercial airline pilot, likewise used ladybirds in this manner, as clearly evidenced in family business records.

[25] Munyan, A.T. Circa. 1929/1930. The ninety-nines. Museum of Women Pilots. *No publication title*/1930: 120.

work. It has often been pointed out that it is more usual to move the controls a fractional part of an inch than three inches".[26] In the hands of the ladybird, flying transformed: no longer a strenuous, perilous task requiring bravery and mastery but a safe and simple pastime – a graceful, artful activity at best. Is it really "work" at all?

These competing images did no favors for the struggling *commercial* airline industry, which teetered on the brink of failure by the late 1920s, despite federal airmail subsidies. Industry constituents understood both options to pose serious liabilities. How can the public conceive of flight as a viable mode of transportation when pilots are either extreme daredevil-heroes or untrained, whimsical scatterbrains?

In an urgent move to grow a passenger base, several airlines colluded with the budding pilot union in a different campaign that sought to refashion the identity of airline flying as complex technical-scientific work done by reliable experts. Commercial fliers were swiftly reborn as a new figurative practitioner – the dependable professional airline pilot, with a culminating rank of Captain – in three main maneuvers[27]: (a) a full-body makeover that muffled the raw physicality of the "grease-monkey-playboy" pilot (picture: leather flying suit and goggles, a potent image of the time) with a military-professional uniform modeled after that of naval officers; (b) avid marketing of the pilot's scientific knowledge and technical skill, materialized in a navigation kit housing technical manuals and resembling a briefcase, as well as in the proliferation of dazzling cockpit instruments and intensified education and training requirements; and (c) explicit training of pilots to perform as omniscient fathers in flight, enabled by a new intercom system broadcasting the invisible voice of authority[28]. Here again, related developments unfolded in Europe, albeit with significant cultural nuances. In the UK, for example, the figurative airline pilot was born on the backs of, and in contrast to, a distinctive array of surrounding masculinities, including the conventional "butler" imagery associated with the airline stew*ard*.[29]

In such ways, and with regional variations, the figurative airline pilot was redrafted (in both senses, redrawn and recruited) around a specific breed of white professional masculinity: commanding, civilized, rational, technical scientific, paternal, and tastefully heterosexual. In the USA, the ladyflier image served up a perfect foil for his makeover. Against her compulsory hyperfeminine embodiment, the professional airline pilot emerged as the only logical steward of the cockpit, served and supported by his stewar*dess* in the cabin. And this new figurative practitioner – airline stewardess, the pilot's alluring "better half" in the back of the plane – became the fate of the ladyflier. Women pilots would not be allowed back in the US airline cockpit for nearly 40 years.

[26] Martyn, T.J.C. 1929. Women find a place among the fliers. *The New York Times*, August 27.

[27] Hopkins 1998.

[28] Kurtz, Howard G. 1953. The common man up in the air. *The Airline Pilot*: 22: 18–21.

[29] Mills, Albert J. 1998. Cockpits, hangars, boys and galleys: corporate masculinities and the development of British Airways. *Gender, Work and Organization* 5: 172–188.

9.3 Privilege by Dis/Association? The Evolution of the Figurative ICT "Professional"

We now turn our focus to examine the dynamics at play in a more recent case study: the evolution of occupational identity in the ICT professions, integrating and interpreting historical research as documented thus far by other scholars. We are particularly interested in what we might learn from some of the key similarities and differences by which both of these occupations came to be characterized as "technical" and closely aligned with white masculinity – lessons we detail further in the conclusion.

In the early 1940s, in both the USA and in Europe, computing was initially envisioned as relatively low-status labor, involving rote, deskilled tasks closely aligned with clerical work. In fact, technical work was often explicitly positioned in opposition to the intellectual and highly skilled work of more established engineering and managerial occupations.[30] As a result, computing and programming were often framed as especially conducive for women – as something that could be done at home while caring for children or as something akin to "following a recipe" or "planning a dinner".[31]

Despite their relatively low status, however, these new occupations also afforded new frontiers for women. And, in fact, many employers, practitioners, and marketers also touted the exciting opportunities for advancement and greater equity endemic in these jobs, especially when compared to other occupations available to women at the time. Likewise, many women themselves experienced these benefits early on. As a result, and in contrast to aviation, women were relatively prevalent in computing from its very inception.[32] As we shall see, this early feminization of the field later presented some unique difficulties that had to be actively overcome in order to recruit men who would be able to fill these rapidly increasing and important occupations.

Beginning with the now renowned (but once forgotten[33]) "ENIAC girls," it soon became apparent that, despite earlier perceptions, these emerging computing jobs actually involved a great deal of highly skilled numerical analysis, program-

---

[30] Ensmenger 2010b; Hicks 2010.

[31] Ensmenger 2010a.

[32] Ensmenger 2010a; Hicks 2010; Light, Jennifer. 2003. Programming. In *Gender and technology: a reader*, ed. Nina E. Lerman, Ruth Oldenziel, and Arwen P. Mohun. Baltimore: The Johns Hopkins University Press.

[33] Light 2003 illustrates how the contributions of the ENIAC women were virtually erased from history. In almost all of the press reporting the success of the ENIAC, only the male engineers were mentioned. While the *New York Times* article reporting on the project's success alluded to the help of "many others," it also hinted at the fact that these anonymous helpers were men, noting that the machine was "doing easily what had been done laboriously by many trained men." This was typical of the press of the day. The few cases where the presence of female workers was acknowledged described them as anonymous groups of workers. As a result, none of the women were ever interviewed or invited to talk about their contributions.

ming, and related kinds of technical problem solving. This recognition began to give rise to new characterizations (but not new realities) of the work. By the mid-1950s, computing jobs were garnering a somewhat mysterious aura as few people understood the nature of the work or what was required to complete it. As[34] observes, "programming began to acquire a reputation for being incomprehensible to all but a small set of extremely talented insiders." Indeed, during the late 1940s and 1950s, these careers were often framed as a sort of "black art," rather than a science, and only those who mysteriously and naturally had "what it takes" could adequately fill these positions. To be clear, in many cases, it was not that the realities of the work and its associated tasks that changed but rather the representations of this work.

These characterizations began to contribute to a more "masculine" construction of computing – that of the "lone wolf" who programmed in a dark room or garage and worked magical feats of genius.[35] In some ways, this image was not unlike the early images of pilots noted above, embodying a "rogue," primarily white, masculinity – albeit a more mental and eccentric one rather than a physical and daring one. As one analyst of the time reported, programmers are "often egocentric, slightly neurotic, and border upon a limited schizophrenia. The incidence of beards, sandals, and other symptoms of rugged individualism or nonconformity are notably greater among this demographic group".[36] Whereas the "lone wolves" in aviation conjured up images of hypermasculine, sexually potent lovers, these "lone wolves" invoked images more akin to awkward, antisocial, "geeky" geniuses. Later, we return to explore some of the potential ramifications of these different masculine representations. For now it is worth noting that throughout the 1950s and 1960s, these two images – the image of computing as hyperfeminized women's work and that of the highly masculinized magical "lone wolf" – collided and circulated alongside each other.

It soon became clear, however, that both of these images were bad for business – especially as computing jobs multiplied, significantly increasing the demand for labor. Although it differed from daredevil pilot images in its particular iteration of masculinity, the "lone wolf" or "geeky," eccentric programmer also did not readily resonate with most men, making wider recruitment efforts difficult. Likewise, the industry grew increasingly concerned about the associated perception that these occupations required mysterious, magical, or idiosyncratic kinds of knowledge, as this perception made it difficult to standardize the credentials necessary for the job and develop certification programs that would attract and train a larger candidate pool. The image of the profession as "women's work" also did not bode well for attracting more men or for raising the status of the field. Nor did the fact that many

---

[34] Ensmenger 2010a: 125.

[35] Ensmenger 2010a, b; Mody, Rustom P. 1992. Is programming an art? *Software Engineering Notes* 17(4): 19–21.

[36] Brandon as cited in Ensmenger 2010a: 128.

of these occupations still involved aspects of menial, rote, low-status work and afforded few managerial opportunities.[37]

As a result, the late 1950s and 1960s gave rise to intense efforts to "rebrand" and professionalize computing occupations. To varying degrees, practitioners expressed an implicit or explicit understanding that in order to recruit more men, computing would need to acquire the typical trappings of a professional occupation, with formal certification programs, professional associations, higher salaries, and opportunities for advancement and management. Similar trends surged through Europe as well.[38] For example, in 1955, the British Aeronautical Research department reported, "Boys generally prefer laboratory work to computing … this might be due in part to the absence of any recognized career in computing and of any suitable specialist courses or qualifications; if this be true it may be possible to make computing into an attractive career for some boys".[39] Of course, today, this idea that it *might be possible* to *make* computing into an attractive career for boys or men is ironic to say the least. The striking contrast to the way this work is characterized today highlights how the nature of work and its associated tasks are highly malleable and cannot simply be taken at face value as having inherent properties.

In order to attract more men to computing, governments and industry throughout the USA and Europe began to take measures to raise the status of computing, imbuing it with long-term career potential. Characterizations of computing began to incorporate more managerial and administrative responsibilities with opportunities for advancement. In particular, Hicks[40] illustrates how British organizations began recruiting from the managerial "executive class" to fill these new kinds of computing positions. Often, however, these men had very little, if any, prior programming or computing experience and would be initially trained by some of the women who had been filling these positions previously. These women would receive a temporary raise in pay but would not be promoted to these positions themselves because they were not perceived to be capable of managerial responsibilities, especially if it involved supervising other men. Ironically, then, given arguments made today, it was a woman's lack of managerial, "*non*technical potential" that "scuttled her chances of ever being on an equal footing with her new trainees".[41] Indeed, questions about women's "technical competence" were rarely, if ever, an issue during these early decades. This, however, did not prevent women from ultimately being relegated to lower status positions or being cut out of the field altogether – a point we will return to in the conclusion.

---

[37] Ensmenger 2010a, b; Hicks 2010; Misa, Tom. 2010. Gender codes: lessons from history. In *Gender codes: why women are leaving computing*, ed. Tom Misa, 251–264. Hoboken: Wiley Press.

[38] Corneliussen, Hilde G. 2010. Cultural perceptions of computers in Norway 1980–2007. In *Gender codes: why women are leaving computing*, ed. Tom Misa, 165–186. Hoboken: Wiley Press; Hicks 2010.

[39] As cited in Hicks 2010: 100.

[40] Hicks 2010.

[41] Hicks 2010: 101.

As the 1960s wore on, the computing industry burgeoned, sparking significant alarm about tech labor shortages and promoting much public conversation about an impending economic crisis. While employers increasingly desired male candidates to fill these higher-status computing jobs, practical necessity made efforts to hire a gender-diverse technical workforce more attractive.

For example, as late as 1968, IBM Corporation unveiled its "Meet Susie Meyers" marketing campaign suggesting that even a "young girl" with "no previous programming experience" could use their new programming language.[42] This was a slightly different twist on the original association of women with computing. Like the ladyflier, such images suggested not so subtly that if even these attractive, young ladies with their long, blond hair and no prior programming experience could occupy these positions, *anyone* can – "come on, give it a try." Of course, in contrast to aviation, these images didn't arise out of a concern about "safety" – or out of a concern related to consumers at all – but rather in response to an increasing demand for computer workers wherever they could be found.

In the USA and Europe, similar campaigns sprung up in an attempt to simultaneously appeal to women and to communicate the idea that anyone could enter a computing career. For example, around this time, the British government ran an ad campaign that included taglines such as "Know Nothing About Computers? Then We'll Teach You (and pay you while doing so)".[43] Employers' attempts to cast computing in this light were, of course, at odds with the interests of computing academics and practitioners who were trying to professionalize these occupations by identifying the prerequisite body of knowledge and skills necessary for such careers and developing the necessary academic and certification processes by which to obtain these skills. These three competing messages – that anyone can compute, that only those eccentric wizards with the "right stuff" can compute, or that only those with rigorous training and certifications can compute – circulated alongside each other in the public discourse. The economic conditions at the time temporarily ushered in an era particularly receptive to the "anyone can compute" message, facilitating more concentrated efforts to hire both women and men into these occupations.

This era, however, proved to be short lived. By the early 1970s, concerns over shortages began to settle down, facilitating the decline of the "anyone can compute" campaigns and their associated gender-diverse hiring efforts in favor of hiring and promotion practices that favored male candidates.[44] As a result, women increasingly remained in lower status positions or began to decline entering the field altogether.

What remained unsettled – and continues so to this day – is the tension between the primarily white masculine images of the eccentric genius of the "lone wolf" versus the rigorously trained, analytical, technical discipline of the IT professional. Indeed, the notion that computing is an art that requires those born with that "something special" remains a widely accepted truism, though also a matter of contentious

---

[42] Ensmenger 2010a.
[43] Hicks 2010.
[44] Ensmenger 2010b; Hicks 2010.

debate.[45] In contrast to aviation, where the boundaries of work and paths to certification are relatively clear, the boundaries of the ICT professions remain highly permeable and varied, as do the pathways for obtaining these jobs.[46] This ambiguity creates nuanced challenges, vulnerabilities, and insecurities (e.g., claims that it is not really scientific, that it is not a "real" profession, that it does not require an elite university degree). At the same time, however, this ambiguity also affords unique advantages in that, to date, it is also a more agile profession. In some ways, then, it is potentially more easily redefined and reimagined, albeit in more fractured ways. It is these possibilities for reimagining the profession that we now turn to in our concluding remarks.

9.4   Conclusion

In the above case comparison, we have illustrated how, amidst a host of possibilities, these two professions acquired their status as "elite, technical" work naturally aligned with particular bodies. We suggest that, taken together, these two cases sharpen the limitations of the three traditional explanations for the work-body relation. As noted earlier, the first explanation suggests that "bodies define work." In both cases, however, male and female practitioners were, at one point, plentiful. Indeed, in the case of computing, women occupied a prominent part of the workforce early on, yet this did not ultimately serve to define the nature of computing work. On the contrary, active efforts ensued to reorganize tasks into different assemblages, ultimately defining the work *against* the actual bodies originally occupying these jobs. Likewise, in the case of aviation, we have seen how the definition could have been, and indeed often was, framed in terms of either female and male bodies.

The second explanation suggests that "work summons bodies." Yet in both cases presented here we see the malleable nature of work and its associated tasks – that is, the same tasks can be framed and assembled in many different ways, and no single framing can be taken at face value as the natural order of things. In the first case, the social characterizations of flight varied greatly – from daring, physically and technically challenging pursuit to an intuitive and artful pastime. Likewise, in the case of computing, characterizations ranged widely from relatively mundane, clerical work to mysterious, beguiling art to scientific, rational, and academic pursuit.

---

[45] Ashcraft, Catherine, Elizabeth Eger, and Michelle Friend. 2012a. *Girls in IT: the facts*. Boulder: National Center for Women & Information Technology, Ashcraft, Catherine, Wendy DuBow, Elizabeth Eger, Sarah Blithe, and Brian Sevier. 2013. *Male advocates and allies: promoting gender diversity in technology workplaces*. Boulder: National Center for Women & Information Technology; Ensmenger 2010a, b; Mody 1992.

[46] Kaufman, Ron. 1992. NRC Report Sparks Debate Among Computer Scientists. *The Scientist*, November 9, 1992; Tynan, Dan. 2011. IT turf wars: the most common feuds in tech. *InfoWorld*, February 14.

The third explanation, "mutual influence," comes closer to accounting for the dynamics at play. In this explanation, work initially takes on tangible characteristics derived from its *typical* practitioner, and these characteristics, in turn, tend to take hold and close the occupation to different kinds of potential practitioners. But as these cases illustrate, what this explanation fails to account for is that this process first requires the construction of a *figurative* (or symbolic) practitioner that then summons the typical practitioner, which, in turn, fortifies belief in the accuracy of the construction. In the case of computing and aviation, for example, the work did not take on its current character and status because men were in these occupations; these occupations were actively constructed, drawing upon narratives of gender, race, and other differences in order to create certain kinds of figurative male practitioners that would attract men to these positions and then later make this association seem natural (e.g., the techno-professional pilot complete with navigation kit and uniform; infusing computing with long-term career potential, managerial opportunities, and prestige). It is this process of constructing the figurative practitioner that the "glass slipper" explanation aims to capture. With its sharper eye for the symbolic, the glass slipper highlights this historical and ongoing social construction as a key mediator in the work-body relationship. In other words, in these and similar cases,[47] professionalization and status are indeed secured *through* segregation (as the third explanation also suggests), but this is only made possible by a social construction battle over the relationship between bodies and work.

Reading these cases alongside each other also helps to sharpen our understanding of the complex and myriad roles figurative practitioners can play in constructing the work-body relation. For example, in the case of aviation, the competing figurative practitioners we have discussed arose from a need to create new markets because "business was bad," whereas these discursive efforts in computing were primarily used to create new sources of labor (because arguably business was quite good). Recognizing the different stimuli or motivations behind the development of figurative practitioners, as well as the different ends to which these symbolic representations are put, enriches our understanding of these dynamics. For example, this cross-case analysis helps prevent the potential misconception that we are immune to these constructions in times when business is good or the labor supply plentiful. The juxtaposition of these two professions also underscores the significance, prevalence, and tenacity of these processes – that is, understanding how similar negotiations unfolded in two seemingly very different situations helps to illuminate the powerful role these systems of privilege and disadvantage play in the construction of occupational identity across contexts.

In comparing these cases, we also see the vast variation in the ways that figurative practitioners draw upon and reinscribe different representations of gender, race, and other aspects of difference. While in some ways, this also calls attention to the tenacity of these narratives it also points to their simultaneous fragility, helping us to understand their particular vulnerabilities – vulnerabilities that make these images and narratives both available for and resistant to reimagining and reconstruction.

---

[47] See also Hearn 1982; Kirkham and Loft 1993.

Consider, for instance, the different masculinities of the hypermasculine, sexually potent airmail pilot versus the eccentric nerdy genius of the lone programmer. On a ladder of heterosexual masculinities, the latter arguably claims a lower rung, at least in heterosexual contexts or relationships. Such differences can have important implications for diversification efforts, especially when it comes to gender. For example, even if the presence of women begins to become a threatening force professionally, the more virile identity of the airline pilot allows for opportunities to validate one's masculine status in other arenas (e.g., the ability to successfully date, seduce, partner with, or marry women). The more eccentric masculinity of the nerd genius, at least figuratively, if not in actuality, possesses less access to this strategy, making the professional realm the most likely, or perhaps *only*, arena for reaffirming one's "masculine credentials." Indeed, in the US context, we suggest that this dynamic may help explain the rise of the "brogrammer" image in the mid-2000s[48] as one attempts to claim some of the benefits of this more virile masculinity. The relative insecurity around "masculine credentials" may also help to explain some of the recent vitriolic backlash to diversifying the computing field, as evidenced in recent events such as Gamergate.[49] Understanding the nuances in these constructions is important then for breaking or dismantling the glass slipper – that is, understanding and unmasking the subtle processes by which systems of privilege and disadvantage are wielded to construct these occupational identities. We contend that doing so is crucial for the study of work and, in our case, the study of technical-scientific work.

We also suggest that understanding these nuances is an important prerequisite for designing and implementing meaningful diversity programs. Indeed, as noted earlier, we suggest that it is irresponsible, no matter how well intentioned, to usher new bodies or task representations into an occupational rebranding effort without an attention to this historical, social construction. And this is perhaps a particularly timely recommendation in the case of computing and information technology. The past decade has ignited increasing concern over the underrepresentation of women in the ICT profession, sparking an array of urgent public rhetoric and a flurry of diversification efforts, both in the USA and in Europe. As a result, this is also an especially crucial time for understanding the historical evolution of the profession if these rebranding, recruiting, and retention strategies are to be successful in ways that transform rather than reproduce existing social inequities. We suggest then, that the above analysis points to several important implications for the success of efforts to diversify ICT professions.

First, if anything, this analysis should give those of us engaged in occupational rebranding and diversity efforts cause to question some of our current strategies. For example, examining the historical evolution of ICT calls attention to the limitations of current efforts aimed at addressing existing biases and stereotypes (e.g., related to women's technical acumen). While these strategies may be important, clearly

---

[48] Macmillan, Douglas. 2012. The rise of the brogrammer. *Bloomberg Business*, March 1.

[49] See Suellentrop, Chris. 2014. Can video games survive? The Disheartening GamerGate Campaign. *New York Times*, October 25 for a recap of the Gamergate controversy.

they are not enough and in fact, even if successful, may have little impact on the occupational identity of computing. As noted earlier, in the early years, women's technical acumen was rarely, if ever, called into question but this did not ensure equal footing for women. Historical precedent indicates that mitigating these biases can simply spark new avenues and strategies for differentiations that maintain existing inequalities.

Examining the historical case of computing also raises additional concerns about an argument commonly used to promote diversity – that is, rationales rooted in the potential for a diverse workforce to alleviate so-called labor "shortages" and difficulties in finding qualified applicants. Of course, in light of rhetoric around labor shortages in science and technology, a number of economists and other scholars have questioned the legitimacy of these shortages,[50] calling into question the ways in which hiring difficulties are sometimes falsely equated to labor shortages. This analysis, however, points out that whether these shortages are "real" or not, using them to justify diversification efforts is a perilous strategy, at best, and a counterproductive one, at worst.

Finally, as part of our endeavors to diversify the workforce, change agents, practitioners, and others, particularly in USA and European countries, are often interested in looking to countries or regions with high levels of female participation in computing with an eye to identifying strategies that seem to be "working" in these countries.[51] But, of course, this very question assumes an ahistorical and acultural lens in the analysis of these dynamics. As we have seen, the mere presence of women, even in large numbers, does not necessarily mean that the current strategies are "working" – if by working we mean transforming existing inequities and fostering meaningful participation of diverse groups. As the "glass slipper" illustrates, more careful attention to the social construction of the relationship of the work-body relationship is needed.

In addition to interrogating our existing diversification strategies, this analysis also highlights two important strategic interventions we might incorporate. The first, and perhaps most obvious course of action, is unmasking and raising awareness about the historical evolution of specific occupational identities. Diversification efforts would do well to employ a sort of "history as strategy," illuminating the processes by which these identities were constructed, troubling the taken-for-granted assumptions and associations of particular body-work relationships. We also suggest that *shifting reconstructions of an occupation's figurative practices must accompany, if not precede, efforts to diversify its actual, usual, or even figurative practitioners.* Typically, diversity interventions seek to multiply the figurative and typical *practitioners* associated with and able to access a particular profession. When framed this way, however, the goal remains focused on individuals and

---

[50] E.g., Berliner, David C., and Bruce J. Biddle. 1995. *The manufactured crisis: myths, fraud, and the attack on America's public schools*. Reading: Addison-Wesley.

[51] Ashcraft, Catherine. 2014. *Increasing the participation of women and underrepresented minorities in computing: missing perspectives and new directions*. Orlando: National Science Foundation Computer Science Education Summit.

individual bodies, but this is likely to stabilize the association of occupational identity with discrete bodies, ultimately favoring some over others. We suggest what is needed is the ability to shift the spotlight toward actual work *practices* and, more specifically, pursue a tactic of shifting plural reconstructions of practice (i.e., clutter or oversaturate the field with an almost dizzying array of figurative practices, task alignments, and associations). Doing so can help position and depict technical work in more complex, multifaceted ways – that is, as having promiscuous, hybrid, and somewhat perplexing or disrupting gender-race affiliations. That our diversity interventions begin with and incorporate such strategies is vital if we are to loosen existing body-work relations in ways that foster more transformative social relations.

References

Abbott, Andrew. 1998. Professionalism and the future of librarianship. *Library Trends* 46(3): 430–443.

Ashcraft, Karen Lee. 2005. Resistance through consent? Occupational identity, organizational form, and the maintenance of masculinity among commercial airline pilots. *Management Communication Quarterly* 19: 67–90.

Ashcraft, Karen Lee. 2006. Back to work: sights/sites of difference in gender and organizational communication studies. In *The SAGE handbook of gender and communication*, ed. Bonnie Dow and Julia T. Wood, 97–122. Thousand Oaks: Sage.

Ashcraft, Karen Lee. 2007. Appreciating the "work" of discourse: occupational identity and difference as organizing mechanisms in the case of commercial airline pilots. *Discourse & Communication* 1: 9–36.

Ashcraft, Karen Lee. 2013. The glass slipper: "incorporating" occupational identity in management studies. *Academy of Management Review* 38(1): 6–31.

Ashcraft, Catherine. 2014. *Increasing the participation of women and underrepresented minorities in computing: missing perspectives and new directions*. Orlando: National Science Foundation Computer Science Education Summit.

Ashcraft, Karen Lee, and Dennis K. Mumby. 2004. *Reworking gender: a feminist communicology of organization*. Thousand Oaks: Sage.

Ashcraft, Catherine, Elizabeth Eger, and Michelle Friend. 2012a. *Girls in IT: the facts*. Boulder: National Center for Women & Information Technology.

Ashcraft, Karen Lee, Sara Louise Muhr, Jens Rennstam, and Katie R. Sullivan. 2012b. Professionalization as a branding activity: occupational identity and the dialectic of inclusivity-exclusivity. *Gender, Work and Organization* 19(5): 467–488.

Ashcraft, Catherine, Wendy DuBow, Elizabeth Eger, Sarah Blithe, and Brian Sevier. 2013. *Male advocates and allies: promoting gender diversity in technology workplaces*. Boulder: National Center for Women & Information Technology.

Berliner, David C., and Bruce J. Biddle. 1995. *The manufactured crisis: myths, fraud, and the attack on America's public schools*. Reading: Addison-Wesley.

Britton, Dana M. 2000. The epistemology of the gendered organization. *Gender and Society* 14: 418–434.

Charles, Maria, and David B. Grusky. 2004. *Occupational ghettos: the worldwide segregation of women and men*. Stanford: Stanford University Press.

Corn, Joesph J. 1979. Making flying "unthinkable": women pilots and the selling of aviation, 1927–1940. *American Quarterly* 31: 556–571.

Corneliussen, Hilde G. 2010. Cultural perceptions of computers in Norway 1980–2007. In *Gender codes: why women are leaving computing*, ed. Tom Misa, 165–186. Hoboken: Wiley Press.

Ensmenger, Nathan. 2010a. Making programming masculine. In *Gender codes: why women are leaving computing*, ed. Tom Misa, 115–142. Hoboken: Wiley.

Ensmenger, Nathan. 2010b. *The computer boys take over: computers, programmers, and the politics of technical expertise*. Cambridge: MIT Press.

Hearn, Jeff. 1982. Notes on patriarchy: professionalization and the semi-professions. *Sociology* 16(2): 184–202.

Hicks, Marie. 2010. Meritocracy and feminization in conflict: computerization in the British government. In *Gender codes: why women are leaving computing*, ed. Tom Misa, 115–142. Hoboken: Wiley.

Hopkins, George E. 1998. *The airline pilots: a study in elite unionization*. Cambridge, MA: Harvard University Press.

Kaufman, Ron. 1992. NRC Report Sparks Debate Among Computer Scientists. *The Scientist*, November 9, 1992.

Kelan, Elisabeth K. 2008. Emotions in a rational profession: the gendering of skills in ICT work. *Gender, Work and Organization* 15(1): 49–71.

Kirkham, Linda M., and Anne Loft. 1993. Gender and the construction of the professional accountant. *Accounting, Organizations and Society* 18(6): 507–558.

Kurtz, Howard G. 1953. The common man up in the air. *The Airline Pilot*: 22: 18–21.

Lay, Beirne Jr. 1941. Airman. *Fortune*: 23: 122–123.

Light, Jennifer. 2003. Programming. In *Gender and technology: a reader*, ed. Nina E. Lerman, Ruth Oldenziel, and Arwen P. Mohun. Baltimore: The Johns Hopkins University Press.

Macmillan, Douglas. 2012. The rise of the brogrammer. *Bloomberg Business*, March 1.

Martyn, T.J.C. 1929. Women find a place among the fliers. *The New York Times*, August 27.

Mills, Albert J. 1998. Cockpits, hangars, boys and galleys: corporate masculinities and the development of British Airways. *Gender, Work and Organization* 5: 172–188.

Misa, Tom. 2010. Gender codes: lessons from history. In *Gender codes: why women are leaving computing*, ed. Tom Misa, 251–264. Hoboken: Wiley Press.

Mody, Rustom P. 1992. Is programming an art? *Software Engineering Notes* 17(4): 19–21.

Munyan, A.T. Circa. 1929/1930. The ninety-nines. Museum of Women Pilots. *No publication title*.

Suellentrop, Chris. 2014. Can video games survive? The Disheartening GamerGate Campaign. *New York Times*, October 25.

Tynan, Dan. 2011. IT turf wars: the most common feuds in tech. *InfoWorld*, February 14.

Chapter 10
Gender-Technology Relations in the Various Ages of Information Societies

Delphine Gardey

Abstract From "domination" to empowerment, gendered uses of information technologies appear in a variety of situations and interpretations. What is added to the history of technology by their social studies, and what is offered otherwise by the critical input of feminism on this field, is the idea that relations between humans and technologies (gender relations among them) are never set in advance but instead the object, as much as the end game of the analysis, as shown by Judy Wajcman. Yet the "seamless fabric" (with reference to Hughes' work) interweaving the social and the technological and tying together gender and power relations is enduring; the role of historians is to acknowledge its lasting existence.

10.1 What ICTs, What History?

Information and communication technologies? Society of information, of knowledge? Communication, networks and digital and virtual economy? ICT?

Certain words and phrases penetrate the vernacular with an ease that hints at suspect self-evidence: it certainly is the case for the acronym "ICT." What those letters cover is a domain embracing such varied technologies as the telegraph, the telephone (before it became cellular), the typewriter, the radio as well as punch-card systems, and computers (before they became personal). The age of mechanical data processing was superseded by the age of computing, itself followed by the era of communication. Having barely incorporated the newly institutionalized[1] terms of a "society" and an "economy" of "information" and "communication," our lexicon is

---

[1] A comparative European history of the transitions from the field of "communication" to that of "information" and then of "the digital" is still to be written. The creation of a research unit on "TIC et société" ("ICT and Society") at the French *Centre National de la Recherche Scientifique* (CNRS) can be seen as evidence of such institutionalization (Brousseau, Eric, and Frédéric Moatty. 2002. La création du Groupe de recherche 'TIC et société' au CNRS. *Réseaux* 2(112–113): 395–398).

D. Gardey (✉)
Gender Institute, The Geneva School of Social Sciences, Geneva University, Bd du Pont-d'Arve 40, 1211 Geneva, Switzerland
e-mail: Delphine.gardey@unige.ch

© Springer International Publishing Switzerland 2015
V. Schafer, B.G. Thierry (eds.), *Connecting Women*, History of Computing,
DOI 10.1007/978-3-319-20837-4_10

157

fed with the new concepts of a digital revolution, a society of "knowledge", and a "cyber world" – of a virtual or "augmented" reality.

How the history of technologies is told is contingent on the times. The history of computer systems was for a long while drafted without any consideration for mechanical data processing as a technico-social system able to process and produce data on a large scale.[2,3] Computer science was included in the genealogy of leading-edge technology, and its history was that of concepts and formalism. As such, the writing of its history is a manifestation of what "technology" is; the prevalent technological internalism or naturalism sides with a "male," "hard(ware)" element, with innovation and the radically new – as feminist researchers offer to describe the social and cultural existence of technology in the West.[4] Postwar computers as technical and conceptual systems could only have the noblest of origins. The French history of computer science, putting emphasis on the emergence of national "science" and "industry," has computer science find its "origin" in the analog computers used for scientific calculation between the World Wars.[5] The acknowledgment of punch-card systems as part of that genealogy is fairly recent[6] and a critical turning point for historiography.[7]

It certainly is significant that an approach of information technologies as socio-technical systems allows a reconnect between the past and the future of computer science and technologies. The explicit relation between the socio-technical infrastructures of the interwar years and postwar computer science takes the spotlight from innovation and shines it on the usage and forms of continuity. It helps to better consider the historical, political, and social (and gender) contexts of the development of machines; it furthermore allows to integrate the history of computing into a broader, newly formulated history of information technologies, as Giuditta Parolini offers in this book.

This connection of the past and future, a new reading of what information technologies are and can become, is carried out at a specific time in the history and the development of Western capitalist societies. In the age of the Internet bubble and the apparent cultural, technological, and economic hegemony of the digital world, the meaning we give to the present questions the past in new ways and may reinforce

[2] Gardey, Delphine. 2008. *Ecrire, calculer, classer. Comment une révolution de papier a transformé les sociétés contemporaines (1800–1940)*. Paris: La Découverte.

[3] See in particular Chap. 7, *"Traiter l'information : de l'économie au gouvernement"*: 243–278.

[4] Cockburn, Cynthia. 1983. *Brothers: male dominance and technological change*. London: Pluto Press; Wajcman, Judy. 1991. *Feminism confronts technology*. Cambridge: Polity Press; Oldenziel, Ruth. 1996. Objections: technology, culture and gender. In *Learning from things. Method and theory of material culture studies*, ed. David Kingery, 55–69. Washington, DC: Smithsonian Institution Press.

[5] Mounier-Kuhn, Pierre-Eric. 2010. *L'informatique en France de la seconde guerre mondiale au Plan Calcul. L'émergence d'une science*. Paris: Presses universitaires de la Sorbonne.

[6] In the French context, an interesting contribution to that acknowledgment in the perspective of an essentially technical and industrial history of technologies is that of Pierre-Eric Mounier-Kuhn.

[7] Krige, John, and Eda Kranakis. eds. 1994. Information technologies and socio-technical systems. *History and Technology*, 1(1). New York: Routledge.

the hypotheses of today. Laymen and expert alike seem to describe the 1990s and 2000s as the era of the emerging "network society," "knowledge economy," "information society," and "digital economy": this raises with rare necessity the question of the descriptions of the past. What name is to be given to the society replaced by the "knowledge society?" How to quantitatively measure and study the "rise of the knowledge worker"[8]? Once identified and represented under different terms, these mutations are revisited in order to institute a form of continuity and historical trend.

One such rewriting effort was undertaken in the volume edited by Alfred Chandler and James Cortada in 2000. Its focus was on finding, in the history of the United States since colonial times, "how a nation was transformed by information" and how "information has shaped the United States" while reading the history of technologies and capitalism through this prism.[9] The obscure research of historians interested in disused techniques and poorly visible economic and social fields gain a new life, new potential value on the market of scholarship, and refreshed academic legitimacy. Yet, this movement is not without its issues. How faithful to the worldview of contemporary stakeholders are the sets, systems, and genealogies constituted and enriched by today's researchers? How can today's research not attribute meaning and purpose against original, now veiled significance once embodied by certain technologies? What of the forgotten lineage and of the once available, used, then forgotten scripts[10,11]? What is to be done about the diversity of technico-human arrangements that follow national contexts, industrial specificities, and local settings?

10.2   Technology Yesterday, ICTs Today?

My research on the "arts of doing"[12] concerning the administration of men and things[13] has led me to describe the various regimes of the use of technology in the protean space of the office throughout its long history. Rather than a teleological

---

[8] Cortada, James (ed.). 1998. *Rise of the knowledge worker*. London: Routledge.

[9] Chandler, Alfred, and James Cortada (eds.). 2000. *A nation transformed by information. How information has shaped the United States from colonial times to present*. Oxford/New York: Oxford University Press.

[10] Akrich, Madeleine. 1992. The de-scription of technical objects. In *Shaping technology-building society: studies in sociotechnical change*, ed. Wiebe E. Bijker and John Law, 205–224. Cambridge, MA: MIT Press.

[11] My work on the movement of mechanization of writing before and after the invention, production, and penetration as an office tool of Sholes's typewriter by Remington aims to recapture forgotten intentions, usefulness, and scripts. One aspect of usefulness is here the intention to help teach writing to the blind, an effort carried on by several generations of inventors and users (Gardey, Delphine. 2001. Mechanizing writing and photographing the word: utopias, office work, and histories of gender and technology. *History and Technology* 17: 319–335).

[12] De Certeau, Michel. 1990. *L'invention du quotidien. 1. Arts de faire*. Paris: Gallimard.

[13] Gardey 2008.

approach, I chose to account for the knowledge and the know-how put into practice by workers for the completion of traditional administrative duties (writing, counting, filing, computing) while facing the development and intensification of these tasks as both tools and products of a mutating economy. I was able to show, with other historians, that mechanization was not the sole motivator for the intensification of work: during the same period and within one same company, a great variety of processes involving men, women, traditional know-how, individual skills, ancient devices, and/or new technologies can coexist.[14]

Practices such as hand calculations and the acknowledgment of qualified employees as a resource were, in many places and for a long time, resisting their replacement by artifacts (calculators and later tabulating machines). Martin Campbell-Kelly pointed out this phenomenon in his work on insurance company Prudential[15]: between the 1880s and the 1920s, in London and in the United States, actuarial work involved organizational, technical, and human solutions to the problem of the rapidly rising volume of calculations to be done. In the London offices, the skills of the employees (who were predominantly male, a fact beside the scope of Campbell-Kelly's study) remain a resource in the long term, in spite of available technological alternatives which are only put in action after 1911. In contrast, US branches turn very readily to punch-card systems.

When considering, over a long historical period, a variety of channels involving practices and knowledge, without prejudice on the types of techniques implemented, one may write a history that is not inflected by the knowledge of the current state of the world. With a focus on gestures, actions, questions, and solutions to actual problems, it becomes possible to account for the organization of the competition between human (mind and body) knowledge and qualifications, tools and cognitive systems, and technical artifacts and machines. The very definition of what is understood with the term "technology" is modified and broadened.

While this approach is a necessary condition of historical research, scholars must also know to detect "turning points," the key moments when consequential transformations take place, accelerations appear, and options become irreversible choices[16]. Studying the formalization and stabilization of such social and technical configurations is crucial in that they may be the stage for gender arrangements, which may take hold and be transmitted.

The economy of European countries underwent deep transformations between 1890 and the 1920s. A new material economy was established over these decades: a new economy of the written word and of data and information processing, signing

---

[14] Gardey, Delphine. 2006. Culture of gender, culture of technology: the gendering of things in France's office spaces between 1890 and 1930. In *Cultures of technology*, ed. Helga Novotny, 73–94. New York: Berghahn Books.

[15] Campbell-Kelly, Martin. 1992. Large scale data processing in the prudential 1850–1930. *Accounting Business and Financial History* 2(2): 117–139.

[16] On this approach, and a discussion of elements of path dependency theory and the role played for this model by the case of the typewriter keyboard, see Gardey, Delphine. 1999. The standardization of a technical practice: typing (1883–1930). *History and Technology* 15: 313–343.

the opening of the contemporary era. This "administrative" or "informational" "white-blouse revolution"[17] was based on significant changes in the domains of writing, computing, filing, and data processing, as well as on the technological convergence of newly redefined domains. Fairly diverse economic fields (from government to commerce and banking, to insurance, and to the industrial sector) started then to share a need for the constant processing of a greatly increased volume of documents, with an emphasis for some sectors on direct output.[18] Maybe just as much as the period of intensification of technological, social, and economic transformations of the late twentieth and early twenty-first centuries, this era can be described as a capitalistic turning point.[19]

10.3   Gender Infrastructures of the Information Age

Between the world wars, offices became a laboratory for this first informational modernity. There, in order to process the ever more abundant data (and in particular the mass of individualized alphanumerical data), an anonymous and *mechanical* space of production, designed for large-scale, human and nonhuman data processing was invented.[20] Hardware use rests on intensive, specialized women labor: typing pools (and less common but equally female computer pools) were a staple of the modernity and proletarianization of office work. Through these rooms, the lasting assignment of women to office machines was introduced, as well as a regime of machine use intensified by workstation equipment and "systematic" layout.[21] A first form of computational machinery is thus created through the interweaving of women, machines, and space-regulating flows. Under this very specific political economy, the vanishing of the qualifications and personalities of the female workers is operated, generating unprecedented productivity. The output of accounting machines and punch-card systems is entirely dependent upon the mobilization of human resources.

The studies presented in this book offer to revisit this section of the history of information and its technologies: beyond the days of machine accounting, after World War II, the determining years of expansion of the 1950s and 1960s (Parolini, Morley, and McDonnell). One significant tool here is the understanding of space as

---

[17] Gardey 2008; Anderson, Gregory (ed.). 1989. *The white blouse revolution. Female office workers since 1870*. Manchester: Manchester University Press.

[18] Gardey 2008.

[19] Yates, Joan. 1989. *Control through communication. The rise of system in American management.* Baltimore/London: John Hopkins University Press.

[20] Akrich, Madeleine, Michel Callon, and Bruno Latour (eds.). 2006. *Sociologie de la traduction: textes fondateurs.* Paris: Mines ParisTech/Les Presses; Latour, Bruno. 1996. *Aramis or the love of technology.* Boston: Harvard University Press.

[21] Bernasconi, Gianenrico, and Stephan Nellen. eds. 2015 (Forthcoming). *The office as interior (1880-1960).* Bielefeld: Transcript.

machinery (inside and outside). The transformation of technologies into artifacts combining the machine and the human, as highlighted by the works of Jennifer Light,[22] Janet Abbate,[23] and Chantal Morley and Martina McDonnell in this volume, is a notable specificity of the first age of information processing. Asking "Who is the computer?" is the most sarcastically incisive way of questioning the elements at stake. The infrastructural and mixed extent of the first computers is a reality. The bodies of women (their hands and arms but also their skills[24]), forgotten for long, now reappear: the return of corporeality is necessary to the understanding of what comprises the economic, social, and political make up of the institutions of today[25]. As a valuable resource, corporeality helps appreciate the complexity with which the contemporary world engages with technology and to discern the specificity of Western modernity.

Another, earlier example of the intense mobilization of women's body in the "informational" context can be found in the telephone industry. In the early days of the twentieth century, this industry is compelled to develop technico-social infra-structures able to meet the demand at minimal cost. One of the first responses is the hiring of white, educated women as switchboard operators. This response, in the American context, frames the service offered to white social classes in terms of gender, race, and class. With intensifying work demand, more women gain access to employment, but this happens in contradiction with the social definition of the industry, as a service provided to an upper class of (white) businessmen.[26] The extension of the benefits of telephone use to upper-class women, as discussed by Dominique Pinsolle in this book, as well as the recruiting of lower-class black women as operators,[27] appear as disruptive elements in the social and political econ-omy of the previous technico-social arrangements.

Two lessons can be gained from the historiographies of the telephone exchange and the office.

---

[22] Light, Jennifer. 1999. When computers where women. *Technology and Culture* 40(3): 455–483.

[23] Abbate, Janet. 2012. *Recoding gender. Women's changing participation in computing.* Cambridge, MA: MIT Press.

[24] One important point made in this volume (Ashcraft, Karen Lee and Catherine Ashcraft. 2015. Breaking the "glass slipper": What diversity interventions can learn from the historical evolution of occupational identity in ICT and commercial aviation. In *Connecting women*, ed. V. Schafer and B.G. Thierry, 137–156. Dordrecht: Springer) based on "Occupational Identity," is in contrast with older discussions on the social construction of skill.

[25] For a proposed material and "corporeal" reading of democratic institutions, and in particular of the French *Assemblée Nationale* since the Revolution, see Gardey, Delphine. 2015. *Le linge du Palais-Bourbon. Corps, matérialité et genre du politique à l'ère démocratique.* Bordeaux: Le Bord de l'Eau.

[26] Fisher, Claude. 1992. *America calling. A social history of the telephone to 1940.* Berkeley: University of California Press; Green, Venus. 1995. Race and technology: African American women in the bell system, 1945–1980, technology and culture. *Technology and Culture* 36(2): 101–143.

[27] Green 1995.

The history of the phone industry and the arbitration regarding the types of female workforce (as well as the choice to use this workforce of not) are reminiscent of the social and racial hierarchies made invisible by the ordinary use of information and communication technologies. Production processes keep managers arbitrating between technology and work and innovation and mobilization of workers. From the example of American Telephone & Telegraph, Kenneth Lipartito[28] showed that women's labor acted as a sustainable substitute for a purely technological intensification of the socio-technical system of the telephone industry: automated switchboards were met with highly competitive human "switches," and operators gained the industry's favor against innovation. An important reason behind this preference is that these women *are* the innovation. Yet, as is the case in histories of typing, this is never really a matter for consideration – not unlike the general part played by women as agents of the history and changes in economy and technology. The economic performance of these systems incorporates the work and skills of women while making them invisible. It is one of the "matrices" of the information economy, worth noting and remembering.

Another bit of knowledge is provided by the history of the office: like the history of earlier workshops, it allows a better understanding of how "social relation can be expressed within space, but [how] space is also active in determining social relation".[29] Such is the reason for the importance of wondering "how politically active is a space." These are elements for analysis when the transition is made, for example, from the socio-technical infrastructure of the "pool" to that of the "open-plan office" to the more recent "cybertariat." Such issues, as control, power, agency, empowerment, and domination, seem to remain underrepresented in the investigation of the more contemporary forms of organization of the technical and cognitive space of information processing. However, one can hardly study these transformations without considering the distribution of agency and control among humans and nonhumans, among social groups, among men and women, and among local and outsourced workers.

Both of these elements should be considered in a contemporary context of global transactions and international forms of gender and social distribution of labor. In 2003, Donna Haraway already attempted to raise awareness on these issues with her famous *Cyborg Manifesto*.[30] Behind the smoothed-out world of our computer screens are invisible infrastructures and an international economy of social and gender relations, founded on the hackneyed social forms of "pools" – fragmented, automated, repetitive activities located for the main part in "emerging" economies. Who operates the mass digitization of the virtual libraries now accessible online? The

---

[28] Lipartito, Kenneth. 1994. When women were switches: technology, work and gender in the telephone industry (1890–1930). *American Historical Review* 99(4): 1075–1111.

[29] Hoskyns, Teresa. 2005. Designing the Agon: questions on architecture, space, democracy and "the political". In *Making things public: atmospheres of democracy*, ed. Bruno Latour and Peter Weibel, 798–803. Cambridge/Karlsruhe: The MIT Press/ZKM Center for Art and Media.

[30] Gardey, Delphine. 2009. Au cœur à corps avec le Manifeste Cyborg de Donna Haraway. *Esprit*: 208–217.

difference must be emphasized between the ideology of virtuality (free, open, and equal access, transparency) and the reality of its political economy. There are no connections between the "virtual world" and the "real world" when the "real work" of those who make it a reality is forgotten.[31]

10.4   ICT as Technology and as Culture

The latter point draws our attention to the conjointly functional and utopian dimensions of these socio-technical systems. As much as they are material, corporal, inscribed within the real space, which they help circumscribe, information and communication technologies are also promises[32] and utopias. Typing pools were rationalist utopias' and productivist's nightmares; the open-plan office is a paradoxical form of the utopia of a nonhierarchical, nonformal, cooperative workplace, but where control over work and interactions is multiplied by the organization of space and flows. The spaces devoted to the economy of knowledge after World War II are examples of the generative function ascribed to architecture. Martin Reinhold shows how the corporate space successfully tackles the daunting task of combining "new managerial protocols, new networks of power and new esthetics problems".[33] Analyzing the office of the second half of the twentieth century as a "laboratory," he studies the "topologies of knowledge" implemented in the works of such architects as Eero Saarinen, Louis Kahn, Robert Venturi, and Denise Scott Brown. Each of the laboratories they design is an "organizational complex" intended to provide added innovation and knowledge value through their very arrangement. What are then the corporate spaces of the high-tech, digital economy? This question must be raised in connection with the language used by leading companies on their products and on the culture they offer to share with customers and into which they mobilize the personalities of their employees. Physicality and discourse – utterly ordinary economic reality and the most trivial ideology – while two separate domains, may together offer an interesting object of study.

Their technological nature does not keep ICTs from having their own culture. As part of the ever-renewed culture of novelty, they are akin to so-called "material" technologies. In the contemporary history of technology, the rhetoric of progress and of the never-seen-before is ubiquitous, in spite of the prevalent and obvious

---

[31] Huws, Ursula. 2003. *The making of cybertariat. Virtual work in real world.* New York: Monthly Review Press.

[32] Haraway, Donna. 1992. The promises of monsters: a regenerative politics for inappropriate/d others. In *Cultural studies*, ed. Lawrence Grossberg, Cary Nelson, and Paula A. Treichler, 295–337. New York: Routledge.

[33] Reinhold, Martin. 2009. Unpublished paper. Von Herrmann, Hans-Christian and Sven Spieker (org.). *The office in the studio. The administration of modernism.* International conference, 23–24 January 2009. Medien Wissenschaft, Friedrich-Schiller Universität Jena.

coexistence of several generations of technologies.[34] As underlined by David Edgerton's research, the "shock of the old"[35] is rarely fully measured, when observers are absorbed by the promotion of eternal novelty. This does not appear to be a trait specific to ICTs.

Information and communication technologies, like most technologies, are also subjected to ambivalent "projections" concerning their potential positive and harmful effects. Steve Woolgar sees this as a constant in the history of technology, both before and after the advent of ICTs. His call for a "technography" of technologies underlines how debates on "new" technologies tend to include ideas on possible alternatives on a social level – discussing technology is discussing the future. The focus of such debates is on what the manufacture and organization of society can be and must be. Whether tangible or immaterial, technologies are thus essentially "theoretical"[36]: they are artifacts and they are discourse, materiality as much as language. In other words, technologies convey the vernacular speech, but also scholarly dissertations, which contribute to their socialization and usage. Social sciences are now among the forms of technical, social, and political significations of technology.

The euphoria exhibited in certain periods of the history of technology (or rather in the history of the discourse on technology, as offered in public and academic spaces) is a ready target for retrospective irony. It would be easy enough to have century-old praise for the telegraph pass as a demonstration of enthusiasm for the Internet, uttered 20 years ago. The language of the innovator is not too different from that of the general public or the expert. In social sciences, even in their more critical forms, technological optimism is a noticeable feature of the 1990s and 2000s. It appears in the feminist infatuation for digital technologies, itself a cultural and social phenomenon worthy of extensive research. Ripe with promises (not only those of monsters) to paraphrase Donna Haraway, ICTs have aroused unprecedented passion. Some feminists saw them as exacting a positive transformative influence on gender relations[37]; "technophilia" is the term used by Judy Wajcman[38] to describe this era.

I proposed the term of "technopportunism" to describe how Donna Haraway reconstructs political struggles and feminism at the turn of the millennium with the

---

[34] Edgerton, David. 1998. De l'innovation aux usages. Dix thèses éclectiques sur l'histoire des techniques. *Annales Histoire, Sciences Sociales* 53(4–5): 815–837.

[35] Edgerton, David. 2007. *The shock of the old. Technology and global history since 1900.* Oxford: Oxford University Press.

[36] Woolgar, Steve. 2000. Virtual technologies and social theory: a technographic approach. In *Preferred placement. Knowledge politics on the web*, ed. Richard Rogers. Maastricht: Jan Van Eyck Akademie Editions.

[37] Kirkup, Gill, et al. 2000. *The gendered cyborg: a reader.* London: Routledge.

[38] Wajcman, Judy. 2007. From women & technology to gendered technoscience. *Information, Commnication & Society* 10(3): 287–298.

figure of the cyborg.[39] The analysis of individual and collective subjectivities in the era of biotechnologies and "global" information processing takes the form of a prophecy. The epistemic and political impact of Haraway's trailblazing research is still to be fully grasped; it allows to see how ICTs are the possible implements of reallocations, new connections, and disembodiment – which all are precisely what cyberfeminism, as a practice of technology and as a technical culture, aims to achieve. One may thus see in cyberfeminism a stage of feminism, and one of its form, the purpose of which is the material, technical, and theoretical exploration of means to start "gender trouble"[40]: questioning contingent forms of embodiment, investigating the social and technical modes of our relation to the others and to the world, and exploring relationality and possible connections in their variety[41]. Cyberfeminists have taken full advantage of the array of possibilities offered by ICTs.

Should the "technophiliac" euphoria remain a valid viewpoint today? One incisive remark from Judy Wajcman puts it into perspective: "However, for all the hype about the network society, the internet does not automatically transform every user into an active producer, and every worker into a creative subject".[42] I have proposed a synthesis of English language academic works on the issue of social and gendered uses of ICTs created in the 1980s to the 2000s.[43] In addition to the study of the thematic evolution of the research, my work offers a contradictory and paradoxical summary of the emancipating or constraining nature of gender-technology relations as they appear in the surveyed research. From "domination" to empowerment, gendered uses of information technologies appear in a variety of situations and interpretations. What is added to the history of technology by their social studies, and what is offered otherwise by the critical input of feminism on this field, is the idea that relations between humans and technologies (gender relations among them) are never set in advance but instead the object as much as the end game of the analysis.[44]

[39] Haraway, Donna. 1985. (Reed. 2003). A cyborg manifesto: science, technology and socialist-feminism in the 1980s. In *The Haraway Reader*, 7–40 London/New York: Routledge; Gardey, Delphine. 2014. The reading of an Oeuvre. Donna Haraway: the poetics and politics of life. *Feministische Studien, Zeitschrift für interdisziplinäre Frauen- und Geschlechterforschung* 32(1): 86–100.

[40] Butler, Judith. 1990. *Gender trouble. Feminism and the subversion of identity*. 2nd ed. 1999. New York: Routledge.

[41] These are discussed in our soon-to-be-published volume: Gardey, Delphine, and Cynthia Kraus (eds.) 2015 (Forthcoming). *Politics of coalition. thinking collective action with Judith Butler*. Geneva and Zürich: Seismo Verlag.

[42] Wajcman, Judy. 2006. New connections: social studies of science and technology and studies of work. *Work, Employment and Society* 20(4): 773–786.

[43] Gardey, Delphine. 2003. De la domination à l'action: quel genre d'usage des technologies de l'information? *Réseaux Communication, technologie, sociétés* 21: 87–117.

[44] Wajcman 2007.

Yet the "seamless fabric"[45] interweaving the social and the technological and tying together gender and power relations is enduring; the role of historians is to acknowledge its lasting existence. José Emilio Pérez Martínez's contribution, on free (and feminist) radio, reminds us of a simple but important truth: the difference between those who design and decide and those who listen and consume – and as consumers are modeled – was and still is a major aspect of the history of technology and consumption. The laboratory of the immaterial is still a space for unmixed masculinity. Women are only marginal contributors to the design of the cultural, technological, and social worlds where our daily lives are carried out. Technologies are thus shaped by gender considerations just as much as they help reorder and shape gender as a social and political field. There may lie one reason why the social and sexual definition of what technologies pertaining to the ICTs is such an important matter. As illustrated by the works of Lie, gender is a marker when it comes to the borders between "high-tech," "low-tech," and "no-tech".[46]

Lastly, the comparative study of representations in the French and German press of the relations between male and female teenagers and ICTs insists on the concrete modes of the shaping and modeling at play (Dalibert and De Julio in this book). A question of specific import for young women is that of the possible identification with role models who may advertise their technology literacy. Such issues remind us how age and gender categories are historically defined by the relation to technologies on the individual and subjective level, as much as collectively. While technologies have been exclusively and for a long time "what men do," being a preteen in today's societies means entertaining a number of social and technological relations to oneself and to others. The "becoming technological" of individual and social identity is one significant aspect of the impact of ICTs, as "relational artifacts",[47] on the world and on our ability to live in it and contribute to it.

References

Abbate, Janet. 2012. *Recoding gender. Women's changing participation in computing*. Cambridge, MA: MIT Press.

Akrich, Madeleine. 1992. The de-scription of technical objects. In *Shaping technology-building society: studies in sociotechnical change*, ed. Wiebe E. Bijker and John Law, 205–224. Cambridge, MA: MIT Press.

Akrich, Madeleine, Michel Callon, and Bruno Latour (eds.). 2006. *Sociologie de la traduction: textes fondateurs*. Paris: Mines ParisTech/Les Presses.

Anderson, Gregory (ed.). 1989. *The white blouse revolution. Female office workers since 1870*. Manchester: Manchester University Press.

---

[45] Hughes, Thomas P. 1983. *Networks of power. Electrification in Western Society, 1880–1930*. Baltimore: The John Hopkins University Press.

[46] Lie, Merete. 2003. Gender and ICT – new connections. In *He, she and IT revisited: new perspectives on gender and information society*, ed. Merete Lie. Oslo: Gylendal Akademish.

[47] Turkle, Sherry. 1984. *The second self: computers and the human spirit*. London: Granada.

Ashcraft, Karen Lee and Catherine Ashcraft. 2015. Breaking the "glass slipper": What diversity interventions can learn from the historical evolution of occupational identity in ICT and commercial aviation. In *Connecting women*, ed. V. Schafer and B.G. Thierry, 137–156. Dordrecht: Springer.

Bernasconi, Gianenrico, and Stephan Nellen. eds. 2015 (Forthcoming). *The office as interior (1880-1960)*. Bielefeld: Transcript.

Brousseau, Eric, and Frédéric Moatty. 2002. La création du Groupe de recherche 'TIC et société' au CNRS. *Réseaux* 2(112–113): 395–398.

Butler, Judith. 1990. *Gender trouble. Feminism and the subversion of identity.* 2nd ed. 1999. New York: Routledge.

Campbell-Kelly, Martin. 1992. Large scale data processing in the prudential 1850–1930. *Accounting Business and Financial History* 2(2): 117–139.

Chandler, Alfred, and James Cortada (eds.). 2000. *A nation transformed by information. How information has shaped the United States from colonial times to present.* Oxford/New York: Oxford University Press.

Cockburn, Cynthia. 1983. *Brothers: male dominance and technological change.* London: Pluto Press.

Cortada, James (ed.). 1998. *Rise of the knowledge worker.* London: Routledge.

De Certeau, Michel. 1990. *L'invention du quotidien. 1. Arts de faire.* Paris: Gallimard.

Edgerton, David. 1998. De l'innovation aux usages. Dix thèses éclectiques sur l'histoire des techniques. *Annales Histoire, Sciences Sociales* 53(4–5): 815–837.

Edgerton, David. 2007. *The shock of the old. Technology and global history since 1900.* Oxford: Oxford University Press.

Fisher, Claude. 1992. *America calling. A social history of the telephone to 1940.* Berkeley: University of California Press.

Gardey, Delphine. 1999. The standardization of a technical practice: typing (1883–1930). *History and Technology* 15: 313–343.

Gardey, Delphine. 2001. Mechanizing writing and photographing the word: utopias, office work, and histories of gender and technology. *History and Technology* 17: 319–335.

Gardey, Delphine. 2003. De la domination à l'action: quel genre d'usage des technologies de l'information? *Réseaux Communication, technologie, sociétés* 21: 87–117.

Gardey, Delphine. 2006. Culture of gender, culture of technology: the gendering of things in France's office spaces between 1890 and 1930. In *Cultures of technology*, ed. Helga Novotny, 73–94. New York: Berghahn Books.

Gardey, Delphine. 2008. *Ecrire, calculer, classer. Comment une révolution de papier a transformé les sociétés contemporaines (1800–1940).* Paris: La Découverte.

Gardey, Delphine. 2009. Au cœur à corps avec le Manifeste Cyborg de Donna Haraway. *Esprit*: 208–217

Gardey, Delphine. 2014. The reading of an Oeuvre. Donna Haraway: the poetics and politics of life. *Feministische Studien, Zeitschrift für interdisziplinäre Frauen- und Geschlechterforschung* 32(1): 86–100.

Gardey, Delphine. 2015. *Le linge du Palais-Bourbon. Corps, matérialité et genre du politique à l'ère démocratique.* Bordeaux: Le Bord de l'Eau.

Gardey, Delphine, and Cynthia Kraus (eds.) 2015 (Forthcoming). *Politics of coalition. thinking collective action with Judith Butler.* Geneva and Zürich: Seismo Verlag.

Green, Venus. 1995. Race and technology: African American women in the bell system, 1945–1980, technology and culture. *Technology and Culture* 36(2): 101–143.

Haraway, Donna. 1985. (Reed. 2003). A cyborg manifesto: science, technology and socialist-feminism in the 1980s. In *The Haraway Reader*, 7–40 London/New York: Routledge.

Haraway, Donna. 1992. The promises of monsters: a regenerative politics for inappropriate/d others. In *Cultural studies*, ed. Lawrence Grossberg, Cary Nelson, and Paula A. Treichler, 295–337. New York: Routledge.

Hoskyns, Teresa. 2005. Designing the Agon: questions on architecture, space, democracy and "the political". In *Making things public: atmospheres of democracy*, ed. Bruno Latour and Peter Weibel, 798–803. Cambridge/Karlsruhe: The MIT Press/ZKM Center for Art and Media.

Hughes, Thomas P. 1983. *Networks of power. Electrification in Western Society, 1880–1930*. Baltimore: The John Hopkins University Press.

Huws, Ursula. 2003. *The making of cybertariat. Virtual work in real world*. New York: Monthly Review Press.

Kirkup, Gill, et al. 2000. *The gendered cyborg: a reader*. London: Routledge.

Krige, John, and Eda Kranakis. eds. 1994. Information technologies and socio-technical systems. *History and Technology*, 1(1). New York: Routledge.

Latour, Bruno. 1996. *Aramis or the love of technology*. Boston: Harvard University Press.

Lie, Merete. 2003. Gender and ICT – new connections. In *He, she and IT revisited: new perspectives on gender and information society*, ed. Merete Lie. Oslo: Gylendal Akademish.

Light, Jennifer. 1999. When computers where women. *Technology and Culture* 40(3): 455–483.

Lipartito, Kenneth. 1994. When women were switches: technology, work and gender in the telephone industry (1890–1930). *American Historical Review* 99(4): 1075–1111.

Mounier-Kuhn, Pierre-Eric. 2010. *L'informatique en France de la seconde guerre mondiale au Plan Calcul. L'émergence d'une science*. Paris: Presses universitaires de la Sorbonne.

Oldenziel, Ruth. 1996. Objections: technology, culture and gender. In *Learning from things. Method and theory of material culture studies*, ed. David Kingery, 55–69. Washington, DC: Smithonian Institution Press.

Reinhold, Martin. 2009. Unpublished paper. Von Herrmann, Hans-Christian and Sven Spieker (org.). *The office in the studio. The administration of modernism*. International conference, 23–24 January 2009. Medien Wissenschaft, Friedrich-Schiller Universität Jena.

Turkle, Sherry. 1984. *The second self: computers and the human spirit*. London: Granada.

Wajcman, Judy. 1991. *Feminism confronts technology*. Cambridge: Polity Press.

Wajcman, Judy. 2006. New connections: social studies of science and technology and studies of work. *Work, Employment and Society* 20(4): 773–786.

Wajcman, Judy. 2007. From women & technology to gendered technoscience. *Information, Commnication & Society* 10(3): 287–298.

Woolgar, Steve. 2000. Virtual technologies and social theory: a technographic approach. In *Preferred placement. Knowledge politics on the web*, ed. Richard Rogers. Maastricht: Jan Van Eyck Akademie Editions.

Yates, Joan. 1989. *Control through communication. The rise of system in American management*. Baltimore/London: John Hopkins University Press.

Index

© Springer International Publishing Switzerland 2015
V. Schafer, B.G. Thierry (eds.), *Connecting Women*, History of Computing,
DOI 10.1007/978-3-319-20837-4

Printed in the United States
By Bookmasters